P9-APF-993

LIVE ANIMAL CARCASS EVALUATION AND SELECTION MANUAL

Third Edition

Donald L. Boggs
South Dakota State University

Robert A. Merkel
Michigan State University

KENDALL/HUNT PUBLISHING COMPANY
2460 Kerper Boulevard P.O. Box 539 Dubuque, Iowa 52004-0539

Animal Science Consultant

Marshall Jurgens—Iowa State University

Copyright © 1979, 1984, 1990 by Kendall/Hunt Publishing Company

Library of Congress Catalog Card Number: 89–63383

ISBN 0–8403–5393–6

All rights reserved. No part of this publication may be reproduced, stored in a retrieval system, or transmitted, in any form or by any means, electronic, mechanical, photocopying, recording, or otherwise, without the prior written permission of the copyright owner.

Printed in the United States of America
10 9 8 7 6 5 4 3

Contents

Preface

Livestock selection and evaluation have been largely dependent on subjective appraisal of the animal's merit and/or value. The ultimate goal of the livestock and meat industry is to have a single, accurate objective measurement for assessing the economically important traits in order to determine value or merit, but no one criterion is available. Therefore, a number of criteria are combined to increase accuracy in live animal and carcass evaluation. Although objective measurements are frequently included, subjective evaluation is still widely used in the livestock and meat industry.

This manual was developed to provide the student in animal science with guidelines for evaluation and selection procedures as applied to breeding, feeder and market swine, as well as to beef cattle and sheep. The manual includes a brief discussion of the process of meat animal growth and fattening, the factors affecting growth and fattening, and their effect on body composition. A brief discussion of livestock improvement through selection is included because it is an area in which important progress has been made and because most students haven't had a previous breeding and genetic course. The principles of improvement through aids used in the selection and the evaluation of performance data are also presented. Therefore, the student is not only exposed to market animal evaluation, grading and pricing procedures, but also to the evaluation of performance data. Visual appraisal of breeding stock to determine which animals should be culled and which kept in the breeding herd is also examined. The manual includes the current recommended evaluation and performance procedures, as utilized by the beef cattle, sheep, and swine industries. A brief discussion of the complex pricing procedure used in the livestock and meat industry is also presented.

The authors have assumed that students have had an introductory course in animal science, although the level of presentation in the manual is comprehensible without it.

An appendix is included in the manual to provide scoring procedures, a swine ear notching system and sample live animal and carcass evaluation, and grading and pricing forms. A line drawing of a pig, steer, and sheep with labeled external parts is also provided for reference purposes. An index is included to locate specific subjects and definitions.

Material is presented by species. This manual's order is swine, beef cattle and sheep, but for study purposes this particular sequence does not have to be followed. Additionally, the sections on evaluation of market animals and carcasses are immediately followed by the sections on breeding animals for each species to provide the complete evaluation and selection procedures involved for each one. However, this order also does not have to be followed. Covering the market animal evaluation sections of all three species prior to covering the breeding animal evaluation sections or vice versa is recommended. It is recommended, however, that the first four sections be covered before any one species section. The manual is also designed so that the sections on evaluation of market animals and their respective carcasses can be studied with either the live animal section or the corresponding carcass section, depending on the preferred starting point for evaluation. However, because of this flexibility some repetition between the live animal and carcass sections of each species will occur. Despite this limitation, we have retained this format because both approaches are used and often the repetition is necessary.

Although the authors wish to emphasize that this is *not* a livestock or meat judging manual, it *is* an integrated approach to the principles and procedures involved in the evaluation, grading, and selection of meat animals and their carcasses for the Animal Science student. Therefore, the principles and procedures presented in this manual provide the basic background for livestock and meat judging, and ideally the student should enroll in judging courses after having a course covering the material in this manual.

Donald L. Boggs
Robert A. Merkel

Acknowledgments ━━━━━━━━━━━━━━━━

The authors wish to express their appreciation to American Hampshire Herdsman, American Yorkshire Club, National Live Stock and Meat Board, and Food Safety and Quality Service of the U.S. Department of Agriculture for their information and illustrations used in this manual. The authors also wish to acknowledge the photographs taken by Kate Danner, Farabee McCarthy, Sharon Parsons, Matt Parsons, and Lori Nixon; and the illustrations drawn by Marcia Couture and Brenda Murphy. We also wish to express our gratitude to the typists of the material in the manual; namely, Bea Eichelberger, Pat Cramer, Marcia Couture, Fran Vincent, and Debi Beeuwsaert. The authors graciously acknowledge the suggestions and the time spent by the faculty and staff in the preparation and review of the material in this manual, notably Ron Allen, Steve Baertsche, Dan Eversole, Amos Fox, Dave Hawkins, Harold Henneman, George Good, Maynard Hogberg, Bill Magee, Jan Busboom, and Harlan Ritchie. Don Mulvaney's assistance in the preparation and review of several sections of this manual is also greatly appreciated. The extensive contributions to this third edition of the manual by Al Culham, Pete Anderson, Dennis Banks and Aubrey Schroeder are also graciously acknowledged. Finally, the authors wish to thank Dr. Ron Nelson, former department chairman and Dr. Maynard Hogberg, the current chairman, for creating the atmosphere to make the writing of this manual possible and for their support and encouragement of our efforts.

Introduction to Evaluation

Accurately evaluating the breeding or market value of livestock and livestock products is essential to the economic success of any livestock or meat industry enterprise. The farmer or rancher culling his herd or flock and selecting replacements, the feedlot operator selecting feedlot replacements, the livestock buyer purchasing slaughter animals, and the retail or the Hotel, Restaurant and Institution (HRI) meat buyer purchasing carcasses or primal cuts must be able to evaluate correctly the available resources and the market demand. They must then make the proper decisions as to which livestock or carcasses are best for their situation. The student must realize that as market trends, feed sources, and consumer demands change, so do the ideal types or standards of livestock and carcasses.

The animal breeder must make the decision of which animals to keep or cull from the herd or flock and which animals to choose as replacements. The breeder must combine "eyeball" or subjective evaluation with objective methods of evaluation (performance testing, production records, linear measurements, determinants of body composition, etc.) in order to determine which seedstock should be incorporated into the selection program. Breeding livestock evaluation, however, goes beyond just determining the breeding potential of an animal. The breeder must recognize which traits need improving in the breeding herd or flock, must evaluate the economic importance of those traits, and must know which traits can be greatly improved and which traits cannot be greatly altered through selection.

In market animal evaluation, the feeder must be flexible in his preference of feeder types and be willing to change, depending on the demands of the market or feeding situation. He must recognize an animal's performance potential and select the most efficient and profitable feeders for the situation. The feeder, as well as the livestock buyer, must also be able to determine the value of the slaughter animal. This involves a knowledge of the animal's weight, body composition, and estimated carcass quality, as well as an understanding of the market conditions and trends.

A complete understanding of the factors that affect carcass quality and yield grade is essential to every producer, feeder, buyer, and consumer of livestock and meat. Producers, feeders, and buyers must be proficient at visual or subjective evaluation, while incorporating objective tools and aids into their selection programs to improve the accuracy of their evaluations. Remember that accurate evaluation of livestock or carcasses is made only after all possible information is collected, carefully analyzed, and applied to the specific situation.

Technology has been developed that allows objective estimation of the carcass components of live animals within reasonable accuracy levels. Ultrasonic evaluation, electrical conductance, and dilution techniques are some examples of the objective methods being used to measure various carcass characteristics on live animals. Of these, ultrasonic measurements appear to be the most promising for meat animal production. Students should be aware that development and use of these methods does not diminish the value of live animal and carcass evaluation skills. Estimates made by trained evaluators can be as accurate as those made by the newer and more objective methods. Furthermore, the cost of the recently developed equipment and the expertise required to operate and interpret these data makes the on-farm visual appraisal still the most popular method to evaluate meat animals. In addition, visual evaluation remains the only way to appraise important traits such as structural correctness and breed character.

Thus, it is obvious that knowledge of and proficiency in the application of evaluation procedures is an important daily activity in the highly competitive livestock and meat industry. The profits, success and reputation of any livestock or meat industry operation are largely contingent upon the evaluation ability of the individual in the organization performing this function. The principles and some procedures of live animal and carcass evaluation are presented in the subsequent sections of this manual.

Growth, Development, and Fattening of Meat Animals

Animal agriculture depends on the growth and fattening processes and on an understanding of the changes associated with these processes. They are essential to animal science students interested in live animal and carcass evaluation. Growth is an integral part of meat animal production, because rate of growth affects efficiency of production and determines profit or loss during production.

Growth, Development, and Fattening

What is growth? The adult animal is not merely an enlarged newborn; therefore, growth is not simply an increase in size. Not all portions of the body develop equally or at the same time during growth. This growth difference of body parts is called *development*. Development occurs from embryonic stages through maturity. One very recognizable development fact is that the head of all animals comprises a larger portion of the body at birth than at any later stage of its life; hence, its postnatal increase is less than other parts. Likewise, the legs of calves, lambs, and foals comprise a larger proportion of the body at birth than at later stages, and they develop less than other body parts during postnatal growth. In contrast, the legs of pigs show considerably more postnatal growth and development than those of cattle, sheep, or foals.

While growth is difficult to define, true growth is frequently described as an increase in the structural tissues; that is, bone, muscle and the connective tissues associated with muscle. These tissues should be differentiated from fat which develops later during the fattening phase. Even though some fattening occurs during normal muscle and bone growth and development, most fattening occurs after bone development is complete and after muscle is approaching its maximum development. Muscle tissue is very important to animal scientists because this component will ultimately be consumed as meat. But bone, skeletal structure, and soundness are important in order to maximize production efficiency during the growth of the animal. Fat is also important because some fat is necessary in order to ensure an acceptable eating quality. Likewise, fat over the outside of the carcass and primal cuts is necessary to protect them during the normal storage and handling period prior to being cut at the Hotel, Restaurant and Institution (HRI) or retail level.

The Growth Curve

The normal growth curve, as shown in Figure 2.1, is a sigmoidal or S-shaped curve. This curve is idealized because growth of individual animals is usually step-like, but they generally follow this pattern of growth and development, despite size and species. The units are identified as growth units and time units. Depending on the species, the growth units may be grams, kilograms, or pounds; and the time units may be days, weeks, months, or years. With respect to the mature weight of the animal, relatively little growth occurs prior to birth, and the increase in growth units following birth is initially very slow. This is followed by a rather rapid increase in growth units relative to time, and this stage is represented by the steep part of the curve in Figure 2.1. This is the stage when animals make the most efficient gains, because they are growing rapidly in a relatively short period of time. The upper part of the curve shows that the growth rate levels off as the animal approaches mature size. At this upper inflection of the growth curve, all tissues have either ceased or are slowing in their rate of growth and development.

Bone, muscle and fat are the tissues of primary concern for live animal and carcass evaluation purposes. They comprise most of the animal body increase in mass during postnatal growth and development. Growth and development of each of these tissues assumes a sigmoidal shape, and the overall growth curve

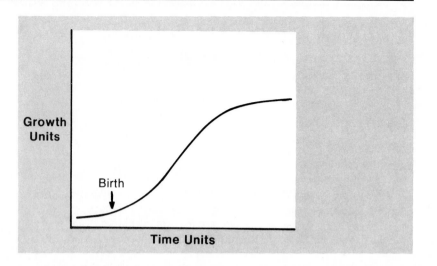

Figure 2.1. An idealized growth curve.

Growth Units

Birth

Time Units

is a summation of their individual growth and that of the more vital tissues of the body. The vital tissues include the brain and central nervous system, cardiovascular system, respiratory system, digestive system, etc. The body tissues differ when they develop in the specific segment of the growth curve. Even the vital tissues differ in the phase of the growth curve when they develop. The brain and central nervous system and the cardio-vascular system are functional in the embryo and are well developed at birth, whereas the respiratory and digestive systems develop early postnatally.

Growth and Development of Bone, Muscle, and Fat

The shape of the curve for muscle, fat, and bone growth and development shown in Figure 2.2 indicates that the curves for muscle and fat are sigmoidal in shape. However, because of the early maturity of bone it has already reached the upper inflection in the growth curve at or about weaning age; consequently, it shows relatively little further increase during the period of maximum growth of muscle and fat. The arrow on the right side of Figure 2.2 shows the approximate point of the Choice quality grade of beef, and at this point on the growth curve their carcasses would have approximately 30% fat.

The efficient production of meat animals with maximum muscle and minimum fat is the major goal of the livestock and meat industry. This goal is consistent with consumer attitudes and their demand for lean meat. The fat associated with meat is generally considered undesirable; and along with bone, it is regarded as waste. However, fat is a component of all cells, and it plays a vital role in metabolism of animals. As mentioned, a small amount of external fat on beef and lamb carcasses is necessary to protect them against dehydration and discoloration during storage and processing. In addition, the fat within muscles (marbling) is an important factor in the quality grade of beef carcasses. It also has impacts on eating quality (i.e., tenderness, juiciness, and flavor of beef, lamb and pork).

Fat is laid down in four major deposits in the carcasses of beef, lamb, and pork. These four deposits are: (1) under the skin or subcutaneous fat; (2) between muscles or intermuscular fat; (3) within muscles or intramuscular fat and (4) around the kidney or kidney fat. *Subcutaneous fat* is measured or estimated on the back of livestock species or their carcasses; consequently, it is referred to as backfat. Measurements or estimates of backfat thickness are included in most evaluation of livestock species because they are easily obtained and highly correlated with yield of retail cuts. Measurements or estimates of backfat are made to evaluate the amount of external fat on carcasses or live animals. *Intermuscular fat* is usually referred to as "seam fat" in the livestock and meat industry. Seam fat is not easily measured or estimated; therefore, it is not included in any of the live animal or carcass evaluation procedures described in this manual. However, the amount of intermuscular or seam fat is a very important factor in the evaluation and pricing of primal, subprimal, and retail meat cuts; but further discussion of this consideration is beyond the scope of this manual. *Intramuscular fat* is referred to as "marbling" by the livestock and meat industry. The degree of marbling is especially important in beef carcass evaluation and grading because it is the major factor

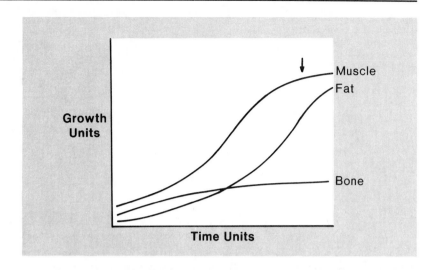

Figure 2.2. Postnatal growth curves of bone, muscle and fat.

in determining the quality grade. Hence, it greatly influences carcass price. Marbling is estimated in the exposed cross section of the ribeye muscle in ribbed carcasses of beef. Marbling also may be evaluated in ribbed lamb and pork carcasses, but it is not included in grading these carcasses. Marbling may also be evaluated in the cut surfaces of other muscles of beef, lamb and pork primal, subprimal, and retail cuts. In conventional packing-house practice, lamb and pork carcasses are not ribbed so marbling cannot be evaluated. Instead of marbling, fat in the flank muscles on the inside of the carcass is evaluated in lamb carcasses. This intramuscular fat is called *flank streaking* and is a factor used in quality grading lamb carcasses. In unribbed pork carcasses, intramuscular fat may be evaluated in the intercostal muscles (i.e., muscles between the ribs on the inside of the carcass). This intramuscular fat deposit is called *feathering*. Feathering is also present in beef and lamb carcasses, but it is seldom evaluated and is not a factor in the carcass grading of any of the species. The deposit of fat in the abdominal cavity that surrounds the kidney is called *kidney fat.* In both beef and lamb carcasses, fat in the pelvic cavity—and in beef carcasses fat in the thoracic cavity surrounding the heart—are also included in this deposit. Heart fat is negligible in lambs. These fat deposits are evaluated to provide an estimate of internal fat in beef and lamb carcasses. Internal fat deposits are not evaluated in swine because they are removed during the slaughter and dressing process, unlike beef and lamb carcasses, where they are left in them. Thus, internal fat in beef carcasses includes an evaluation of kidney, heart, and pelvic fat. In lambs, kidney and pelvic fat are used.

The stage of the fattening phase when these four fat deposits are laid down differs. The earliest developing deposit is the kidney and pelvic fat, and the latest is marbling, with backfat and intermuscular fat being intermediate. Thus, an animal could have a considerable amount of kidney and backfat, yet have very little marbling. Even though these fat deposits grow somewhat independently of each other, they all increase during the fattening phase. In other words, carcasses with high degrees of marbling tend to have greater amounts of kidney and backfat deposits and vice versa; however, exceptions to these trends are common.

The body site of major deposition of subcutaneous fat differs between pigs and cattle and lambs. The pig has the greatest deposit of its subcutaneous fat over the shoulder and has much less fat deposited over the loin and rump regions. The actual backfat thickness measurement at the first rib may be as much as twice the thickness of that found at the last rib or at the last lumbar vertebra. In cattle and lambs the greatest deposit of subcutaneous fat occurs over the center portions of the body (i.e., over the rib and loin regions of the back and over the brisket, plate, and flank in beef; and over the breast in lamb on the belly region of the body). The least subcutaneous fat in cattle and lambs occurs over the shoulders and rounds or legs (lamb), especially on the lateral surfaces.

The distribution of fat differs between these four deposits in the livestock species as shown in Figure 2.3. Subcutaneous fat accounts for 70% of total fat in pork carcasses and 30% and 44% in beef and lamb carcasses. On the other hand, intermuscular or seam fat accounts for 42% of total fat in beef carcasses,

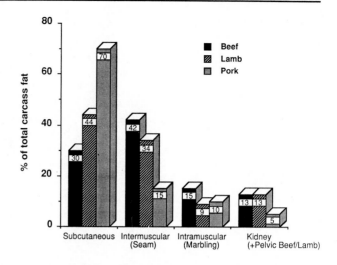

Figure 2.3. A graph showing the distribution of fat between the subcutaneous, intermuscular, intramuscular, and kidney (and pelvic) fat in beef, lamb, and pork carcasses.

34% in lamb carcasses, and only 15% in pork carcasses. Marbling accounts for 15% of total fat in beef carcasses and 9 to 10% in lamb and pork carcasses. The remaining fat is kidney and pelvic fat, which represents 13% of total fat in beef and lamb carcasses and 5% in pork carcasses.

Kidney, pelvic, and heart fat is removed from beef and lamb carcasses either at the slaughter plant when cutting them into primal and subprimal cuts, or when they are cut into retail cuts and HRI portions. The fat surrounding the kidney or leaf fat is removed from pork carcasses during slaughter. Thus, kidney fat (including pelvic fat in lamb, and pelvic and heart fat in beef carcasses) has been removed from all retail cuts and HRI portion cuts. The external or subcutaneous fat is generally trimmed to 1/4 inch of fat or less on beef, lamb, and pork retail and HRI portion cuts. Some retailers trim most subcutaneous fat from retail cuts, especially beef cuts. Intermuscular or seam fat, on the other hand, usually cannot be trimmed from retail cuts. Consequently, seam fat presents the biggest problem to the meat industry because it is the largest fat deposit in beef and the second largest deposit in lamb and pork carcasses. Yet, it can only be removed from a few retail cuts in conventional meat cutting. Seam fat presents the greatest problem in retail cuts from the chuck, brisket and plate in beef; shoulder and breast in lamb; and shoulder and belly (bacon) in pork. Only with *muscle boning* (separation of individual or groups of adjacent muscles) can seam fat be completely removed. Muscle boning is not a common practice in the meat industry. The high degrees of marbling are recognized by most consumers as excessive fat, and retail cuts containing high amounts of marbling and seam fat are obviously objectionable.

The amount of muscle, fat, and bone in the carcasses of cattle, pigs, and lambs—as well as the non-carcass components at weaning and at typical market weight—is presented in Figure 2.4 A (cattle) and B (pigs and lambs). Also shown in Figure 2.4 A and B is the amount of protein in the carcass (total of muscle, fat and bone), which is shown to the right of the main bar. The actual amount of each component (in pounds) is shown within each component of the bars. This figure shows that fat increases the most, while muscle is intermediate, and bone increases least from weaning to typical market weight in all three species. This is consistent with the growth curves for fat, muscle, and bone shown in Figure 2.2 and their relative rates of maturity. It is also obvious from the data in Figure 2.4 that noncarcass components increase dramatically from weaning to market weight. This figure also shows that the increase in total carcass protein from weaning to market weight ranges from approximately two-fold for cattle and lambs to more than ten-fold for pigs.

It also is important for the student of animal production to recognize the daily gain of fat, muscle, bone, and total carcass protein as well as the noncarcass components in relationship to typical live weight gains of cattle, pigs, and lambs from weaning to market weight. This information is presented in Figure 2.5. The actual daily gain of each component in pounds is shown within the bars for the respective components. The daily live weight gain from weaning to market weight for cattle is 2.4 lb., pigs 1.6 lb., and lambs .7 lb. In lambs the daily gain of muscle and fat is nearly equal, and in cattle muscle gain per day

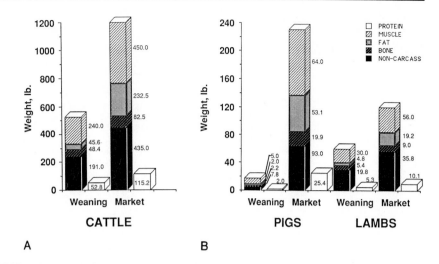

Figure 2.4. A graph showing the amount of muscle, fat, bone and non-carcass components in pounds in live cattle (A), pigs, and lambs (B) at weaning and at market weight. The white open bars to the right of muscle, fat, bone, and non-carcass components shows the protein associated with muscle, fat, and bone in the respective carcasses at weaning and at market weight. Weaning and market weights for cattle are 525 and 1200 lb.; for pigs 17 and 240 lb.; and for lambs 60 and 120 lb., respectively.

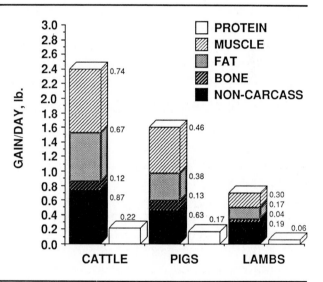

Figure 2.5. A graph showing the gain per day for muscle, fat, bone, and non-carcass components of cattle, pigs, and lambs. The daily protein gain from carcass muscle, fat, and bone are shown to the right of the other components for cattle, pigs, and lambs in the open bars. These daily gains of each component are calculated from weaning to market weight for each species utilizing the data in Figure 2.4. The average daily gain for cattle is 2.4 lb/day, for pigs is 1.6 lb/day, and for lambs .7 lb/day.

slightly exceeds fat gain. In pigs muscle gain per day approaches twice the fat gain. The differences between the species reflect the age at weaning relative to the growth curve. Because of its early maturity, bone gain per day is lower than the other carcass components. Total carcass protein gain per day slightly exceeds the bone gain. The low protein gain per day does not imply early maturity of protein, but occurs because most of the protein synthesized each day is actually broken down or turned over. As can be seen in Figure 2.5, a major proportion of the total live weight gain per day of each species is represented by the noncarcass components.

Physiological Age

Not all animals within species or breeds grow, develop, fatten or mature at the same chronological age. The animal scientist uses the term *physiological age* when referring to this difference in stage of maturity among animals of the same species and chronological age. The term physiological age is somewhat of a nebulous concept, but it refers to the stage of development of an animal. As an indicator of relative age, it is independent of chronological age and only represents identifiable points in the life span of animals from conception to death. Physiological age is usually discussed and compared on the basis of various identifiable stages of growth and development such as the onset of puberty, attainment of maximum body height and weight, various indicators of skeletal maturity, or body composition. Even within groups of

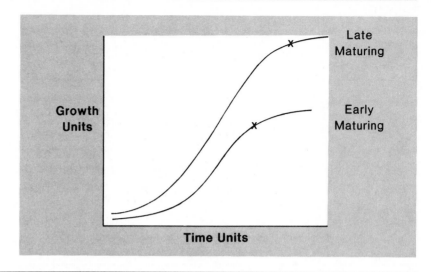

Figure 2.6. Growth curves of early and late maturing animals. The X at the upper inflection of the curves indicates the onset of maturity.

animals of the same species these identifiable stages of physiological age may occur at different chronological ages; consequently, some breeds within species may be described as being either early or late maturing. Conversely, at a given chronological age, animals from a late maturing breed would be physiologically younger than animals from an early maturing breed. Physiological age differs between animal types and sexes within species and will be discussed below in relationship to the growth curve and body composition.

Effects of Maturing Rate on Growth and Development

Within each species of livestock, there are early and late maturing animals. Early maturing animals generally are smaller at maturity than late maturing animals. Conversely, late maturing animals usually are larger at maturity than early maturing animals as illustrated in Figure 2.6. Examples of early and late maturing cattle and sheep are Angus vs. Charolais and Southdown vs. Suffolk. The X near the upper inflection of the growth curve indicates the point where the animal approaches maturity. At this stage of development the epiphyseal cartilage of long bones calcifies or ossifies (i.e., it turns to bone and no further increase in the length of the bone occurs). Considerable cartilage is also associated with the vertebrae of the backbone of young animals, and maturity of beef carcasses is evaluated by the extent of calcification or ossification of these cartilage areas. Color and shape of ribs, as well as the color of lean, are also used to evaluate maturity. At the stage of physiological maturity when bone growth ceases and muscle growth begins to level off, fat continues to increase and may do so for a considerable period of time depending on the energy level fed to the animal.

Figure 2.6 shows that at any given point in chronological age, late maturing animals would be physiologically less mature, heavier, have less fat (including marbling), and therefore quality grade lower than early maturing animals. However, because of less fat, the late maturing animals would have superior yield grades compared to early maturing animals. Late maturing animals reach maturity at a later chronological age than early maturing animals. Thus, late maturing beef cattle, for instance, would be considerably older and heavier than early maturing cattle when they have sufficient marbling for the Choice quality grade. Naturally, intermediate maturing animals would fall between the late and early maturing animals with respect to their growth rate, development, and physiological age.

Effects of Sex on Growth and Development

An animal's sex influences physiological age. Intact males (i.e., bulls, rams and boars) are heavier, leaner, and physiologically less mature than castrate males or females at a given chronological age. This information is shown in Figure 2.7. In cattle and sheep, females reach maturity earlier and at lighter weights or younger chronological ages than males. Additionally in cattle and sheep, castrate males (i.e., steers and wethers) are intermediate between males and females in the time when they reach maturity as shown in Figure 2.7. However in pigs, gilts, and castrate males (barrows) are much closer together in chronological

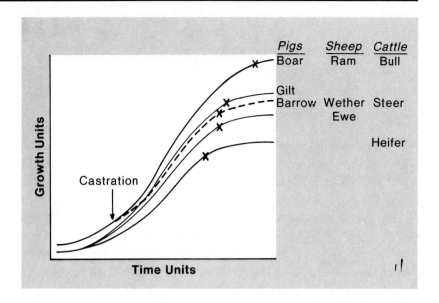

Figure 2.7. Growth curves of the various sexes of pigs, sheep and cattle. The X at the upper inflection of the curve indicates the onset of maturity. The approximate point of castration is indicated by an arrow on the lower left of the figure.

age when they reach maturity than females and castrate males of the other species. Even so, barrows reach maturity slightly earlier than gilts. This is in contrast to cattle and sheep. In these species, females are physiologically more mature than their respective castrate males (Figure 2.7) at given chronological ages.

The curves shown in Figure 2.7 apply best for cattle, because even in sheep the spread in chronological age between wether and ewe lambs when they reach maturity is considerably less than for cattle. However, the spread in chronological age between ewes and wethers is still greater than for gilts and barrows. While the data in Figure 2.7 indicate that males are heavier, leaner, and have less fat at any given chronological age than either of the other sexes, males also have lower quality grades because of the association of marbling with quality grade. In the case of cattle and sheep, the early maturing heifers and ewes are fatter and have higher quality grades at any given chronological age and/or weight than steers and wethers. Because barrows reach maturity earlier than gilts, they also have more fat and less lean than gilts.

Relative Lean-to-Fat Ratio by Species and Sex

The relative *lean-to-fat ratios* by species and sex are shown in Table 2.1. In all instances, males of each species have the highest lean-to-fat ratio (i.e., the most lean in relationship to fat). In the case of cattle and sheep, heifers and ewes have the lowest lean-to-fat ratio. In other words, they have the least lean and most fat. In cattle and sheep, steers and wethers are intermediate in lean-to-fat ratio (i.e., they contain more lean and less fat than heifers and ewes), but have less lean and more fat than the respective males of the species.

With the exception of boars, the sexes of pigs differ from the other two species in their lean-to-fat ratios as can be seen in Table 2.1. Barrows have a lower lean-to-fat ratio than gilts. Consequently, the lean-to-fat ratio of gilts is intermediate to boars and barrows. Thus, barrows are physiologically more mature than gilts at given chronological ages. This is in contrast to steers and wethers because steers and wethers are physiologically less mature than the females of their respective species. There is no known explanation for these species differences in physiological maturity.

The degree of marbling is inversely related to lean-to-fat ratio. Since marbling is the major factor in quality grade of beef carcasses, quality grade is also inversely related to lean-to-fat ratio. Thus, carcasses with high lean-to-fat ratios usually have low degrees of marbling; and in the case of beef specifically, but generally lamb carcasses as well, they quality grade lower than carcasses with low lean-to-fat ratios. Thus, it should be apparent that knowledge of growth and development of the major tissues (i.e., bone, muscle and fat), as well as the effects of type and sex on physiological age and composition within each species, is extremely important for the student to intelligently approach the evaluation of meat animals.

Table 2.1 Relative Lean to Fat Ratio by Species and Sex at Same Weight or Chronological Age.

Lean to Fat Ratio	Cattle	Sheep	Pigs
Highest	Bull	Ram	Boar
Intermediate	Steer	Wether	Gilt
Lowest	Heifer	Ewe	Barrow

Effects of Nutrition on Growth and Development

All essential nutrients must be available to the animal for optimum growth and development of the tissues. Obviously, if an essential nutrient is limited, then growth and development will be limited. The extent generally varies in direct proportion to the degree that the nutrient is limited. Practical diets fed to livestock usually provide adequate amounts of the essential nutrients so that animals normally grow at or near their genetic potential. The major dietary factors in meat animal production are energy content, and protein content and quality. The specific units of proteins used for growth are the amino acids which make up the proteins in the feed. Feed proteins contain varying proportions of essential to nonessential amino acids. Protein quality refers to the balance of dietary essential amino acids in proportion to the animal's needs. Dietary energy or the calories are derived entirely from the proteins, fats, and carbohydrates in the feed. Carbohydrates provide the major source of dietary energy in livestock feeds. Fifty to 65 percent of the feed energy is required for maintenance in meat animals. Dietary energy or protein in excess of requirements for body maintenance and productive purposes (i.e., for growth in growing animals) is deposited as fat. The growth rate of animals fed excess energy or protein would not be any greater than those fed for optimum performance (i.e., those fed practical livestock diets). Thus, excess energy, in particular, and to a limited extent excess protein fed to growing-finishing animals, results in overly fat carcasses that are inefficiently produced because there is no added improvement in rate of gain.

If the amount of protein in the diet is limited, the rate of gain will be decreased. Muscle will be the major tissue affected, especially in young growing animals when muscle growth is extensive. Other than water, protein is the major component of muscle tissue. Most of the protein in the animal body or carcass is in muscle tissue. Thus dietary protein is absolutely necessary for normal muscle protein synthesis and growth. Logically, lean and fast growing animals would have higher protein requirements than fatter, slower growing animals, especially during the period of extensive muscle growth. This is, in fact, true. Male animals have a higher protein requirement than females and castrates; and bulls, boars and rams are leaner and grow faster than the respective females and castrates of each species (see Figure 2.7 and Table 2.1). The protein requirement of females and castrates of each species also increases as the leanness and growth rate of each increases. Additionally, late maturing animals, which are leaner and grow faster, also have a higher protein requirement than early maturing animals, which are fatter and tend to grow slower. Likewise, the protein requirement of young growing animals is higher than for animals during the finishing phase because muscle growth matures earlier than fat. Thus, dietary protein for meat animals is usually decreased in practical livestock feeding during the finishing period to increase efficiency of production.

Utilization of the amino acids from a poor quality protein by the animal for protein synthesis is limited by the most deficient essential amino acid(s) in relation to the animal's requirements. The excess amino acids, over and above the most limiting one(s), is used for energy metabolism and fat deposition. Thus, feeding poor quality protein not only reduces gains, but also may result in fatter animals. These effects of poor quality protein are most obvious in pigs; they are practically irrelevant in sheep and cattle because ruminant animals are capable of considerable protein synthesis, even from nonprotein nitrogenous compounds, by the microorganisms present in the rumen. However, microbial protein production does not meet all the protein requirements of fast growing animals. Therefore, dietary protein must be supplied and the amount varies with rate of gain and leanness.

Dietary energy restriction not only will reduce gains, but it will also affect the major tissues contributing to composition (i.e., muscle, fat and bone) in reverse order of their development and maturation. In other words, since bone is the earliest maturing of these tissues and fat is the latest (Figure 2.2), the fat content would be the most severely decreased and the amount of bone would be the least affected by dietary energy restriction. If, however, energy restriction occurred early, either during fetal development or the first few weeks after birth, then muscle and bone also would be decreased. Nutrient deprivation via impaired blood supply to the fetus results in "runts," a condition most prevalent among animals with multiple births such as pigs. Not only are runts smaller in size at birth, but they also have less bone, muscle, and fat than their normal littermates. In the litter situation, the runt problem generally is further aggravated during the nursing period. Because of their smaller size, runts are less competitive than their larger littermates, and they are generally forced to select the poorer milk producing sections of the udder. The reduced milk protein and energy intake results in slower gains and some retardation of bone, muscle, and fat development during the nursing period. Following weaning, even though runts are smaller than their littermates, they make "compensatory" or "catch up" gains so that during the growing and finishing period their gains are only slightly less than normal. However, because bone and muscle are early maturing tissues some retardation of these tissues has occurred, and not all is recovered by the compensatory gains during the growing-finishing period. Consequently, runt pigs generally have fatter carcasses at market weight than their normal size littermates. Excessive or compensatory fat deposition occurs during the finishing period because less energy is needed for growth at this point and most dietary energy is then diverted to the fattening process. These same responses occur in calves and lambs if they are stunted in early life.

If dietary energy is restricted to animals during the growing period, then followed by full feeding during the finishing period, the carcasses of such animals are fatter than those that are not restricted. The amount of muscle is affected during the growing period if the energy restriction is severe. Because muscle growth occurs primarily in the growing period, it would undergo little compensatory growth during the finishing period, while the animal would over compensate its fat deposition resulting in a fatter carcass than normal. Thus, management practices should be followed that do not limit dietary energy except during the latter phases of the finishing period when fat deposition is at or near its maximum. Many countries, especially in Europe, advocate restricted dietary energy feeding practices during the finishing period with the expressed purpose of decreasing carcass fat. Restriction of dietary energy during the finishing period has a negligible affect on muscle and bone tissues. While restricted feeding has the advantage of decreasing fat, it should be emphasized that gains are less. Consequently it takes several weeks longer to reach market weight. For this reason and from an overhead standpoint, the practice has not been very widely followed in the United States.

Criteria Used to Evaluate Growth, Development and Fattening

Certain characteristics are subjectively evaluated and others objectively measured to assess growth, development, and fattening. The specific characteristics used for each species will be listed and briefly described below; however, they will be explained in more detail in the discussion of the live and carcass evaluation sections later in this manual.

Weight

The most common evaluation characteristic used throughout the livestock and meat industry is weight. Weight is usually obtained on live animals and carcasses when they are bought and sold. Carcass weight may include either hot or chilled weight, or both. By itself weight gives little indication of the stage of growth, development and fattening, or grade and value. It is almost always used in conjunction with other characteristics (either subjective or objective criteria) to obtain the evaluation endpoint desired. These additional criteria include eyeball evaluations or objective measurements of muscle and/or fat to determine grade and value.

Muscle

Muscle is evaluated in live cattle, pigs, and sheep by assessing the muscling primarily in the round, ham, and leg, respectively. The ribeye area is used in ribbed beef and sheep carcasses to objectively measure muscle. In the unribbed sheep carcass, muscling is assessed by assigning a subjective leg conformation grade or score. In pork carcasses, the loin eye area (when exposed) is used to objectively measure muscle. When the loin eye is not exposed in pork carcasses, muscling is subjectively assessed primarily in the ham, but the loin and shoulder are also included to determine degree of muscling. A procedure has been developed to estimate the percentage of muscle in pork carcasses.

Fat

Fat is primarily evaluated in all species as backfat. In cattle, fat thickness over the ribeye muscle is estimated or measured at the 12th rib. In sheep, the thickness of fat over the ribeye muscle on both the right and left sides of the carcass is also determined at the 12th rib and averaged. In pork carcasses, two different locations for measurement of backfat are obtained. The first and most frequently used measurement is the average of three measurements taken opposite the first rib, the last rib, and the last lumbar vertebra. This is referred to as average backfat thickness. Pork carcasses are also evaluated for backfat thickness by estimating or measuring the amount of fat over the eye muscle at the 10th rib. This latter measurement is used to calculate percentage muscle. Backfat thickness at the last rib is used to determine live hog and pork carcass U.S.D.A. grade.

Internal fat is evaluated in cattle by estimating or weighing and calculating the percentage of kidney, heart, and pelvic fat. In sheep the percentage of kidney and pelvic fat is evaluated. Intramuscular fat is evaluated in beef carcasses by estimating degree of marbling in the exposed ribeye muscle at the 12th rib interface. Marbling is used to determine quality grade in beef carcasses. Degree of marbling is not used in quality grading lamb carcasses because they are not ribbed in commercial practice. Instead, the degrees of flank fat streakings are estimated to determine quality grade. Even though lambs may be ribbed to expose the ribeye muscle at the 12th rib during carcass evaluation, degree of marbling is never used to determine quality grade. Marbling is frequently estimated at the 10th rib interface in ribbed pork carcasses, or in wholesale loins, if it is cut to expose the eye muscle to determine loin eye area and quality of lean. However, marbling is only used to assess quality and is not used in pork carcass grading.

The yield of boneless trimmed retail cuts from the round, loin, rib, and chuck is also used in cattle to indirectly evaluate the retail or edible portion from the carcass. This retail yield is identified as the *yield grade*. Boneless trimmed retail cuts from the leg, loin, rack, and shoulder are also evaluated in lambs and likewise identified as yield grade. Yield grade is much more highly related to the amount of fat in the carcass than to muscle. Thus, yield grades are not good indicators of muscle mass.

The percentage lean cuts, as well as the ham and loin percentages, are used to evaluate value in hogs; but like the yield grades of beef and lamb, these percentages are much more highly related to fat than to muscle. The swine and pork carcass grade standards are based on the expected yield of lean cuts (i.e., the percentage that the ham, loin, picnic and Boston shoulder comprise of the entire carcass).

Livestock Improvement Through Selection

Many traits must be considered in the selection of livestock. The emphasis placed on each trait depends on the relative economic importance of that particular trait and the rate of improvement possible for the trait. The following are the major factors affecting the rate of improvement from selection:

1. Heritability
2. Selection differential
3. Generation interval

Heritability

The expression of a trait is influenced by the heredity and the environment in which the animal is raised. Heritability represents the fraction of the population variation of the expressed trait due to heredity. It is an estimate of the fraction of the phenotypic superiority or inferiority that can be transmitted from one generation to the next. In traits with low heritability estimates (.10–.20), 80 to 90% of the variation is due to environmental factors such as health, nutrition, or weather. Therefore, these lowly heritable traits change slowly in response to selection, and the selection progress is slower than with the more highly heritable traits. Reproductive traits, such as fertility, calving interval, and litter size generally fall into the low heritability category. Ironically, these traits also have the greatest effect on the economic return in a livestock breeding program. By contrast, traits with high heritability estimates (.50–.70), such as carcass characteristics, can be changed more rapidly through selection since as much as 50–70% of their variation is due to actual genetic differences. Unfortunately, many of these highly heritable traits often have a relatively small effect on the economic return. Production traits, such as growth rate and feed efficiency, have moderate heritability estimates (.25–.45). As expected, the rate of progress from selection for these traits is intermediate between the lowly heritable and highly heritable traits. The heritability estimates for some economically important traits are listed in Table 3.1.

Selection Differential

The *selection differential* is the measured difference of a trait between the average of the selected individuals and the herd average. For example, if the herd average for loin eye area (LEA) is 4.5 square inches (in.²), a gilt with a 6.0 in.² LEA would have a larger selection differential (6.0 in.²−4.5 in.² = 1.5 in.²) than a gilt with a 5.0 in.² LEA (5.0 in.²−4.5 in.² = .5 in.²). The greater the selection differential, the more rapidly improvement will be made. Selection differential is usually greatest for those traits which exhibit the most variation within a population. Selection differential can also be increased by selecting from a larger population or by selecting fewer replacements. The example below (Table 3.2) demonstrates how selection pressure, selection differential, and heritability can be used to predict the performance of the offspring in two selection systems.

In the first system, selection of both heifers and bulls is based on average daily gain (ADG) during a post-weaning test. The average selection differential is calculated by averaging the differences in ADG between the selected heifers and the herd average and the selected bull and the herd average. Note that since only one bull is being selected, it is possible to have a larger selection differential for the bull than for the heifers. This should be typical in any type of selection program, since the breeder will almost always save more female replacements than males. The progress from selection is computed by multiplying the

Table 3.1   Heritability Estimates for Beef, Swine and Sheep.

BEEF		SWINE	
Trait	**Heritability Estimates**	**Trait**	**Heritability Estimates**
Birth Weight	.40	Litter Size (weaned)	.12
Weaning Weight	.25	Weaning Weight (3 weeks)	.15
Yearling Weight	.40	Number of Nipples	.25
Feedlot Gain	.45	Age at 220 lb.	.30
Efficiency of Gain	.40	Length at 220 lb.	.50
Fat Thickness	.45	Backfat Thickness at 220 lb.	.45
Ribeye Area	.70	Percentage Carcass Muscle	.50

SHEEP	
Trait	Heritability Estimates
Number Born	.13
Weaning Weight (90 days)	.30
Yearling Weight	.40
Post-Weaning Daily Gain	.40
Efficiency of Gain	.22
Fleece Weight	.40
Milking Ability	.25
Fat Thickness	.25
Ribeye Area	.45

Table 3.2   Selection System.

	Heifers and Bulls	**Bulls Only**
Average Daily Gain (ADG) of Herd	2.00	2.00
ADG of Selected Heifers	2.40	2.00
Selection Differential (SD) for Selected Heifers	.40	.00
ADG of Selected Bull	3.00	3.00
SD for Selected Bull	1.00	1.00
Average SD	.70	.50
Heritability Estimate (HE) for ADG	.45	.45
Progress from Selection (HE × D)	.32	.22
Predicted ADG of Offspring	2.32	2.22

average selection differential by the heritability estimate for ADG. Adding the progress from selection to the herd average gives the predicted ADG of the offspring from the selected replacements. Note the difference in progress from selection when selection pressure for ADG is applied only in the selection of the bull. This should illustrate the importance of not only using performance tested bulls, boars, or rams, but also applying some performance criteria to the selection of replacement females.

Generation Interval

Naturally, little progress is made each year because a complete annual turnover of the breeding herd is not practical. To calculate the annual progress from selection, divide the calculated progress from selection by the *generation interval*. The generation interval equals the average age of the parents in the herd. The shorter the generation interval, the more rapid the improvement through selection. In beef cattle herds, the average generation interval is a relatively long 4 to 5 years compared to only approximately 2 years in swine.

OTHER FACTORS AFFECTING SELECTION PROGRESS

Number of Traits Selected

The number of traits being selected in a breeding program also affects the rate of progress from selection. As the number of traits included in a selection program increases, the progress made in any one trait decreases.

Genetic Correlation Between Traits

The genetic correlation between traits also influences selection progress. For example, the external fat on an animal is highly correlated to carcass quality grade. Thus, selecting for low external fat and high carcass quality grade would be essentially selecting in opposite directions and little progress would be made in either trait. By contrast, selecting for low external fat and increased efficiency of gain would allow for greater progress from selection, since these traits are positively correlated.

Accuracy of Records

The selected traits must also be measurable, and the measurements must be accurate. Many traits, such as breed character and masculinity, are not measurable and are difficult to improve through selection. The more objective traits, such as weaning weight and rate of gain, are easily measured and more usable in a selection program. As with any records, the more accurate the information, the more successful the program. For example, records of litter size and number of lambs born are more easily and accurately measured than records of feed efficiency.

Selection Systems

There are three basic types of selection systems. *Tandem selection* involves selecting for only one trait while disregarding all others. This is the simplest selection system, and rapid progress can be made in improving the selected trait. However, profitable livestock production involves many areas, and no one trait is a good indication of overall production.

Independent culling levels are widely used in the livestock industry and involve the establishment of levels of achievement for each trait included in the selection program. To be selected as a replacement, an individual has to surpass all of the established performance standards. This system allows for the inclusion of more than one trait into the selection program. The major disadvantage of this system is that an outstanding performance in one trait cannot overcome a slightly sub-standard performance in another trait.

The third system for selecting replacements is called the *selection index*. The index allows the producer to place added emphasis on the more economically important traits, but still maintain some selection pressure on the traits less important to his program. The following is an example of how a selection index might be used in selecting a boar.

$$\text{Index} = 250 + (\text{litter size} \times 10) + (\text{ADG} \times 50) - (\text{backfat} \times 40)$$

Since larger litters and higher ADG are advantages to the boar, they are added to the index; and because increased backfat is a disadvantage to the boar, it is subtracted from the selection index. From a performance standpoint, the boar with the highest index would be the most desirable.

The amount of emphasis a trait receives is determined by the variation in the trait as well as the regression coefficient (constant by which the trait is multiplied) as illustrated by the following selection index.

$$\text{Index} = (\text{Yearling Weight} \times 1) + (\text{ADG} \times 10)$$

The emphasis on yearling weight is much greater than the emphasis on ADG. This is because yearling weights will sometimes vary 300 to 400 lb., whereas ADG will usually vary only 1 to 2 lb. per day. Thus, even though the regression coefficient is greater for ADG, it is not large enough to overcome the difference in trait variation.

Any one or any combination of these types of selection systems can be used successfully in improving a given livestock production program. Typically, a producer may establish independent culling levels for one or two especially critical traits, then use a selection index to rank the individuals that surpass the culling levels on the other important traits. However, no one system is the best selection program for all situations. Thus, the producer must be able to recognize those traits that are economically important to his particular livestock enterprise, have a general estimate of the heritability for these traits, and then adapt his breeding program to most efficiently select for those traits.

Supplemental Aids in Livestock Selection

4

Visual evaluation has long been used as the method for appraising an animal's breeding or market value. Proficient visual evaluation requires the ability to make accurate and complete observations of an animal's traits and characteristics and to compare these qualities against an ideal. The stockman must then be able to use these observations and comparisons to make the important decisions of selecting livestock for the breeding or feeding program. These are vital decisions in developing a successful livestock program and require a high level of accuracy and competency. While many individuals are highly skilled at visual evaluation, the visual observations are subjective measures, and this subjectivity can possibly lead to error and inconsistency in the selection system. Thus, the stockman should consider the use of some of the following aids as supplements to visual appraisal in making final selection decisions. It must be recognized that these aids should be used as supplements to, and not replacements for, visual evaluation.

Aids in Determining Growth

Weight

Livestock weights will be important as long as livestock and meat products are marketed on a per pound basis. While many producers become proficient at estimating weights, scales are a valuable tool for the livestock enterprise. They increase the accuracy and completeness of weight information in the selection program. Therefore, the producer should consider obtaining a small, portable set of scales for measuring birth weights and a larger set of scales for measuring weaning, yearling, market and mature weights. The importance of measuring weights at these specific times will be discussed in subsequent sections.

Frame Size

Although weight is a very important factor in the selection and production of livestock, it can be misleading because it fails to indicate the composition of the animal. In other words, some animals may be heavy simply because they are fat. Frame size, on the other hand, is an indirect indicator of composition, since larger framed animals are leaner at a given weight. Therefore, when used together, weight and frame size indicate both the growability and the relative composition of the animal. Even though frame size is important in all species of livestock, measurement of frame size is most common in beef cattle. Thus, the remainder of the discussion will concentrate on aids for determining frame size in beef cattle, although the principles would be applicable to other species as well.

1. *Body Type Score.* A subjective system of measuring frame size was developed at the University of Wisconsin to represent the range in body types of cattle involved in their body type research projects. The outlines in Figure 4.1 represent the seven body type scores currently being used in most performance testing programs.

Body type 1 cattle are the smallest framed and earliest maturing cattle. Body type 7 represents large framed and late maturing cattle. Due to the incorporation of extremely large exotic breeds and dairy breeds into the United States beef cattle population, body type scores 8 and 9 are necessary to accurately categorize these larger framed cattle. Presently, most British breed cattle will be body types 2 through 7, and most of the exotic or continental European breeds of cattle will be body types 4 through 9. Body type scores and their relationship to final market weights of steers and heifers will be discussed in Section 17.

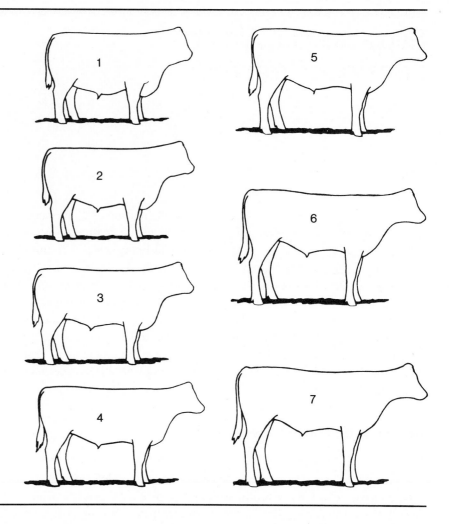

Figure 4.1. Outlines representing the body types of cattle fed in the Wisconsin body-type studies.

While the determination of the body type score system is efficient from a time and labor standpoint, the subjectivity of the system does allow for error. It is difficult to standardize the scoring system from one evaluator to another, and it is difficult for the same person to be consistent in scoring cattle between locations. Also, certain color patterns and depth versus length relationships create optical illusions which lead to human scoring errors.

2. *Linear Measurements*. Linear measurements are more objective and repeatable than body type scores and other subjective evaluations. Linear measurements provide a more consistent method for comparing cattle at different locations and between herds. However, as with other performance measurements, they are used most effectively on a within herd basis. However, there are disadvantages. The time and labor required to take linear measurements may limit their use in large herds.

Several linear measurements are popular among cattle and sheep breeders. Height, measured at either the withers (shoulder) or over the hooks (hip), is the most accurate and repeatable measure of frame. Figure 4.2 shows the proper method for measuring height at the hip. The calf should be standing with its head at a normal height and its legs positioned squarely in a near-normal stance. The calf should be restrained to prevent as much movement as possible. The surface under the calf should be hard and level. Since it is difficult to define the skeletal reference points for the measurements, it is best for *one* individual to take all of the cattle measurements in the group being compared. Height at the hip is the most common measurement of height in beef cattle. Tables 11.1 and 11.2 (Section 11) show the Beef Improvement Federation recommendations for relating hip height, measured from the ground to the top of the hook bone, to frame scores for bulls and heifers. Sheep producers more commonly record shoulder height which is measured from the ground to the highest point of the withers. Body length, measured from the point of the shoulder to the pin bone, is also an indicator of an animal's skeletal size. Heart girth circumference is measured by

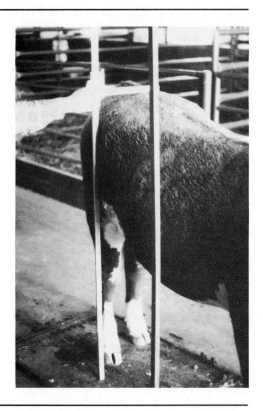

Figure 4.2. Illustration showing the proper method for measuring hip height on cattle.

encircling a tape around the girth of the animal posterior to the shoulder at about the fourth or fifth rib. Heart girth circumference is an indicator of the chest capacity of the animal and can also be used to estimate the animal's weight if scales are not available. Measurements of body length and heart girth circumference are less repeatable than height measurements, and they are more likely to be influenced by the amount of fat and fill.

Performance Testing

The important performance traits for each species will be discussed in subsequent sections. However, it is appropriate at this time to consider the advantages and disadvantages of performance testing and the use of performance records in a selection program. In developing a performance testing program, the producer should remember that the purpose of a testing program is to locate the highest producing females and males within the herd or flock. One should also realize that no performance testing program contains all of the answers to accurate livestock selection. A breeder must use a combination of visual appraisal and performance data to develop a complete selection program. Probably the biggest advantage of performance testing is that it forces the producer to keep records on the herd or flock. On too many occasions when records are not kept, a poor producing, or sometimes nonproducing, animal may be kept in the breeding program simply because of style or type, when a quick look at the records of performance would certainly indicate that it should be culled. On the other hand, there are times when economics may dictate keeping an animal with superior type, but lower production, because his or her offspring may bring a premium due to their superior type. Thus, it is evident that using visual selection and performance selection together is superior to either system used by itself.

Comparing livestock from performance data is most effective and accurate when the livestock have been raised in the same or similar environments. It should be recalled from Section 3 that most of the important traits in a selection program have heritability estimates of .10 to .50. Thus, 50% to 90% of the variation in a trait is due to the animal's environment. Therefore, we should refrain from turning performance testing into a competition between producers and keep the testing programs at their most effective level on a within herd or flock basis for culling females and selecting replacements.

Central Test Stations

In many areas, central testing stations are available to evaluate the performance traits of potential sires from different herds or flocks tested under uniform conditions. For the most part, these stations provide performance information on the developing sire prospect. One should remember that these tests do not estimate genetic differences in the herds, but only in the individual representatives from the different herds. A few of the available tests are for progeny of the potential sires. While these progeny tests are certainly more accurate in determining genetic differences between potential sires, they are more costly, require more animals, and necessitate a good deal of time to adequately prove a sire.

While central test stations do help minimize the effects of various feeding and management systems, there are still some important considerations a buyer should take into account before purchasing from a test station. One consideration is that the performance, while on test, is greatly influenced by the handling and management of the animal prior to the start of the test. Therefore, it is necessary that an adequate pre-test or adjustment period is conducted prior to the actual test to minimize these pre-test differences. The producer should also determine that the performance traits being measured are the ones economically important to his own production system. Finally, a producer should try to find a test station that has nutritional and environmental conditions similar to his production system. Remember, the high-performing bull, boar, or ram under one set of conditions may not be the high-producing sire in a completely different management or environmental situation.

Contemporary Index or Ratio

A popular and relatively simple method of comparing animals in the same herd or contemporary group is by the *index,* or *ratio method.* The index is calculated as follows:

$$\text{Index} = \frac{\text{Individual Performance Trait}}{\text{Herd Average for the Trait}} \times 100$$

In the following example, the herd average for adjusted weaning weight is 500 lb., and three calves in the herd (A, B, C) had adjusted weaning weights of 450 lb., 500 lb., and 600 lb., respectively. By examining the weaning weight ratios

$$\text{Index of calf A} = \frac{450 \text{ lb.}}{500 \text{ lb.}} \times 100 = 90$$

$$\text{Index of calf B} = \frac{500 \text{ lb.}}{500 \text{ lb.}} \times 100 = 100$$

$$\text{Index of calf C} = \frac{600 \text{ lb.}}{500 \text{ lb.}} \times 100 = 120$$

of the calves, the producer can readily see that calf B had performed equally with the herd average, while calf A had performed 10% below the herd average, and calf C 20% above the herd average. An index is especially useful when comparing large numbers of contemporaries.

Many livestockmen feel that performance differences between herds or flocks are due mainly to environment and management differences. Therefore, contemporary index or ratio systems should be used when comparing animals from different herds or flocks. For example, ram A weighed 290 lb. at one year of age and was from a flock with an average yearling weight of 250 lb., while ram B weighed 300 lb. at one year of age with a flock average of 275 lb. Upon examining the weights, one would conclude ram B was the superior ram for yearling weight (300 lb. vs. 290 lb.). However, if a ratio system was used to minimize the influence of environmental factors, it would then appear that ram A was superior, since he indexed at 16% above the average, while ram B indexed only 9% above average in their respective flocks.

$$\text{Ram A} = \frac{290 \text{ lb.}}{250 \text{ lb.}} \times 100 = 116$$

$$\text{Ram B} = \frac{300 \text{ lb.}}{275 \text{ lb.}} \times 100 = 109$$

Aids in Determining Body Composition

Ultrasonic Instruments (Sonoray)

Ultrasonic instruments are used to estimate backfat thickness and longissimus muscle area in an animal, without sacrificing the animal. Ultrasonic measurements are most commonly used to estimate the carcass characteristics of breeding animals. Ultrasonic instruments give relatively accurate measurements of backfat and longissimus muscle area of potential seedstock, and they help eliminate the costly testing of littermates and half-sibs.

While there are many different types of ultrasonic instruments on the market, they operate on the principle of sound waves creating an echo when they hit a dense surface. In livestock, the dense surfaces are the skin, the membrane between fat layers, the membrane between fat and muscle, and the muscle and bone. For example, with one type of ultrasonic device, the scanoprobe, an ultrasonic or high frequency sound is directed into the animal's skin or hide. Some of the sound is reflected when it hits each dense surface but the rest of the sound continues on through to the other dense surfaces. The scanoprobe translates these echoes into light signals on a calibrated ruler. Hence, the fat depth and loin eye depth can be read directly from the calibrated ruler. Since the loin eye is measured as square inches of loin eye area, a conversion factor of 2.54 is multiplied by the loin eye depth to calculate loin eye area. As one would expect, the scanoprobe is much more accurate for measuring backfat than for estimating loin eye area.

However, recent developments in ultrasonic technology have helped to overcome the drawbacks and insufficiencies of the earlier ultrasonic instruments. Real-time ultrasound equipment can provide a cross-sectional image of the longissimus muscle. With real-time ultrasound, both backfat thickness and loin eye area can be accurately measured in a live animal. The application of real-time ultrasound is illustrated in Figure 4.3A on a lamb and on a pork carcass in figure 4.3B. The image of the ribeye muscle and fat thickness of a pork carcass is shown on the screen in Figure 4.3C. The actual measurements of ribeye area and fat thickness are calculated from the image on the screen by applying a conversion factor determined during calibration of the instrument before measurements are taken. Though not as accurate, some scientists are using this technology to predict marbling or intramuscular fat in live animals and unribbed carcasses. Further development of this technology will enhance the accuracy and efficiency of marketing both slaughter animals and carcasses.

Unfortunately, the cost of the equipment prohibits most producers from purchasing ultrasonic instruments. In some states ultrasonic equipment is available through the Cooperative Extension Service. Several breed associations and commercial organizations also offer sonoray services for a nominal fee.

Backfat Probe, Swine

The steel backfat probe was one of the first mechanical aids to be developed and used for livestock selection. While the probe can be used in any species of livestock, it is most commonly used to determine the average backfat thickness of swine. Backfat measurements are taken at three probe sites and then averaged. The probe sites are: (1) parallel to the midpoint of the front foot; (2) just in front of the hind foot; and (3) mid-way between these two points (Figure 4.4). These locations correspond to the first rib, last rib, and the last lumbar vertebra which are the sites of the carcass backfat measurements. A small incision in the skin is made at a point approximately 2 inches laterally from the dorsal midline at each probe site (Figure 4.5). The steel probe is inserted into each incision and the ruler is read when the steel probe touches the longissimus (loin eye) muscle (Figure 4.6). Care must be taken to ensure that the probe has penetrated the trapezius muscle over the shoulder (first rib site only) and is in contact with the longissimus muscle. The average backfat measurement should then be adjusted to a 230 lb. live weight basis (Section 7).

Backfat Probe, Cattle

The use of a backfat probe to measure fat thickness in beef cattle is becoming increasingly popular and important. Many of the central bull testing stations are now including backfat probe measurements as a part of their final production test report. The use of this tool also has on-farm application in the selection of replacement breeding stock.

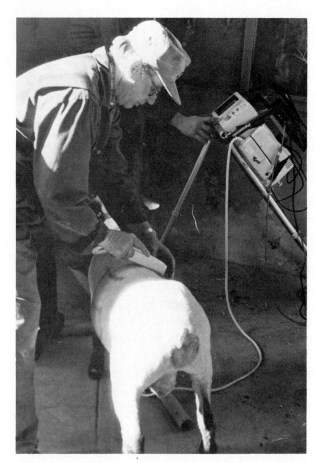

A

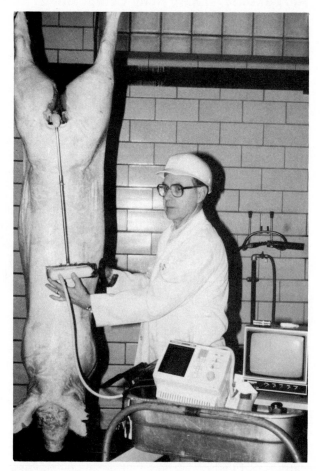

B

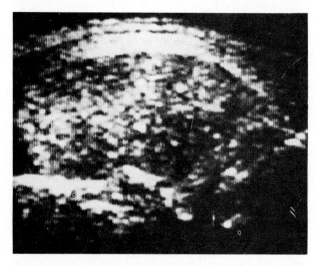

Figure 4.3. An illustration showing the application of real time ultrasound to a lamb (A) and a pork carcass (B). An image of loin eye muscle and backfat of a hog is shown on the screen in C. The top layer on the screen in C represents the skin of the hog and below it are the several layers of backfat. The outline of the eye muscle is visible below the backfat on the screen.

C

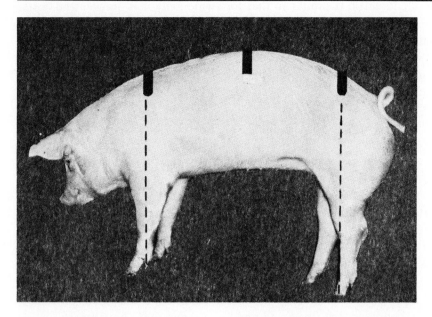

Figure 4.4. Illustration showing the location of probe sites for determining average backfat on a live hog as viewed from the side.

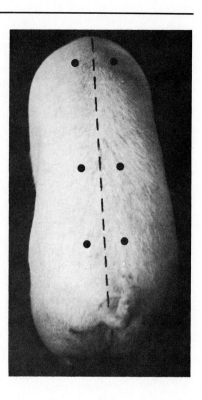

Figure 4.5. Illustration showing the location of probe sites on both the right and left side approximately 2 in. laterally fron the dorsal midline (dotted line) for determining average backfat thickness on a live hog as viewed from the rear.

Figure 4.6. Illustration showing the backfat thickness measured with a probe on a carcass at the 10th rib approximately 2 in. from the midline indicated by P. The backfat thickness measurement at the 10th rib is shown to the right of the probe site.

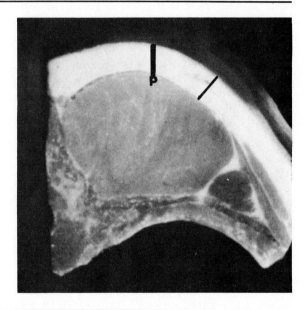

The procedure for using the probe in cattle is similar to that for swine, only it is quicker and easier because only one measurement is taken per animal. The location for this measurement is approximately 2 inches on either side of the dorsal midline, immediately above the 12th rib. This location is shown in Section 9 in Figure 9.1. An incision is made at this site with a specialized trocar, and the probe is inserted until it touches the lean of the longissimus muscle and the fat depth is read. Care must be taken not to puncture this muscle when inserting the probe.

Body Condition Scores

A simplified approach to categorizing beef cattle by their body condition has been established. This system uses visual evaluation of fat depots and external palpation (handling) of the animal to determine body condition. This system is relatively simple and easy to use. While it does not provide an exact measurement of fat or an estimate of body composition, it is useful as a management tool for grouping cows, heifers, or steers by their approximate body condition. Because body condition of cows at various times in the reproduction cycle affects reproductive efficiency, this system is most commonly used in beef cows. Illustration of body condition scores 2, 4, 6, and 8 are shown in Figure 12.16. The following are the descriptions for the nine body condition scores (BCS) in this system.

BCS 1—EMACIATED—Cow is extremely emaciated with no detectable fat over spinous processes, transverse processes, hip bones, or ribs. Tail-head and ribs project quite prominently.

BCS 2—POOR—Cow still appears somewhat emaciated but tail-head and ribs are less prominent. Individual spinous processes are still rather sharp to the touch but some tissue cover exists along spine.

BCS 3—THIN—Ribs are still individually identifiable but not quite as sharp to the touch. There is obvious palpable fat along spine and over tail-head with some tissue cover over dorsal portion of ribs.

BCS 4—BORDERLINE—Individual ribs are no longer visually obvious. The spinous processes can be identified individually on palpation but feel rounded rather than sharp. Some fat cover over ribs, transverse processes, and hip bones.

BCS 5—MODERATE—Ribs no longer visible, hooks, pin bones, and point of shoulder are less prominent. Little evidence of fat in the brisket and around the tailhead. Upon palpation, fat cover over ribs feels spongy and areas on either side of tail-head now have palpable fat cover.

BCS 6—HIGH MODERATE—Firm pressure now needs to be applied to feel spinous processes. A high degree of fat cover is palpable over ribs and around tail-head.

BCS 7—GOOD—Cow appears fleshy and obviously carries considerable fat. Very spongy fat cover over ribs and over and around tail-head. In fact "rounds" or "pones" beginning to be obvious. Some fat around vulva and in crotch.

BCS 8—FAT—Cow very fleshy and over conditioned. Spinous processes almost impossible to palpate. Cow has large fat deposits over ribs, around tail-head, and below vulva. "Rounds" or "pones" are obvious.

BCS 9—EXTREMELY FAT—Cow obviously extremely wasty and patchy and looks blocky. Tail head and hips buried in fatty tissue and "rounds" or "pones" of fat are protruding. Bone structure no longer visable and barely palpable. Animal's mobility may even be impaired by large fatty deposits.

Live Hog Evaluation, Grading, and Pricing

Live market hog evaluation is essentially an estimation of important carcass characteristics. The specific characteristics evaluated are those that provide an indication of amount of fat and/or muscle which, in turn, determines carcass value. Live value can then easily be calculated from estimated carcass value. A definition, brief description, ranges, and the mechanics used in estimating each carcass characteristic are presented in this section. The student should familiarize him or herself with the normal ranges and the mechanics involved for evaluation of each characteristic.

Evaluation

Weight

Definition: Live weight is the actual weight of the hog at the time of evaluation or slaughter. Carcass weight may be either hot (dressed carcass just prior to chilling) or chilled (after carcass chilling) weight. Both are used in the industry. Hot carcass weight can be calculated by multiplying chilled carcass weight by 101.5%. If hot carcass weight is available and chilled carcass weight is needed, multiply hot carcass weight by 98.5%.

Live weight

Extreme Range:	180–300 lb.
Normal Range:	190–270 lb.
Average:	245 lb.

The information given below for each characteristic is most applicable to hogs that are approximately 190 to 265 lb. live weight.

Dressing Percentage

Definition: (Chilled carcass weight ÷ live weight) × 100.

Extreme Range:	65–80%
Normal Range:	68–77%
Average:	72%

The major factors affecting dressing percentage of hogs in order of their relative importance are: (1) amount of fill (contents of the stomach and intestines); (2) degree of muscling (heavy muscled vs. light muscled hogs); and (3) degree of fatness. Fill has the greatest effect on dressing percentage; and as fill increases, dressing percentage decreases. Thus, hogs that are held off feed for 12 to 24 hours before slaughter have less fill and a correspondingly higher dressing percentage than hogs that are fed up to the time of slaughter.

For hogs with the same fill, heavily muscled hogs will dress 2 to 3% more than those that are light muscled. Fatness of the hog has little affect on dressing percentage. Only when very fat hogs are compared to lean hogs is dressing percentage higher in the fat hogs, but generally the difference is less than 1%. Dressing percentage is lowest in young, light weight hogs and increases as they increase in age and weight.

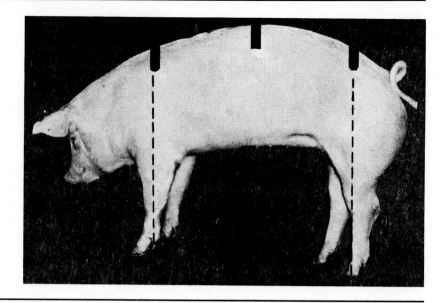

Figure 5.1 Location of sites for estimation or probe of average backfat thickness on the live hog corresponding to the first rib, last rib and last lumbar vertebra on the carcass.

As hogs increase in age and weight, viscera becomes a progressively smaller proportion of the body and dressing percentage increases. Dressing percentage is receiving increasingly less emphasis by most packer buyers of hogs. However, it will be used in the procedures described in this manual to determine the live price of hogs.

Backfat Thickness

Definition: Thickness of fat, including skin, dorsal to the surface of the loin eye muscle (live hog probe) or dorsal to the surface of the vertebrae (carcass measurement). It may be a single measurement (e.g., last rib) or an average of three measurements taken opposite the first rib, last rib, and last lumbar vertebra as shown in Figure 5.1.

Extreme Range:	.5–2.5 in.
Normal Range:	.7–1.8 in.
Average:	1.3 in.

Figure 5.1 shows where backfat thickness is measured on the live hog. The three locations are: (1) parallel to the mid longitudinal axis of the front foot; (2) just in front of the hind foot; and (3) midway between these two points as shown in Figure 5.1. These three locations on the live hog correspond approximately to the first rib, last rib, and last lumbar locations of the carcass. A single backfat measurement or estimate opposite the last rib is used to determine pork carcass grade.

Backfat thickness is a valuable tool for the improvement of hogs. It is easy to measure, as well as having a high inverse relationship to total carcass muscling. The live probe is slightly more highly correlated with lean cut percentage than the carcass backfat measurement.

10th Rib Backfat Thickness

Definition: Depth (including skin) of a single backfat measurement at the 10th rib, 3/4 the lateral length of the eye muscle measured perpendicular to the skin surface as shown in Figure 5.2.

Ranges: Essentially the same as for the average of three backfat measurements.

Measurement of backfat at the 10th rib is more accurate than average or last rib backfat thickness measurements because of the flat smooth surface of the fat where the 10th rib measurement is taken. The demarcation of the fat layer adjacent to the eye muscle is more well defined than for backfat measurements taken along the dorsal midline, particularly in unevenly split carcasses.

Figure 5.2. A. The dark line on the back indicates the location of the 10th rib on a live hog. **B.** Cross section of the longissimus muscle showing the procedure for backfat thickness measurement at the 10th rib.

A

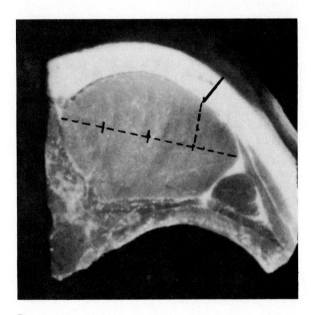

B

Tenth rib backfat thickness is slightly more highly related to lean cut or ham and loin percentages than average backfat thickness. It is used to calculate percentage carcass muscle, but it necessitates the carcass being "ribbed" or the loin being "cut" at the 10th rib to expose the eye muscle. This procedure is not widely used except for carcass shows or other evaluation purposes since eye muscles are normally not exposed in commercial practice because of devaluation of the wholesale loin and belly.

Average backfat thickness may be used to estimate 10th rib backfat during live hog evaluation. The adjustments of average backfat to estimate 10th rib backfat for carcasses differing in muscling and average backfat are shown in Table 5.1. Loin eye area is a good indicator of muscling; thus, the estimates of loin eye area and average backfat are used to adjust average backfat to 10th rib backfat. The appropriate adjustments shown in Table 5.1 are added to or subtracted from estimated average backfat. An example of how the 10th rib estimate is obtained follows. Assume you estimated 1.5 in. of average backfat and a loin eye area of 4.5 in.². The adjustment for this hog is −.1 (Table 5.1). Therefore, the estimated 10th rib backfat measurement for this hog is 1.4 in. The fat thickness measurement at the last rib generally is about

Table 5.1   Adjustments of Average Backfat Estimates to Estimate 10th Rib Backfat.

Average Backfat Thickness	Muscling (evaluated as loin eye area)		
	Light ≤ 3.9 in.²	Average 4.0-4.9 in.²	Heavy ≥ 5.0 in.²
Estimate	Adjustment		
≤ 1.1 in.	− .1 in.	− .2 in.	− .3 in.
1.2-1.6 in.	− .1 in.	− .1 in.	− .2 in.
≥ 1.7 in.	+ .2 in.	+ .1 in.	+ .1 in.

.2 inch less than average backfat thickness when the average measurement is 1.0 inch or less. For average backfat thicknesses of 1.1 inches or more, fat thickness at the 10th rib will be about .3 inch less than the average of the 3 measurements.

Length

Definition: Measured from the cranial edge of the first rib to the cranial edge of the aitch bone (pubic symphysis) on the hanging carcass.

Extreme Range:	26–36 in.
Normal Range:	28–34 in.
Average:	31.0 in. (varies by breed and type)

On live hogs, length is estimated from the midpoint of the longitudinal axis of the front foot to the midpoint of the longitudinal axis of the hind foot when the hog is standing with all four feet placed squarely under it. These two reference points approximate the first rib and cranial edge of the aitch bone on a live hog. Because of the normal arch to the back when the hog is standing squarely on all four feet, length from the reference point on the front foot to the reference point on the hind foot will be 4 to 6 in. less than the carcass length. Thus, judgment is needed to assess the amount of deviation from linearity due to arch of back. The reference points for estimating length on the live hog as well as arch of back are shown in Figure 5.3.

Loin Eye Area

Definition: Area of the longissimus muscle measured at the 10th rib.

Extreme Range:	3.0–8.5 in.²
Normal Range:	3.5–7.0 in.²
Average:	4.8 in.²

Loin eye area is quite highly related to total carcass muscling in hogs. Loin eye area is easily obtained and accurately measured in the carcass. On the live hog, it can be measured ultrasonically with a fair degree of accuracy. In "eyeball" estimation, width and depth of loin are used to evaluate the loin eye size because area is largely determined by these two dimensions. Ham muscling is also frequently used to estimate loin eye area because there is a relatively good correlation between muscling in one part of the carcass and another. Ham muscling is easier to evaluate than loin muscle in live hogs and unribbed pork carcasses. It should also be emphasized that muscling and backfat are inversely related and that thickness, fullness, and plumpness due to fat must be taken into account when estimating muscling or loin eye area. The location of the 10th rib is shown on the live hog in Figure 5.2. The loin eye area is shown in Figure 5.4.

Figure 5.3. Reference point for length estimation on the live hog; _____ length disregarding arch of back; - - - length including arch of back.

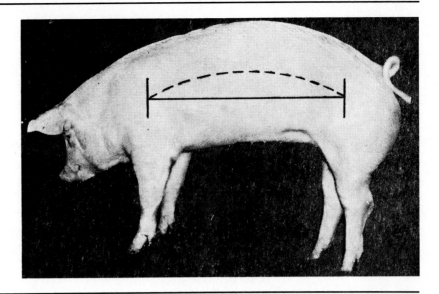

Figure 5.4. An illustration showing loin eye area. The eye (longissimus) muscle is darkened around its perimeter to distinguish it from adjacent muscles.

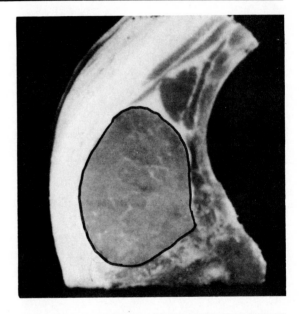

Cutability

The following four estimates of carcass cutability are used to varying degrees in the pork industry to evaluate grade and/or value. The four estimates of pork carcass cutability include: (1) percentage carcass muscle; (2) percentage lean cuts; (3) percentage ham and loin; and (4) percentage ham. The current live hog and pork carcass grade standards and some live hog buying procedures are based on estimated yield of lean cuts. Ham and loin percentage or percentage ham are used in carcass evaluation programs and to some extent in hog buying procedures. Estimation of percentage carcass muscle is gaining in acceptance for pork carcass evaluation programs and in live hog buying procedures.

Percentage Carcass Muscle

Definition: (Weight of total muscle in the carcass including 10% intramuscular fat ÷ hot carcass weight) × 100.

Extreme Range: 42–68%
Normal Range: 45–64%
Average: 52%

The ultimate objective of the pork industry is the production of maximum quantity of high quality muscle per unit of energy input. The other estimations of cutability are not accurate enough indicators of total carcass muscle to assess quantity of muscle because of cutting and trimming variation and amount of intermuscular fat that cannot be removed in normal cutting operations. Thus, a regression equation was developed to estimate carcass muscle percentage. This equation estimates the pounds of muscle containing 10% intramuscular fat (equivalent to about a "small" to "moderate" amount of marbling). The percentage muscle is then obtained by dividing the pounds of muscle by adjusted hot carcass weight and multiplying by 100.

Regression Equation

Pounds of muscle containing 10% fat = 10.5 + (.5 × adjusted hot carcass wt., in pounds)*
+ (2 × loin eye area, in square inches)
− 14.9 × 10th rib fat thickness, in tenths of inches)

$$\% \text{ Muscle} = \frac{\text{pounds of muscle}}{\text{adjusted hot carcass weight}} \times 100$$

*If only chilled carcass weight is available, it can be converted to hot carcass weight by dividing by .985 (most pork carcasses shrink about 1.5% during the chilling process). For skinned carcasses, adjust to a skin-on basis by dividing hot carcass weight by .94 (skin represents about 6% of the carcass). If the jowl(s) was (were) removed because of abscesses or if muscle, fat, and bone have been removed because of bruises or localized infections, the weight of the removed portion(s) should be accurately estimated and the hot carcass weight adjusted accordingly.

Percentage of Lean Cuts

Definition: (Weight of the 4 trimmed lean cuts ÷ chilled carcass weight) × 100. The lean cuts include the trimmed ham, loin, picnic shoulder, and Boston shoulder and are shown on the live hog in Figure 5.5.

Extreme Range: 50–68%
Normal Range: 54–66%
Average: 59%

Lean cut percentage is primarily influenced by fat and secondarily by muscling. In fact, fat has a *much* greater effect (3 to 4 fold greater) than muscling on percentage lean cuts.

Percentage of Ham and Loin

Definition: (Weight of the trimmed ham and loin ÷ chilled carcass weight) × 100. The ham and loin are shown on the live hog in Figure 5.5.

Extreme Range: 38–55%
Normal Range: 40–50%
Average: 45%

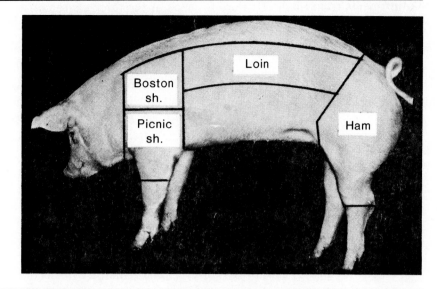

Figure 5.5. Illustration showing the location of the ham, loin, picnic shoulder and Boston shoulder on a live hog.

Like the lean cuts, fat has a much greater effect than musling on ham and loin percentages. Ham and loin percentage is frequently used instead of lean cuts as a basis of evaluation because (1) it entails less labor; (2) it involves less cutting and trimming error; and (3) it is composed of the two highest priced wholesale cuts of pork.

Percentage of Ham

Definition: (Weight of the skinned ham ÷ chilled carcass weight) × 100. The ham is shown on the live hog in Figure 5.5.

Extreme Range:	16–30%
Normal Range:	18–28%
Average:	24%

Like the lean cuts and ham and loin percentage, fat has a much greater effect on percentage ham than does muscling. Ham percentage has the same advantages listed above for ham and loin percentage. In fact, the ham is subject to the least trimming and cutting variation of the four lean cuts. In estimating lean cuts, ham and loin or ham percentage, muscling in each of the areas being evaluated should be appraised and trimness also taken into account because fat is highly inversely related to these cutout percentages.

Working Formula for Estimating Percentage Muscle

To simplify the above equation, a working formula is used in practical everyday situations because it requires less calculations and it is much faster to use. The working formula gives the results directly as percentage muscle without any further calculations. To use the working formula, begin with a base of 53% muscle which is adjusted up or down for the variation above or below the base value for either live weight or hot carcass weight, loin eye area, and 10th rib backfat thickness. The base of 53% muscle (containing 10% fat) is equivalent to a hog with:

Base
1. 240 lb. live wt. or 180 lb. hot carcass wt. (240 live wt. × .75, i.e., the dressing percentage)
2. 5.0 in.² loin eye area
3. 1.0 in. backfat, 3/4 lateral length of eye muscle at 10th rib

Adjustments from the base values for each of the three characteristics are made as described in the following three steps:

Step 1

Live weight—for every *25 lb.* increase or decrease from 240 lb. live weight, add or subtract .2% muscle to or from the base of 53% muscle, *or* hot carcass weight may be used instead of live weight if preferred. However, the working formula is usually used only for evaluating live hogs; the regression equation is used to determine percent muscle in pork carcasses because it is more accurate than the working formula.

Adjusted hot carcass weight—for every *10 lb.* increase or decrease from 180 lb. hot carcass weight, add or subtract .1% muscle to or from the base of 53% muscle.

Step 2

Loin eye area—for every *.1 in.^{2}* increase or decrease from 5.0 in.^{2} loin eye area, add or subtract .133% muscle to or from the % muscle after adjusting for weight in step 1.

Step 3

10th rib backfat thickness—for every *.1 in.* increase or decrease from 1.0 inch of 10th rib backfat thickness, add or subtract .8% of muscle to or from the percentage muscle in step 2.

From the above adjustments, it is readily apparent that 10th rib backfat thickness has the greatest effect on the percentage muscle. Live or hot carcass weight has the least effect and loin eye area is intermediate in its effect on percentage muscle in the carcass.

To describe the use of the working formula, the following two hogs are used as examples.

	Hog A	Hog B
Live wt., lb.	265	215
Loin eye area, in.^{2}	6.3	4.0
10th rib backfat thickness, in.	.8	1.4

Hog A:

This hog is 25 lb. heavier than the base of 240 lb. Since each 25 lb. is equivalent to .2% muscle, the total adjustment for live weight is .2% (1–25 lb. increment $\times$ .2%). The .2% adjustment is subtracted from the base of 53% muscle to give 52.8% after adjusting for live weight. Each .1 in.^{2} of loin eye from the base of 5.0 in.^{2} is multiplied by .133% muscle. Since hog A has 1.3 in.^{2} more than the base, the adjustment is 1.7% muscle (13−.1 in.^{2} increments $\times$ .133%). The 1.7% adjustment is added to the 52.8% (% muscle after adjusting it for live weight) to give 54.5% muscle after adjusting for live weight and loin eye area. Each .1 in. of 10th rib backfat thickness deviation from the base of 1 in. is multiplied by .8% muscle. Since hog A has .2 in. less backfat than the base, the adjustment is 1.6% muscle (2−.1 in. increments $\times$ .8%). The 1.6% adjustment is added to 54.5% (% muscle after adjusting for live weight and loin eye area) to give 56.1% muscle in hog A after all adjustments have been made. If the regression equation was used instead of the working formula, the percentage muscle would be 55.8%.

Hog B:

This hog weighs 25 lb. less than the base of 240 lb. live weight, thus the base percent muscle is adjusted by .2% muscle (1–25 lb. increment $\times$ .2%) to give 53.2% muscle after adjusting for live weight. The loin eye area adjustment for hog B is 1.3% muscle (10–.1 in.^{2} increments $\times$ .133%) when subtracted from 53.2% = 51.9% muscle after adjusting for live weight and loin eye area. The adjustment for 10th rib backfat is 3.2% (4–.1 in. increments $\times$ .8%) which is subtracted from 51.9% (% muscle after live weight and loin eye area adjustment) to give 48.7% muscle after all adjustments have been made. If the regression equation was used instead of the working formula, the percentage muscle would be 48.6%.

From the two examples given above, the percentage muscle in the carcass can be quite accurately estimated (within .3%) by the working formula. The working formula underestimates the percent muscle by about 2% for light weight pigs (around 200 lb. live weight) that have very low backfat ($\approx$.5 in.) and very large loin eye areas ($\approx$7 in.^{2}). On the other hand, the working formula overestimates the percent muscle by about 1% of medium weight pigs (220–250 lb. live weight) that are very fat ($\approx$2.0 in. backfat). Adjustments in the percent muscle obtained by the working formula should be adjusted accordingly. It is also apparent that weight, loin eye area, and 10th rib fat thickness are objective measurements that can be accurately and easily obtained; and they are highly related to cutability or percentage muscle. This information reflects value and is useful in determining live or carcass price.

Facts to Remember

1. The adjustment for live or hot carcass weight above the base weight of 240 lb. or 180 lb. is subtracted from the base percentage muscle, while adjustments for live or hot carcass weights below the base weight are added to the base percentage muscle.
2. Hot carcass weight is obtained by multiplying live weight by .75 (75% dressing percentage). Hot carcass weight is always used to calculate the percentage or pounds of muscle with the regression equation.
3. The adjustment for loin eye area above the base loin eye area of 5.0 in.^{2} is added to, and that below 5.0 in.^{2} is subtracted from the base percentage muscle. It is obvious that as loin eye area increases so does total carcass muscle, hence the reason for adding or subtracting the adjustment.
4. The adjustment for 10th rib backfat thickness is added to the base percentage muscle when the measurement is below the base of 1.0 in. of 10th rib backfat and subtracted when the measurement exceeds the base of 1.0 in. of backfat. Again this reflects the fact that fat and muscle are inversely related.
5. The pounds of muscle obtained by using the regression equation can be converted to percent muscle for the respective carcass by dividing by its hot carcass weight. However, for comparative purposes the percent muscle on all carcasses may be adjusted to a 160 lb. hot carcass weight basis, which provides a more appropriate basis for comparison among carcasses. Thus, when comparison of carcasses is necessary, the pounds of muscle from the regression equation is divided by the 160 lb. hot carcass weight. However, it should be emphasized that this comparison on a weight constant basis is only useful in classroom evaluation programs and quality pork contests. Packers must merchandize each carcass or its primal cuts on the basis of the actual weight, and since prices of pork primal cuts are based on weight, packers are primarily concerned with actual hot or chilled carcass weights. It should be obvious that the final calculation of percentage muscle (whether divided by actual carcass weight or all adjusted to a 160 lb. carcass weight basis) depends on the objectives of the carcass evaluation program.

A brief discussion of the procedure for estimating the lean pork (percentage muscle containing 10% fat) gain per day on test is presented in Section 7 with other evaluations of swine performance data.

Adjustments for Sex Differences

Usually gilts are leaner and more muscular than barrows of the same weight. These differences must be considered when both sexes are represented. Below is a summary of the average differences between gilts and barrows of the same weight (240 lb. average ± 20 lb.):

% Lean Cuts: Gilts 2 to 6.0% higher than barrows
% Ham and Loin: Gilts 2.0 to 5.0% higher than barrows
% Ham: Gilts 1.0 to 4.0% higher than barrows
% Muscle: Gilts 1.5 to 5.5% higher than barrows

Average Backfat, Last Rib Backfat or 10th Rib Fat Thickness: Gilts .1 to .2 in. less than barrows
Loin Eye Area: Gilts .3–.7 in.^{2} more than barrows
Length: Gilts .2–.5 in. longer than barrows

Live Hog Grading

Hogs are graded U.S. No. 1, U.S. No. 2, U.S. No. 3, U.S. No. 4 or U.S. Utility. The grades of slaughter hogs are intended to be directly related to the grades of the carcasses they produce. To accomplish this, the slaughter grades of live hogs are predicted on the same two general considerations that provide the basis for the grades of pork carcasses. These considerations are: (1) quality which includes characteristics of the lean, and firmness of fat, and (2) characteristics related to the combined carcass yield of the four lean cuts (ham, loin, picnic shoulder, and Boston shoulder).

Two general levels of quality are considered: (1) hogs with characteristics which indicate that the carcass will have acceptable belly thickness, lean quality, and acceptable firmness, and (2) hogs with characteristics which indicate that the carcass will have unacceptable belly thickness, lean quality, and/or firmness of fat. The bellies of carcasses with acceptable quality are at least slightly thick overall and are not less than 0.6 inches thick at any point. Carcasses with bellies less than 0.6 inches are too thin to be suitable for bacon production. Live hogs that weigh 215 lb. or more should not have bellies that are too thin. Since carcass indices of lean quality, which include marbling, color and firmness, are not directly evident in live hogs, other factors must be used to evaluate quality. Therefore, the amount and distribution of external finish and indications of firmness of fat and muscle are used as quality-indicating factors.

Hogs with characteristics which indicate unacceptable belly thickness or quality of lean are graded U.S. Utility. Also graded U.S. Utility are hogs with indications that their carcasses will have oily or less than slightly firm fat.

The grades of hogs are based almost entirely on the expected yield of the four lean cuts. The grade standards described in this manual are applicable to barrows and gilts and no distinction is made for class (sex). Hogs differ in yield of the four lean cuts because of differences in degrees of fatness, muscling, and thickness of muscling in relation to skeletal size. Fatness is assessed by estimating backfat thickness at the last rib as illustrated in Figure 5.1. Since last rib backfat thickness has been found to be a good indicator of lean cut yield, it—together with degree of muscling—is used to determine the grades. Backfat thickness is most highly related to yield of lean cuts, and degree of muscling accounts for a much lower relationship than does backfat. The degrees of muscling in the grade standards ranked from the heaviest muscled to the lightest muscled hog are: (1) thick; (2) average, and (3) thin. Hogs representative of each of the three degrees of muscling are shown in Figure 5.6. The differences in muscling are most obvious in the ham. This portion of the hog receives the most emphasis in evaluating muscling, but the loin and shoulder should also be evaluated to determine the degree of muscling. It is necessary to take into account how much the thickness and plumpness of these regions of the hog are influenced by fat.

In hogs with acceptable quality and with acceptable belly thickness, the preliminary grade is determined from the estimate of backfat thickness as shown in Table 5.2.

Table 5.2   Preliminary Grade Based on Backfat Thickness at the Last Rib.

Backfat Thickness Range	Preliminary Grade
1.00 inch or less	U.S. No. 1
1.00 to 1.24 inches	U.S. No. 2
1.25 to 1.49 inches	U.S. No. 3
1.50 inches & over*	U.S. No. 4

*Carcasses with last rib backfat thickness of 1.75 inches or over cannot be graded U.S. No. 3 even with thick muscling.

Final live hog grade is determined by adjusting for muscling as shown in Figure 5.7. In hogs with average muscling the final grade is the same as the preliminary grade as shown on Figure 5.7. Hogs with thin muscling will be graded one grade lower than indicated by their preliminary grade, based on thickness of backfat over the last rib. Hogs with thick muscling will be graded one grade higher than indicated by their preliminary grade, based on backfat thickness over the last rib, except hogs with 1.75 inches or greater backfat thickness over the last rib must remain in the U.S. No. 4 grade. Hogs with thin muscling cannot be graded U.S. No. 1. The determination of final grade from Figure 5.7 is illustrated by the following two example hogs: the information for these two hogs is presented on the bottom of page 35.

Figure 5.6. An illustration showing slaughter hogs representative of the three degrees of muscling.

Thick

Average

Thin

	Hog C	Hog D
Last rib backfat thickness, in.	1.1	1.4
Muscling score	Thick	Thin
Carcass quality	Acceptable	Acceptable

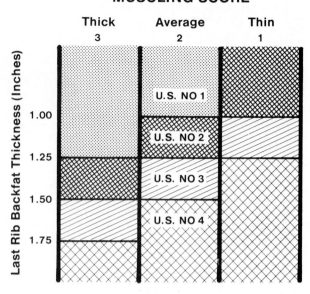

Figure 5.7. Hog grading chart showing the relationship of last rib backfat thickness, and degree of muscling.

MUSCLING SCORE

| Thick 3 | Average 2 | Thin 1 |

Last Rib Backfat Thickness (Inches)

U.S. NO 1

U.S. NO 2

U.S. NO 3

U.S. NO 4

1.00

1.25

1.50

1.75

The preliminary grade for hog C is U.S. No. 2 (Table 5.2). However, because it has thick muscling it is graded U.S. No. 1, as can be seen from Figure 5.7. The preliminary grade for hog D is U.S. No. 3 (Table 5.2). Because hog D has thin muscling along with 1.4 inches of last rib backfat thickness, it is graded U.S. No. 4 as is evident from Figure 5.7. If either of these hogs or any hog has unacceptable quality and/ or belly thickness that is too thin, then they would be graded U.S. Utility.

The grade of slaughter hogs with indications of acceptable quality can also be determined by use of the following equation:

Grade = 4 × backfat thickness in inches at the last rib − (minus) 1 × muscling score

Muscling score is based on:

Thin = 1
Average = 2
Thick = 3

Using this equation for hog C:

$$4 \times 1.1 = 4.4$$
$$-1 \times 3 \;\; = \underline{3.0}$$
$$1.4 \text{ or U.S. No. 1 grade}$$

Hog D:
$$4 \times 1.4 = 5.6$$
$$-1 \times 1 \;\; = \underline{1.0}$$
$$4.6 \text{ or U.S. No. 4 grade}$$

This equation estimates grade to the nearest .1. Thus, it is the preferred procedure used to calculate grade in live hog and carcass evaluation courses and intercollegiate competitions.

Photographs of live hogs representative of the U.S. No. 1, No. 2, No. 3, No. 4 and Utility grades are shown in Figure 5.8. These photographs provide the student with a guide to the appearance of hogs representative of each grade. However, final live grade of the hogs evaluated is based on estimated last rib backfat thickness and degree of muscling using the diagram in Figure 5.7.

Figure 5.8. An illustration showing slaughter swine representative of each of the U.S. grades.

U.S. No. 1

U.S. No. 2

U.S. No. 3

U.S. No. 4

U.S. Utility

Pricing Live Hogs

On Percentage Muscle Basis

The percentage muscle basis is used to illustrate the procedure for pricing live hogs and pork carcasses in evaluation courses and will be described in sections 5 and 6. However, this method is not widely used by the pork industry. Pricing live hogs and/or pork carcasses on the basis of lean pork value is relatively new. However, because of its accuracy and ease of application, it is gaining acceptance by the pork industry.

Using the percentage muscle basis, the live price per hundred weight is determined from the percentage muscle estimated as previously described in this section and from the estimated dressing percentage. For purposes of illustration in this section and in section 6, the base percentage muscle of 53% has been arbitrarily chosen for determining carcass price/cwt. However, any base percent muscle between 50 and 60% may be used. The carcass price/cwt varies with daily market fluctuations, but for purposes of explaining the procedures involved in pricing live hogs, a carcass price of $70.00/cwt will be used for hogs with the base of 53% muscle. For each 1% muscle above or below 53% muscle, add or subtract $1.00 to or from the carcass price/cwt. The $1.00 adjustment of carcass price/cwt for each 1% muscle above or below the base of 53% also was arbitrarily chosen for illustration purposes only. The actual adjustment varies with market hog prices, but adjustments of $.50 to $1.50 for each 1% of muscle are typical. If the percentage muscle is below the base, subtract $1.00 for each 1% below 53% and for each 1% above 53%, add $1.00 to $70.00, which is the carcass price/cwt with 53% muscle. To calculate the live price/cwt, multiply the carcass price/cwt, after adjusting for percentage muscle, by the estimated dressing percentage.

To illustrate the pricing procedure, refer to hogs A and B previously used to estimate percentage muscle. Hog A had 56.1% muscle which is 3.1% above the base of 53% muscle (56.1–53.0). Each 1% muscle is equivalent to $1.00/cwt: therefore, 3.1 × $1.00 = $3.10/cwt is the carcass price adjustment necessary for this hog. The $3.10 adjustment is added to the $70.00 (base price for 53% muscle) to equal $73.10/cwt which is the carcass price/cwt for a carcass with 56.1% muscle. Let us assume the dressing percentage for this hog was estimated at 72.5%, then $73.10/cwt × .725 = $53.00 which is the live price/cwt for hog A using these prices and base percent muscle. The live price/cwt should always be rounded to the nearest dime but no rounding is necessary in this example.

Hog B had 48.7% muscle as described earlier, which is 4.3% below the base of 53% muscle (53.0–48.7). Each 1% = $1.00; therefore, 4.3 × 1.00 = $4.30/cwt is the adjustment for carcass muscle percentage. The $4.30/cwt is subtracted from the base price of $70.00/cwt, which equals $65.70/cwt ($70.00–$4.30) for hog B with 48.7% muscle. If the dressing percentage of hog B was estimated to be 73.4%, the live price/cwt of this hog is $48.22 ($65.70 × .734)/cwt or $48.20 when rounded to the nearest dime.

Estimating Carcass Traits of Live Market Hogs

The major carcass traits evaluated in market hogs are muscle (loin eye area), fatness (average backfat and 10th rib fat thickness), and frame (carcass length). These traits can then be used to predict percentage carcass muscle and U.S.D.A. grade. Estimates of these traits are made by studying the relationships of live weight to frame and thickness. These relationships are derived from the concepts of growth and development discussed in Section 2 where large framed, late maturing animals are leaner than small framed, early maturing animals of the same weight.

In classroom and contest situations, live weights usually are provided. However, in many production situations, weights are not known; thus, the student should try to develop some aptitude for estimating live weights. For purposes of this discussion, the five market hogs (E, F, G, H and I) in Figure 5.9 are assumed to have a constant weight of approximately 230 lb. This will allow us to make estimates of their carcass characteristics by evaluating differences in their conformation.

When viewing the gilt (E) in Figure 5.9 (top left) and the barrow (F) in Figure 5.9 (top right), the evaluator should get an overall impression that E is leaner and larger framed than F. E stands on more length of leg and appears to be longer sided. She is trimmer in the jowl, elbow pocket, and flank. E is also leaner over the loin, loin edge, and shoulder and should show more shoulder blade movement at the walk.

Gilt E

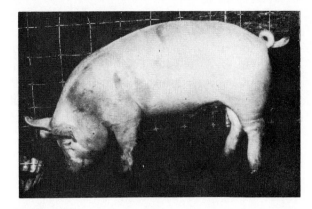

Barrow F

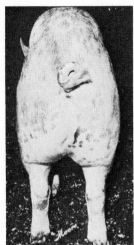

Figure 5.9. Photographs of five market pigs (showing two side and three rear views) illustrating differences in muscle, fat, frame and thickness. These photographs are intended to aid the student in his/her initial attempt at estimation of carcass charatericstics in live hogs.

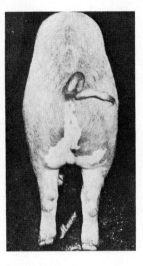

Barrow G   Barrow H   Barrow I

She should measure approximately 33 in. long and have about 1.1 in. of average backfat. F is shorter legged and shorter sided than E. Thus, at the same weight he will be fatter. He is wastier through the jowl and middle and appears to have more fat over the shoulder. This barrow should measure approximately 31 in. long and have about 1.5 in of average backfat. If these two hogs were heavier than 230 lb., one would estimate them to be both longer and fatter. Likewise, if they weighed less than 230 lb., one would estimate them to be shorter and have less fat.

Differences in both muscle and backfat are easily detected among barrows G, H, and I (lower half of Figure 5.9). Muscle differences can be seen by looking at the turn over the loin, the definition of the ham-loin junction, the thickness of rump, the bulge through the center of the ham, and the thickness and firmness at the base of the ham. Fat differences can be seen by looking at the turn over the top, the seam fat, and the firmness at the base of the ham. While a system for predicting 10th rib thickness from average backfat thickness is presented earlier in this section, 10th-rib fat can be estimated directly when viewing the hog from behind.

G (Figure 5.9, lower left) appears to be a lean, heavy muscled barrow. G stands wide and has a very bulging, expressively muscled ham. He has a very distinct ham-loin junction and a very muscular turn of top. In addition, G is lean over the loin edge and trim through the seam and base of the ham. He will have about 6.0 in.^{2} of loin eye area and about .6 in. of 10th rib fat thickness.

H (Figure 5.9, lower center) appears to be a lean barrow with average muscling. He is much less expressive at the ham-loin junction and has less bulge and flair to the ham. While he does have some seam fat, he is still very lean over the edge of the loin. H will have about 5.0 in.^{2} of loin eye area and approximately .9 in. of 10th rib fat thickness.

I (Figure 5.9, lower right) appears to be fat and light muscled. I stands narrow and is very flat in the shape of his ham. He is also wasty through the seam of the ham and shows very little distinction of ham-loin junction. Whereas, barrows G and H were "turned" over their tops, I is fat at the loin edge and very "square" over his top. I will have approximately 4.0 in.^{2} of loin eye area and 1.5 in. of fat at the 10th rib.

Pork Carcass Evaluation, Grading, and Pricing

Pork Carcass Evaluation

The porcine species is subdivided into kinds and classes. The kinds include slaughter hogs and feeder pigs (Table 6.1). The material in this section will be confined to slaughter hogs. The classes of slaughter hogs include barrows, gilts, sows, stags and boars (Table 6.1); however, the discussion of slaughter hogs in this section will be limited to barrows and gilts. The classes of feeder pigs include barrows, gilts, and boars but will not be discussed further here but in Section 17.

Table 6.1   Market Kinds, Classes and Grades of Swine.

Kind	Class	Grade
Slaughter Hogs	Barrow[1]	U.S. No. 1, U.S. No. 2, U.S. No. 3, U.S. No. 4, U.S. Utility
	Gilt[1]	U.S. No. 1, U.S. No. 2, U.S. No. 3, U.S. No. 4, U.S. Utility
	Sow[2]	U.S. No. 1, U.S. No. 2, U.S. No. 3, U.S. Medium, U.S. Cull
	Stag	none
	Boar	none
Feeder Pigs[3]	Barrow	U.S. No. 1, U.S. No. 2, U.S. No. 3, U.S. No. 4, U.S. Utility
	Gilt	U.S. No. 1, U.S. No. 2, U.S. No. 3, U.S. No. 4, U.S. Utility
	Boar	U.S. No. 1, U.S. No. 2, U.S. No. 3, U.S. No. 4, U.S. Utility

1. Slaughter barrows and gilts are graded without regard for differences in characteristics due to class (sex).
2. Sow carcasses are graded on different standards than those applicable to slaughter barrows and gilts.
3. Feeder pigs are graded without regard to class because they are almost always graded as feeders before sexual maturity.

Determination of Class

The grade standards for barrow and gilt carcasses apply regardless of class (sex condition) and will be discussed later in this section. Even though no class distinction is made for grading barrow and gilt carcasses, the student should learn to recognize the differences and be able to identify carcass class. The classes of slaughter hogs and distinguishing characteristics are as follows:

1. Barrow carcasses are identified by the presence of a small pizzle eye (severed attachment of the penis) located dorsally from the aitch bone. In addition, the exposed gracilis muscle ventral to the aitch bone is relatively small in size and partially covered with fat. These identifying features are shown in Figure 6.1. A pocket on either side of the split belly surface where the preputial sheath was removed may also be apparent. The latter is the least reliable feature to positively identify barrow carcasses.
2. Gilt carcasses are identified by the absence of a pizzle eye. The exposed gracilis muscle is considerably larger, bean shaped, and has very little fat covering compared to that of barrows. These identifying features are shown in Figure 6.1. The split belly has a smooth surface compared to the sheath pocket present in barrows. The latter is not a good identifying characteristic of gilt carcasses. Gilt carcasses have no mammary development.

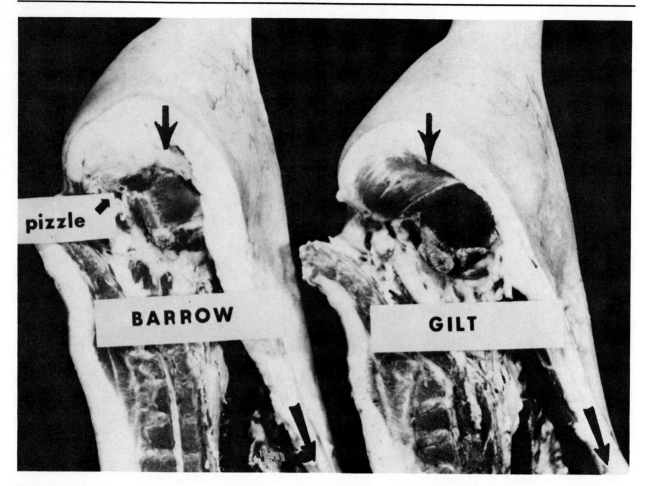

Figure 6.1. Illustration of a barrow (left) and gilt (right) showing the pizzle eye (small arrow dorsal and caudal to the aitch bone) in the barrow carcass. The large lean gracilis muscle (arrow on the ham facing) is evident in the gilt carcass as well as presence of less fat in this area compared to the barrow carcass. The arrows on the belly indicate the area of removal on the sheath in the barrow carcass compared to smooth ventral fat surface of the gilt.

3. Sow carcasses are identified by the same characteristics as those described for gilts. However, they can be distinguished from gilts because of their developed mammary tissue associated with lactation or advanced stages of pregnancy. In addition, sow carcasses usually are heavier than gilts.

4. Stag and boar carcasses are identified by the same characteristics as those described for barrows. However, the pizzle eye of stags and boars is larger and more prominent than in barrows because of sexual maturity. The shoulders of stags and boars are heavier muscled with larger bones and joints, and the skin over the shoulders is somewhat thicker and the color of lean is darker compared to barrows. Stags and boar carcasses are usually heavier and more mature in appearance than barrows.

Weight

Hot carcass weight is almost always obtained on pork carcasses just prior to chilling, and chilled carcass weight is usually calculated from hot carcass weight in commercial practice because chilled weight is usually not obtained. If chilled carcasses are weighed, they are weighed just prior to cutting the wholesale cuts. In practice, hot carcass weight is shrunk 1.5% (hot carcass wt. × .985 = chilled carcass wt.) to obtain chilled carcass weight. When chilled carcass weight is obtained and hot carcass weight is not, the latter can be calculated from chilled weight by multiplying chilled carcass weight by 101.5%. Hot carcass weight is based on a packer style of dressing (i.e., the carcass is split down the backbone, jowls are attached but

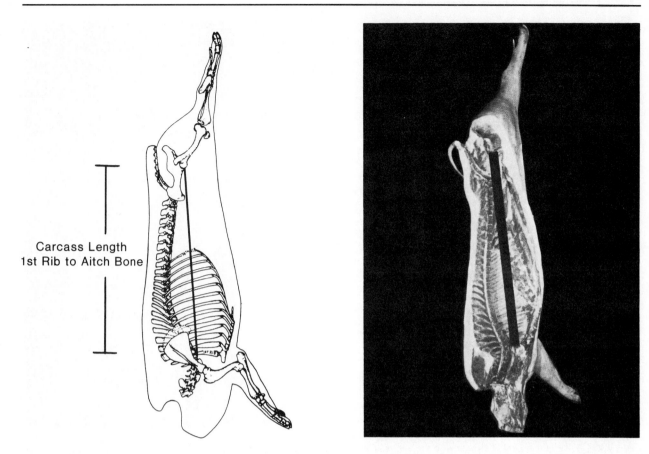

Figure 6.2. A skeletal diagram (left) showing the anatomical reference points and a carcass (right) showing the carcass length measurement (black line).

the head and leaf fat are removed). Chilled carcass weight is used to calculate dressing percentage of hogs by dividing by the live weight and multiplying by 100. If the carcass has been skinned, either hot or chilled carcass weight on a skin-on basis can be calculated by dividing the weight available (hot or chilled) by .94 (skin represents about 6% of the carcass). If the jowl(s) and other parts have been removed from the carcass during the slaughter operation, an accurate estimate of the removed part(s) should be made in terms of pounds and added to the weight to obtain either the hot or chilled carcass weight.

Length

Carcass length is measured with a metal tape or may be estimated on the hanging carcass from the cranial edge of the first rib adjacent to the backbone to the cranial edge of the aitch bone (pubic symphysis) as shown in Figure 6.2. Usually only one side of each carcass is measured, but both sides may be measured and then averaged.

Average Backfat Thickness

Thickness of backfat, including skin, is estimated or measured to the dorsal surface of the spinous processes at the first rib, last rib, and last lumbar vertebra as shown in Figure 6.3. Either the estimate or measurement at each of the three anatomical locations is made to the nearest .1 in. and then averaged to obtain average backfat thickness. Backfat measurements are generally taken with a metal ruler. Usually only one side of the pork carcass is used to obtain average backfat thickness, but in the case of uneven splits, both sides should be estimated or measured. If a portion of the backfat was trimmed away from one side during the slaughter process at the site where the estimates or measurements are obtained, then the opposite side is used. A single measurement opposite the last rib is used to determine pork carcass grades.

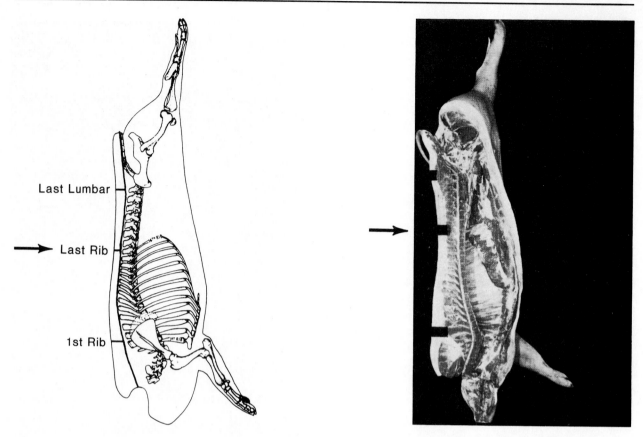

Figure 6.3. A skeletal diagram (left) showing the anatomical reference points and a carcass (right) showing the three backfat measurements (black areas) opposite the first rib, last rib and last lumbar vertebra. Only the last rib measurement (indicated by the arrow) is used to determine pork carcass grades and lean guide to pork value.

Ribbing Pork Carcasses

Pork carcasses are seldom ribbed (cut between the 10th and 11th rib to expose the loin eye muscle and 10th rib backfat) in commercial practice. The pork carcass grade standards are designed for use on unribbed carcasses. However, to facilitate the maximum learning experience in meat evaluation courses, pork carcasses are frequently ribbed at the 10th rib interface to expose the loin eye muscle and backfat. Carcass length must be estimated and/or measured on the carcass before ribbing. Loin eye area and backfat thickness at the 10th rib may also be estimated or measured on the loin during the cutting of wholesale cuts but prior to trimming the loin and removing the fatback from it.

In pork carcasses, only one side and usually the right side, is ribbed. The 10th rib is located by counting from the first rib. It is not recommended to count from the last rib because of the variable number of ribs in pork carcasses. After locating the cranial edge of the 11th rib at its dorsal attachment at the 11th–12th thoracic vertebrae junction, saw through the vertebra just cranial to the 11th rib holding the saw perpendicular to the longitudinal axis of the vertebral column. After sawing, use the knife and continue to cut through the skin, fat and muscle perpendicular to the vertebral column to make a perpendicular cut across the longissimus muscle. Avoid following the curvature of the 10th rib and do not cut through the 10th rib. The knife cut should not be extended more than 1 inch laterally to the longissimus (loin eye) muscle to avoid cutting into the belly.

10th Rib Backfat Thickness

The depth of subcutaneous fat, including skin, is estimated or measured in tenths of inches at the 10th rib interface, ¾ the lateral length of the eye muscle perpendicular to the skin surface as shown in Figure 6.4. The 10th rib interface may be exposed on either the ribbed carcass or on the untrimmed loin

Figure 6.4. A skeletal diagram (left) showing the location of the 10th rib and a cross section of the loin at the 10th rib (right) showing the procedure for measurement of backfat thickness at this location.

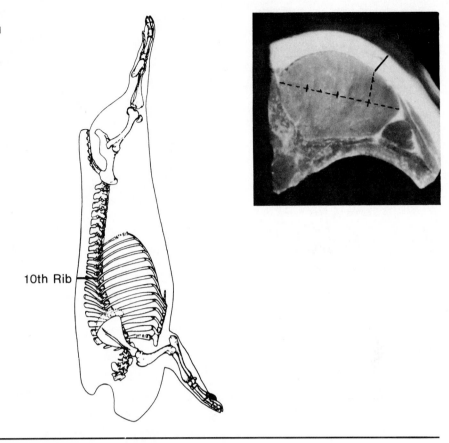

10th Rib

(fatback left on it). The 10th rib backfat is a more accurate measurement of subcutaneous fat than average backfat thickness because it is not influenced by variation in carcass splitting and trimming.

Loin Eye Area

Area of the longissimus (eye) muscle is either estimated or measured in square inches (in.^{2}) on the cross section of the muscle at the 10th rib interface (Figure 6.5A). A large (6.8 in.^{2}) and a small (3.8 in.^{2}) loin eye area are shown in Figure 6.5B. The 10th rib interface may be exposed on either the ribbed carcass or on the untrimmed loin. Area is determined either with a plastic grid or from a tracing of the eye muscle with a compensating polar planimeter. The plastic grid method is most frequently used in carcass evaluation.

When estimating area of the eye muscle on the ribbed carcass or loin, the easiest method is to estimate length (lateral dimension) and width (ventral-dorsal dimension) in inches and multiply them to obtain the area in square inches. Since length $\times$ width is the formula for determining area of a rectangle and since no eye muscle is perfectly rectangular in shape, an adjustment for the deviation from the rectangular shape is necessary to avoid overestimating the area. With limited experience this method is more accurate than "just guessing" at the area of eye muscle.

When using the plastic grid, place it on the eye muscle with either the 2, 3, or 4 in.^{2} circumscribed area within the perimeter of the eye, depending on which one lies entirely within the eye. Then count all the dots outside the 2, 3, or 4 in.^{2} circumscribed area used, but within the perimeter of the eye muscle. If one or two dots of the circumscribed area lies outside the perimeter of the eye muscle, subtract these one or two dots from the total dots counted. Count only the dots within the perimeter of the eye muscle while being careful not to include adjacent muscles. In the case of dots that are on the exact perimeter of the muscle, count only every other such dot so that area will not be overestimated. After all dots have been counted, divide the total by 20 (because there are 20 dots per square inch). Then add the figure obtained to the circumscribed area that was entirely within the perimeter of the eye muscle. The following example

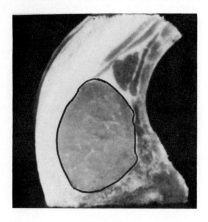
A.

B. Large Loin Eye

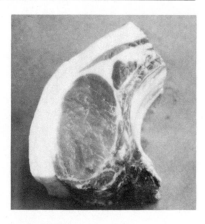
B. Small Loin Eye

Figure 6.5. A. A cross section of the loin at the 10th rib showing loin eye area. The eye muscle (longissimus) is darkened around its perimeter to distinguish it from adjacent muscles. **B.** Cross section of two loins showing a large and a small loin eye area. The loin on the left has a loin eye area of 6.8 square inches and the one on the right 3.8 square inches.

Figure 6.6. A cross section of a loin at the 10th rib with a plastic grid superimposed on the eye muscle for determination of loin eye area. The two in.2 circumscribed area of the grid lies with the darkened perimeter of the eye muscle. All dots on the grid within the perimeter of the eye muscle are counted.

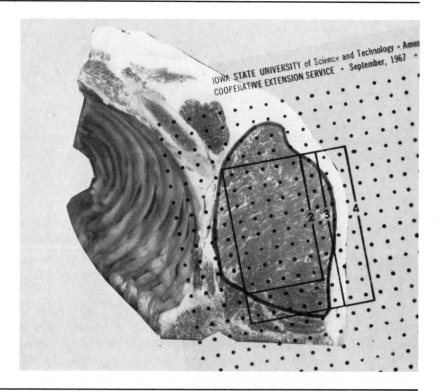

will illustrate the procedure involved. In the example carcass shown in Figure 6.6, 2 in.² area fits within the perimeter of the eye. The number of dots outside the 2 in.² circumscribed area within the perimeter of the eye muscle is counted and they total 30. The 30 dots divided by 20 = 1.5 in.². Add the 1.5 to the original 2.0 in.² of the circumscribed area that was not counted and it equals 3.5 (2.0 + 1.5) in.² of loin eye area for this carcass.

Percentage Carcass Muscle

Percentage carcass muscle containing 10% intramuscular fat can be calculated from a regression equation that was recently developed. The equation includes hot carcass weight, loin eye area, and backfat thickness at the 10th rib and it is as follows:

Pounds of muscle containing 10% fat = 10.5 + (.5 × adjusted hot carcass wt., in pounds)

+ (2 × loin eye area, in square inches)

− (14.9 × 10th rib fat thickness, in tenths of inches)

The pounds of muscle obtained by use of the regression equation can be converted to percent muscle for the respective carcass by dividing by its hot carcass weight. This is the usual manner of carcass evaluation as employed in the industry. However, for comparative purposes the percent muscle of all carcasses may be adjusted to a 160 lb. hot carcass weight basis, which provides a more appropriate basis for comparison among carcasses as explained in section 5. In this case the pounds of muscle is *always divided by the 160 lb.* hot carcass weight as shown below.

$$\% \text{ Muscle} = \frac{\text{pounds of muscle}}{160 \text{ lb.}} \times 100$$

Working Formula

To simplify the above regression equation, a working formula is used in practical everyday situations because it requires less calculations and it is much faster to use. However, the regression equation is more accurate than the working formula and should be used for all carcass evaluation and especially in competitive situations when actual loin eye areas and 10th rib backfat are obtained. Because the working formula may be used in practical everyday market situations when carcasses are not ribbed, it will be presented and illustrated here. The working formula gives the results directly as percentage muscle without any further calculations. To use the working formula, begin with a base of 53% muscle which is adjusted up or down for the variation above or below the base value for either live weight or hot carcass weight, loin eye area, and 10th rib backfat thickness. The base of 53% muscle (containing 10% fat) is equivalent to a hog with:

Base
1. 240 lb. live wt. or 180 lb. hot carcass wt. (240 live wt. × .75 dress. %)
2. 5.0 in.² loin eye area
3. 1.0 in. backfat, ¾ lateral length of eye muscle at 10th rib

Adjustments from the base values for each of the three characteristics are made as described in the following three steps:

Step 1

Hot carcass weight—for every *10 lb.* increase or decrease from 180 lb. hot carcass weight, add or subtract .1% muscle to or from the base of 53% muscle. Every 10 lb. increment of hot carcass weight is used for carcass evaluation, and every 25 lb. increment is used for live weight. The difference between hot carcass weight and live weight represents the dressing percentage (approximately 75%).

Step 2

Loin eye area—for every *.1 in.²* increase or decrease from 5.0 in.² loin eye area, add or subtract .133% to or from the percent muscle after adjusting for hot carcass weight in step 1.

Step 3

10th rib backfat thickness—for every *.1 in.* increase or decrease from 1.0 inch of 10th rib backfat thickness, add or subtract .8% of muscle to or from the percentage muscle in step 2.

From the above adjustments, it is apparent that 10th rib backfat thickness has the greatest effect on the percentage muscle, that hot carcass weight has the least effect, and that loin eye area has an intermediate effect on percentage muscle in the carcass.

To illustrate the use of the working formula, the following two pork carcasses are used as examples.

	Carcass A	Carcass B
Hot carcass wt., lb.	190	150
Loin eye area, in.^{2}	5.8	4.3
10th rib backfat thickness, in.	.7	1.3

Carcass A:

This carcass is 10 lb. more than the base of 180 lb. and since each 10 lb. is equivalent to .1% muscle the total adjustment for hot carcass weight is .1% (1–10 lb. increment × .1%). The .1% adjustment is subtracted from the base of 53% muscle to give 52.9% after adjusting for hot carcass weight. Each .1 in.^{2} of loin eye from the base of 5.0 in.^{2} is multiplied by .133% muscle and since carcass A has .8 in.^{2} more than the base the adjustment is 1.1% muscle (8–.1 in.^{2} increments × .133%). The 1.1% adjustment is added to the 52.9% (% muscle after adjusting for hot carcass weight) to give 54.0% muscle after adjusting for hot carcass weight and loin eye area. Each .1 in. of 10th rib backfat thickness deviation from the base of 1 in. is multiplied by .8% muscle. Since carcass A has .3 in. less backfat than the base, the adjustment is 2.4% muscle (3–.1 in. increment × .8%). The 2.4% is added to 54.0 (% muscle after adjusting for hot carcass weight and loin eye area) to give 56.4% muscle in carcass A after all adjustments have been made. If the regression equation was used instead of the working formula, the percentage muscle would be 56.1%, a difference of .3%.

Carcass B:

This carcass weighs 30 lb. less than the base of 180 lb. hot carcass weight; thus, the base percent muscle is adjusted by .3% muscle (3–10 lb. increments × .1%) to give 53.3% muscle after adjusting for hot carcass weight. The loin eye area adjustment for carcass B is .9% muscle (7–.1 in.^{2} increments × .133%) and when subtracted from 53.3% = 52.4% muscle after adjusting for hot carcass weight and loin eye area. The adjustment for 10th rib backfat is 2.4% (3–.1 in. increments × .8%) which is subtracted from 52.4% (% muscle after hot carcass weight and loin eye area adjustment) to give 50.0% muscle after all adjustments have been made. If the regression equation was used instead of the working formula, the percentage muscle would be 49.8%, a difference of .2%.

From the two examples given above, it can be seen that the percentage muscle in the carcass can be quite accurately estimated by the working formula. The reader is referred to section 5 for a brief discussion of the limitations of the working formula for light weight and very heavily muscled carcasses and for medium weight and very fat pork carcasses. Since weight, loin eye area, and 10th rib fat thickness are objective measurements that can be accurately and easily obtained, and they are highly related to cutability or percentage muscle, the percent muscle procedure provides a very accurate method of pork carcass evaluation.

Facts to Remember

1. The adjustment for hot carcass weight above the base weight of 180 lb. is subtracted from the base percentage muscle, while adjustments for hot carcass weights below the base weight are added to the base percentage muscle.
2. The adjustment for loin eye area above the base loin eye area of 5.0 in.^{2} is added to and that below 5.0 in.^{2} is subtracted from the base percentage muscle. It is obvious that as loin eye area increases so does total carcass muscle, hence the reason for adding or subtracting the adjustment.
3. The adjustment for 10th rib backfat thickness is added to the base percentage muscle when the measurement is below the base of 1.0 in. of 10th rib backfat and subtracted when the measurement exceeds the base of 1.0 in. of backfat. Again this reflects the fact that fat and muscle are inversely related.
4. The pounds of muscle obtained by use of the regression equation usually is converted to percent muscle for the respective carcass by dividing by its hot carcass weight. However, for comparative purposes such as in carcass quality shows, it is appropriate that the percent muscle on all carcasses

be adjusted to a 160 lb. hot carcass weight basis; thus, pounds of muscle is then always divided by the 160 lb. hot carcass weight.

A brief discussion of the procedure for estimating the lean pork (percentage muscle containing 10% intramuscular fat) gain per day on test is presented in Section 7 with other evaluations of swine performance data.

Percentage carcass muscle is a more accurate estimate of carcass cutability than the calculation of percentages lean cuts, ham and loin, or ham because it is based entirely on objective measurements and is not influenced by cutting and trimming variation like the cutout percentages. Thus, the use of percentage muscle to determine carcass and live price is undoubtedly a better indicator of value than cutout percentages.

Percentage Lean Cuts

The lean cuts of pork are the trimmed ham, loin, Boston shoulder, and picnic shoulder as shown in Figure 6.7. The combined weight of these trimmed wholesale cuts is expressed as a percentage of chilled carcass weight. The weight(s) of the individual cuts, as well as combinations of them, are usually also expressed as a percentage of chilled carcass weight. The two most frequently used of these percentages for carcass evaluation and/or pricing are lean cuts and the combined ham and loin. Lean cuts, ham and loin, and ham percentage are inversely correlated with fatness to the extent that backfat thickness is associated with approximately 50% of the variation in these percentages. Thus, fat has a much greater affect on these

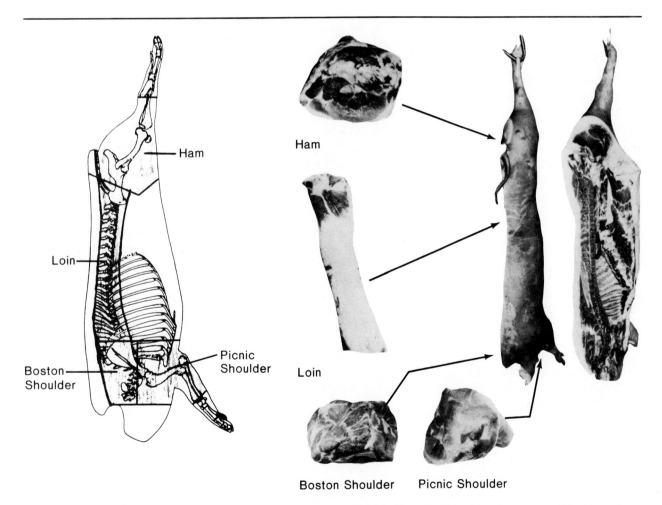

Figure 6.7. A skeletal diagram (left) showing the location of lean cuts. The right illustration shows a pork carcass and the trimmed four lean cuts after removal from the carcass.

percentages than all other factors including muscling. The ranges in percentage lean cuts by pork carcass grade are shown in Table 6.4.

The most limiting factor associated with the use of percentage lean cuts, ham and loin, or ham is the variability due to cutting and trimming. Because of this variability, these percentages are most accurate when used within a given pork cutting operation. Consequently, these percentages vary between plants and with seasonal demands for the respective wholesale cuts. Depending on demand, hams and loins, in particular, may be cut long or short, and the amount of fat left on each cut may also vary. These facts demonstrate the shortcomings of using percentage carcass muscle, lean cuts, ham and loin or ham in pork carcass evaluation, pricing or carcass shows. As a consequence, a procedure for pork carcass evaluation based entirely on objective measurements was developed.

Pork Carcass Grading

Grades for barrow and gilt carcasses are based on two general considerations: quality indicating characteristics of the lean and fat, and expected yield of the four lean cuts (i.e., ham, loin, picnic shoulder, and Boston shoulder).

Quality

Two levels of quality are considered: carcasses with characteristics that indicate the lean has acceptable quality, and carcasses with unacceptable quality of lean. Quality of lean is best evaluated in a cut surface of major muscles. The grade standards describe the quality characteristics of the loin eye muscle at the 10th rib. However, when this surface is not exposed, other exposed major muscle surfaces can be used for the quality determination. When a major muscle-cut surface is not exposed, quality of the lean is evaluated indirectly, based on quality-indicating characteristics in the carcass. These include firmness of the fat and lean, amount of feathering between the ribs, and color of the lean. The degree of external fatness is not considered when evaluating the quality of the lean. However, a pork carcass must have a belly with sufficient thickness to be suitable for bacon production in order to be considered acceptable in quality. Belly thickness is determined by an overall evaluation of its thickness, with primary consideration being given to the thickness along the navel edge and the thickness of the belly (flank) pocket. The minimum belly thickness for acceptable quality is 0.6 inches at any point. The minimum standard for each quality characteristic for unribbed pork carcasses is presented in Table 6.2.

In classroom evaluation procedures the pork carcasses are generally ribbed to expose the loin eye muscle. Quality of lean is usually evaluated in the eye muscle at the 10th rib interface either on ribbed carcasses or on the wholesale loin. Three factors are used to evaluate quality, namely: (1) degree of marbling; (2) color and (3) firmness of lean in the eye muscle at the 10th rib. Each of these quality factors is scored on a numerical basis from 1 to 3 as is shown in Table 6.3. The five degrees of marbling, three marbling scores, and acceptability status are shown in Figure 6.8. Examples of the eye muscle color scores

Table 6.2   Minimum Pork Quality Characteristics in Unribbed Carcasses.

Characteristic	Minimum Standard for Acceptable Quality
Firmness of lean & fat	Slightly firm
Feathering between the ribs	Slight
Color of lean	Grayish pink to moderately dark red
Belly thickness	Not less than 0.6 inches at any point

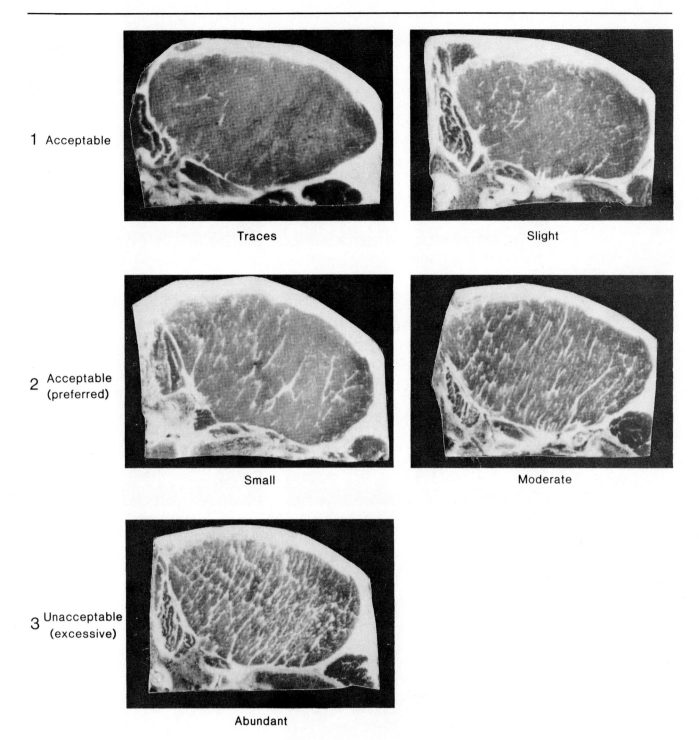

1 Acceptable

Traces

Slight

2 Acceptable (preferred)

Small

Moderate

3 Unacceptable (excessive)

Abundant

Figure 6.8. Illustration of the 5 degrees and 3 scores of marbling in pork and acceptability status.

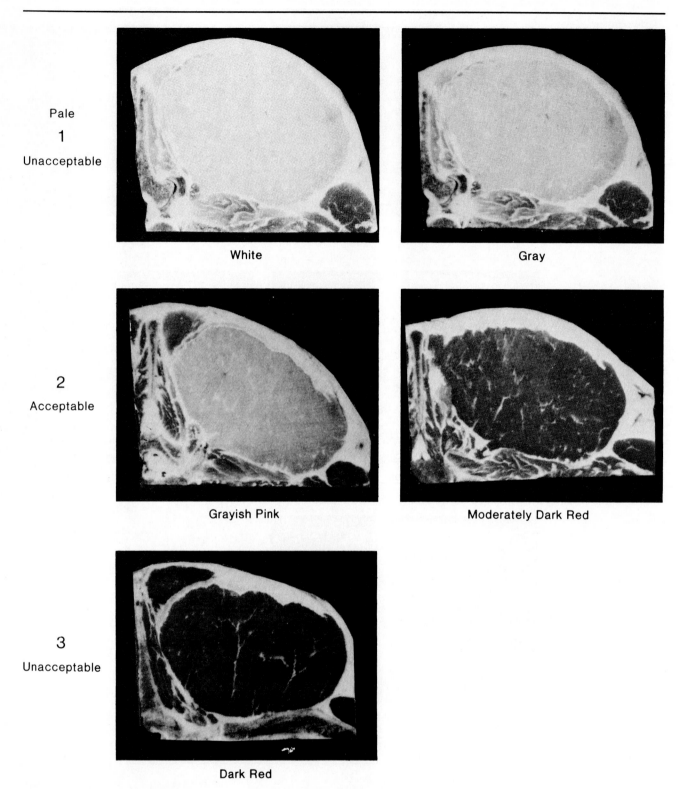

Pale

1

Unacceptable

White

Gray

2

Acceptable

Grayish Pink

Moderately Dark Red

3

Unacceptable

Dark Red

Figure 6.9. Illustration of the color of lean scores in pork and acceptability status.

and acceptability status are shown in Figure 6.9. Even though these photographs are black and white, the relative intensity of color is apparent. Scores and acceptability status for firmness, wateriness, or dryness of lean in the loin eye muscle at the 10th rib—as well as in ham muscles on the cut surface—are shown in Figure 6.10.

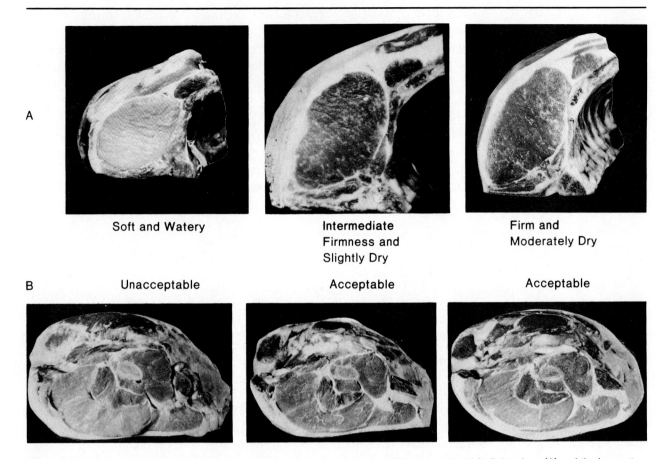

Figure 6.10. Illustrations of three degrees of muscle firmness and wateriness or dryness at the 10th rib interface (A) and the lean cut surface of the ham (B) and the respective acceptability status.

Table 6.3 Pork Quality Characteristics, Scores and Acceptability Status.*

Characteristic	Description	Score	Acceptability Status
Marbling	Traces, Slight	1	Acceptable
	Small, Moderate	2	Acceptable (preferred)
	Abundant	3	Unacceptable (excessive)
Color	Pale (white, gray)	1	Unacceptable
	Grayish Pink to Moderately Dark Red	2	Acceptable (preferred)
	Dark Red	3	Unacceptable
Firmness	Soft and Watery	1	Unacceptable
	Intermediate	2	Acceptable
	Firm & Moderately Dry	3	Acceptable

*These are National Pork Producers Council Quality Standards which have been incorporated into the USDA Grade Standards for pork carcasses. These quality of lean characteristics are described in terms of those observed in the exposed loin eye muscle at the 10th rib.

Carcasses that have indications of acceptable lean quality and acceptable belly thickness are placed in one of four grades, denoted by numbers 1 through 4. These grades are based entirely on the expected carcass yields of the four lean cuts, and no consideration is given to a development of quality superior to that described as minimum for these grades. Carcasses that have characteristics indicating that the lean in the four lean cuts has unacceptable quality or bellies too thin (< 0.6 inches) to be suitable for bacon production are graded U.S. Utility regardless of their combinations of backfat thickness and muscling score. Belly thickness of carcasses that weigh 150 lb. or more (215 lb. live weight or more) should not have bellies that are too thin. Also graded U.S. Utility, regardless of their development of other quality-indicating characteristics, are carcasses that are soft and oily.

When evaluating pork carcasses for percentage muscle and/or pounds of lean pork gain per day of age or per day on test (Section 7), acceptable quality muscle properties are required. Carcasses with unacceptable quality should not be given further consideration in any rankings.

Yield of Lean Cuts

Four grades, U.S. No. 1, U.S. No. 2, U.S. No. 3, and U.S. No. 4 are provided for carcasses that have indications of an acceptable lean quality and acceptable belly thickness. These grades are based entirely on the expected carcass yield of lean cuts, and no consideration is given to a development of quality superior to that described as minimum for the grades. The expected lean cut yield of each grade is shown in Table 6.4.

Table 6.4   Expected Yields of the Four Lean Cuts by Grade.*

Grade	Yield of Lean Cuts
U.S. No. 1	60.4% and over
U.S. No. 2	57.4–60.3%
U.S. No. 3	54.5–57.3%
U.S. No. 4	Less than 54.4%

*Lean cut percentages are based on chilled carcass weight.

These yields are based on cutting and trimming methods used by the U.S. Department of Agriculture in developing the standards. Other cutting and trimming methods may result in different yields. For example, if more fat is left on the four lean cuts than prescribed in the U.S.D.A. methods, the yield of each grade will be higher than indicated. However, such a method of trimming, if applied uniformly, should result in similar differences in yields between grades.

Pork carcasses differ in lean cut yield because of differences in backfat thickness and in degree of muscling (i.e., thickness of muscling in relation to skeletal size). Backfat thickness is most highly related to yield of lean cuts, and degree of muscling accounts for a much lower relationship than backfat. As the amount of external fat increases, the yield of lean cuts decreases. An accurate evaluation of the amount of external fat may be made by measuring the backfat thickness at one or more points on the carcass. In grading barrow and gilt carcasses, the amount of external fat is considered by measuring the backfat thickness (including skin) over the last rib perpendicular to the skin surface as shown in Figure 6.3. The actual measurement, without adjustment, is used for the grade determination, except for carcasses from which the skin has been smoothly and evenly removed. These carcasses will have one-tenth inch added to the measurement to compensate for the skin. Carcasses that have had the skin removed and the fat is rough and uneven, or those that have had more than a slight amount of trimming to remove bruised or otherwise damaged parts, are ineligible for grading. The yield of four lean cuts from skinned carcasses will be higher than those shown in Table 6.4.

The degree of muscling is determined by a subjective evaluation of the thickness of muscling in relation to skeletal size. Since the total thickness of a carcass is affected by both the amount of fat and the amount of muscle in relation to skeletal size, the fatness must also be considered when degree of muscling is evaluated. To best evaluate muscling, primary consideration is given to those parts least affected by fatness, such as the ham. In evaluating the ham for degree of muscling, consideration should be given to both the stifle and back views. The size of the lumbar lean area and the relative width through the back or loin and through the center of the ham are also good indications of muscling.

Figure 6.11 illustrates five degrees of muscling that are assigned to three muscling scores in the pork carcass grade standards. These muscling scores are: thick, average, and thin. These degrees are intended to cover the entire range of muscling in pork carcasses. The carcasses in Figure 6.11 are representative of the degree of fatness normally associated with each degree of muscling shown (i.e., those with the thickest muscling have the thinnest backfat thickness).

Figure 6.11. Illustration showing the degrees and three scores of pork carcass muscling.

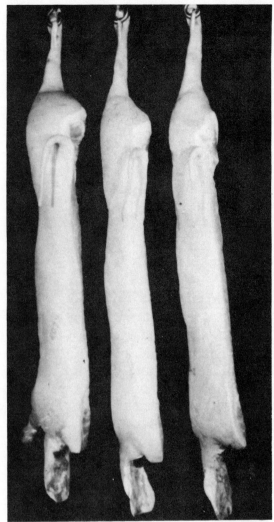

THICK   AVERAGE   THIN
3   2   1

Preliminary pork carcass grade is determined by the last rib backfat thickness as shown in Table 6.5. Final carcass grade is determined by adjusting for muscling score as shown in Figure 6.12. In carcasses with the average muscling score, the final carcass grade is the same as the preliminary grade as shown on Figure 6.12. Carcasses with a thin muscling score will be graded one grade lower than indicated by their

Table 6.5   Preliminary Carcass Grade Based on Backfat Thickness at the Last Rib.

Backfat Thickness Range	Preliminary Grade
1.00 inch or less	U.S. No. 1
1.00 to 1.24 inches	U.S. No. 2
1.25 to 1.49 inches	U.S. No. 3
1.50 inches & over*	U.S. No. 4

*Carcasses with last rib backfat thickness of 1.75 inches or over cannot be graded U.S. No. 3 even with thick muscling.

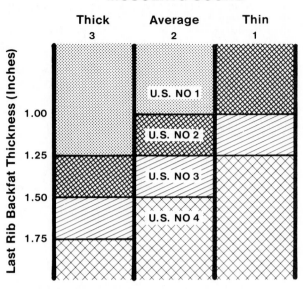

Figure 6.12. Pork carcass grading chart showing the relationship of last rib backfat thickness and degree of muscling score.

preliminary grade, based on thickness of backfat over the last rib. Carcasses with a thick muscling score will be graded one grade higher than indicated by their preliminary grade, based on backfat thickness over the last rib, except carcasses with 1.75 inches or greater backfat thickness over the last rib, which must remain in the U.S. No. 4 grade. Carcasses with a thin muscling score *cannot* be graded U.S. No. 1. The application of determining final pork carcass grade from Figure 6.12 is illustrated by the following two examples:

	Carcass C	**Carcass D**
Last rib backfat thickness, in.	.9	1.4
Muscling score	Thin	Thick
Carcass quality	Acceptable	Acceptable

The preliminary grade for carcass C is U.S. No. 1 (Table 6.5). However, because a carcass with thin muscling cannot be graded a U.S. No. 1, and as can be seen from Figure 6.12, carcass C is graded U.S. No. 2. The preliminary grade for carcass D is U.S. No. 3 (Table 6.5). Because carcass D has thick muscling along with 1.4 inches of last rib backfat thickness, it is graded U.S. No. 2 as is shown in Figure 6.12. If either of these carcasses or any carcass has unacceptable quality (marbling, color, firmness) and/or belly thickness that is too thin ($<$ .6 inches at any point), they are graded U.S. Utility.

The grade of pork carcasses with indications of acceptable quality can also be determined by the following equation:

$$\text{Grade} = 4 \times \text{backfat thickness in inches at the last rib} - (\text{minus}) \ 1 \times \text{muscling score}$$

Muscling score is based on:

Thin = 1
Average = 2
Thick = 3

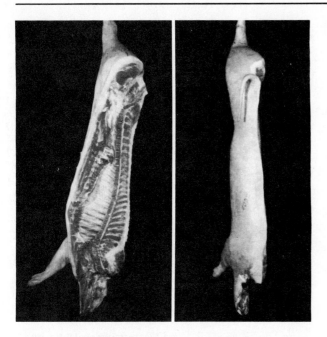

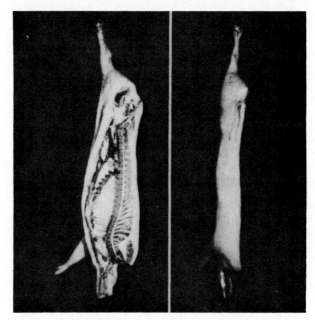

Last Rib Backfat .... .8 Inches
Thickness
Degree of Muscling .... Thick
U.S. No. 1

Last Rib Backfat .... 1.1 Inches
Thickness
Degree of Muscling ...... Average
U.S. No. 2

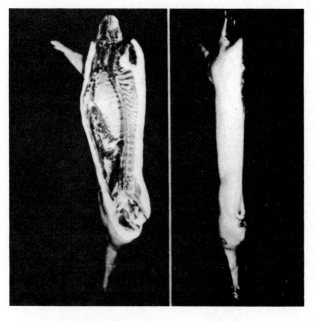

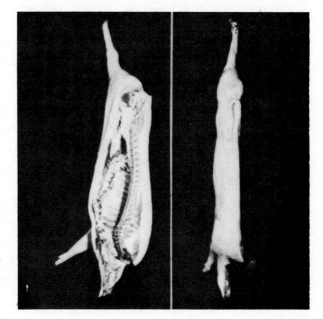

Last Rib Backfat .... 1.3 Inches
Thickness
Degree of Muscling ...... Average
U.S. No. 3

Last Rib Backfat .... 1.6 Inches
Thickness
Degree of Muscling .... Thin
U.S. No. 4

Figure 6.13. Illustrations of the U.S. No. 1, No. 2, No. 3 and No. 4 pork carcass grades.

Using this equation for carcass C:

$$4 \times .9 = 3.6$$
$$-1 \times 1 = \underline{1.0}$$
$$2.6 \text{ or U.S. No. 2 grade}$$

Carcass D:

$$4 \times 1.4 = 5.6$$
$$-1 \times 2 \ \ = \underline{2.0}$$
$$3.6 \text{ or U.S. No. 3 grade}$$

This equation estimates grade to the nearest .1 and is the preferred procedure used to calculate grade in live hog and pork carcass evaluation courses and intercollegiate competitions.

Four of the pork carcass grades are shown in Figure 6.13. The legend accompanying each carcass shows last rib backfat thickness, degree of muscling, and the respective carcass grade.

Pricing Pork Carcasses

On Percentage Muscle Basis

Wholesale carcass price/cwt is calculated by adjusting the base price for 53% muscle to the actual percentage muscle obtained by using the regression equation and the actual carcass data (i.e., hot carcass weight), loin eye area, and 10th rib backfat thickness. The base of 53% muscle for calculating prices was arbitrarily chosen for illustrative purposes but any percentage between 50 and 60% may be used. The pounds of muscle is usually converted to percent muscle by dividing the pounds of muscle in the respective carcass by its hot carcass weight and multiplying by 100. In some evaluation and educational programs it may be desirable to convert the percentage muscle of all carcasses evaluated to a weight-constant basis. In this case the pounds of muscle obtained from the regression equation is converted to percentage by dividing the pounds of muscle by the 160 lb. hot carcass weight and multiplying by 100 to convert all carcasses to a weight constant 160 lb. basis. These procedures are described earlier in the discussion of the calculation of percentage muscle in this section and in section 5. Actual carcass price is obtained by adding or subtracting $1.00 from the base carcass price/cwt for each 1% that the actual percentage muscle deviates from the arbitrarily chosen base of 53%. This procedure is identical to the one described in section 5 for determining the live price/cwt of hogs. The base price of pork carcasses with 53% muscle varies with daily market fluctuations so that the base price/cwt needs to be checked each day before pricing live hogs or pork carcasses. Actual carcass price/cwt is multiplied by actual dressing percentage to obtain the actual live price/cwt. The calculation of live price from actual carcass price is more accurate than that estimated on the live hogs because the factors affecting it can be accurately measured or more accurately estimated on carcasses.

Retail Pricing of Pork

Procedures for determining the retail price of pork will be presented and discussed in Section 18.

Evaluation of Swine Performance Data

A successful swine selection program must focus on sow productivity, structural soundness, performance ability (growth rate and feed efficiency), and product acceptability (carcass merit). Each producer must consider all of the traits included in these major production areas and place emphasis on those traits that have the most significance in his production system. One of the drawbacks to swine production testing programs in the past has been a lack of direction and guidance. In 1975, the National Swine Improvement Federation was established for the purpose of developing more uniform and effective swine testing programs. Many of the procedures recommended by the NSIF will be included in this manual.

Sow Productivity

Sow productivity is essentially a combination of the sow's reproductive efficiency and her milking ability. Conception rate, time required for rebreeding, and litter size are the major traits affecting reproductive efficiency, while milking ability is most accurately estimated by adjusted 21-day litter weaning weights. The economic success of a swine operation is highly dependent on the breeding and preweaning traits which make up sow productivity.

Conception Rate and Time of Rebreeding

These two traits have very low heritability estimates and are basically a function of management and the environment. However, gilts and sows that are difficult to get bred during one breeding period seemingly become the problem breeders in future breeding periods. Thus, the producer should consider culling such females from the breeding herd.

Litter Size

The number of live pigs born per litter appears to be the most accurate measure of prolificacy. While some people feel that the total number of pigs born (alive and dead) is influenced to a lesser extent by environment, researchers at The Ohio State University have found that the number of pigs farrowed alive has a higher heritability than the total number farrowed. While the selection pressure for this trait will vary among producers, gilts should farrow a minimum of eight live pigs per litter and sows a minimum of nine live pigs per litter. The Ohio researchers have also reported a heritability estimate of .35 for the number of stillbirths (i.e., the difference between total born and number born alive). This is rather highly heritable for a reproductive trait, thus they have recommended that selection against stillbirths be added to the selection program.

Teat Count

Teats should be counted on all gilts when they are ear-notched. Gilts that have less than twelve teats should be identified as market gilts and should no longer be considered as replacement prospects. Underlines should be re-examined when replacements are selected. Underline evaluation will be covered in detail in Section 8.

Birth Weight

In swine, as in other species, selection for heavy birth weights can lead to dystocia. However, heavier pigs at birth generally have more strength, liveability, and greater subsequent performance. Birth weights of 2.5 to 4.0 lb. are considered acceptable.

Litter Weight

Litter weight at weaning is an excellent indicator of sow productivity because it reflects both litter size, and mothering and milking ability. Since time of weaning varies between 14 and 21 days, depending on the management system and sow milk production peaks, the NSIF recommends that litter weights be taken prior to weaning and as close to 21 days as possible. Since it is impractical to weigh each litter at exactly 21 days of age, it is necessary to adjust litter weights to 21 days of age by the following equation:

$$\text{21-day litter weight} = b \text{ (actual litter weight)}$$

where b equals one of the following factors depending on the age in days.

Age	b	Age	b	Age	b
14	1.30	19	1.07	24	.91
15	1.25	20	1.03	25	.88
16	1.20	21	1.00	26	.86
17	1.15	22	.97	27	.84
18	1.11	23	.94	28	.82

Parity Adjustments. Parity refers to the number of litters that a female has produced. Thus, a gilt that has just farrowed is considered a first parity sow, whereas a mature sow that has just had her fourth litter is considered a fourth parity sow. Normally a gilt will not reach her maximum level of milk production until her second parity, and her milking ability will start to decline after the third or fourth parity. Likewise, the maximum number of pigs born alive is not reach until the fourth parity and declines with the increase of the sow's age. This decline usually begins at approximately the eighth parity. Therefore, in order to compare sows from different parity groups, it is necessary to adjust both the number of pigs born alive and the 21-day litter weight to a mature sow equivalent by adding the following numbers to the record based on the parity of the female.

Parity	Number born alive	21-day litter weight
1	1.5	6.5
2	.9	0
3	.3	0
4	0	1.5
5–7	0	4.5
8–10	.4	8.5
>10	1.6	12.0

A common management practice is to equalize (standardize) litter size among sows by moving pigs from large litters to sows which had small litters. Standardizing litter size minimizes the adverse effects of raising very large or very small litters. Also, the milking ability of the sows is more accurately estimated when litters are standardized to an equal number nursed. To prevent the discrimination against a sow that has fewer pigs but may be milking well, the adjusted 21-day litter weight should be standardized to 10 pigs by adding the appropriate value from the following.

Number of pigs after transfer	Adjustment of 21-day litter weight
≤3	65
4	50
5	37
6	26
7	17
8	10
9	4
≥10	0

For example, if a first parity sow produced a litter of 8 pigs that weighted 90 lb. at 16 days of age, her adjusted number born alive and adjusted 21-day litter weight would be calculated as follows:

$$\text{Adjusted number born} = 8 + 1.5$$
$$= 9.5 \text{ pigs}$$

$$\text{Adjusted 21-day weight} = (b \times \text{weight}) + \text{parity adjustment} + \text{standardization}$$
$$= (1.2 \times 90) + 6.5 + 10$$
$$= 108 + 6.5 + 10$$
$$= 124.5 \text{ lb.}$$

Sow Productivity Index

Since no single parameter accurately measures overall sow productivity, an index including two or more traits should be used to identify the top producing sows in the herd. In their 1987 recommendations, the NSIF suggested using the following productivity index.

$$\text{Sow Productivity Index} = 100 + [6.5\,(L - \overline{L})] + [1.0\,(W - \overline{W})]$$

where:

L = Adjusted number of pigs born alive for individual sow
$\overline{L}$ = Average adjusted number born alive for contemporary group
W = Adjusted 21-day litter weight for individual sow
$\overline{W}$ = Average adjusted 21-day litter weight for contemporary group
6.5 and 1.0 = Regression coefficients

For example, the Sow Productivity Index (SPI) for the first parity sow from the previous example would be calculated by using her adjusted number born alive of 9.5 and her adjusted 21-day litter weight of 124.5 lb. If her contemporary group averages for these traits were 8.5 pigs and 110 lb., the SPI would be calculated as follows:

$$\text{SPI} = 100 + [6.5 \times (9.5 - 8.5)] + [1.0 \times (124.5 - 110)]$$
$$= 100 + 6.5 \qquad\qquad + \quad 14.5$$
$$= 121$$

Sow Production Breeding Value

To be the most accurate when culling the sow herd, the producer should utilize records from all of the litters each sow has produced. Since not all sows in the herd have produced the same number of litters, a more complex and accurate tool is required to make these comparisons. Whereas the Sow Productivity Index incorporates the records of only a single litter, the Sow Production Breeding Value (SPBV) utilizes records from all of the litters produced as well as the estimates for heritability and repeatability of the traits. Therefore, the SPBV is actually an estimation of the genetic capability for sow productivity that will be transmitted to the sow's offspring. The SPBV is calculated as follows, with C representing the factor for heritability and repeatability.

$$SPBV = 100 + C \text{ (Average Sow Index} - 100)$$

The value of C varies with the number of records for a sow and should be taken from the following table. It should be noted that C increases as the number of records increases. This is because a larger number of records allows for a higher and more accurate measure of repeatability.

Number of Records	C	Number of Records	C
1	.20	4	.46
2	.32	5	.50
3	.40	6	.53

The SPBV for a sow that had produced three litters with indexes of 105, 95, and 115 would be calculated as follows:

$$SPBV = 100 + .4 \left[(\frac{105 + 95 + 115}{3}) - 100 \right]$$

$$= 100 + .4 \, [105 - 100]$$
$$= 100 + .4 \, [5]$$
$$= 100 + 2$$
$$= 102$$

Growth Rate

Growth rate in swine has traditionally been measured as the number of days required to reach a specified weight. The specified weight represents the market weight of the finished pig. Therefore, the fastest gaining pig would require the fewest days to reach market weight. As the size of the breeding stock and the slaughter weight of the market hog have increased, the weight range over which replacements are tested for their growability has also increased. Most producers and test stations presently test gains to 230 lb. While performance and growth rate standards will vary depending upon environment and management, high quality boars should not require more than 160 days to reach 230 lb. and high quality gilts should reach 230 lb. in 170 days or less. Some superior gaining pigs may reach 230 lb. in 140 days or less. Since weighing each pig just as it reaches 230 lb. would be very difficult, an adjustment factor is necessary to calculate the pig's age at 230 lb. One simple adjustment system is to add or subtract 1 day of age for each 2 lb. below or above 230 lb. A more precise adjustment is given in the following formula:

$$\text{Days to 230 lb.} = \text{actual age} + (230 - \text{actual weight}) \left(\frac{\text{actual age} - 38}{\text{actual weight}} \right)$$

For example, a boar weighing 240 lb. at 160 days of age, using the simple adjustment, would have an adjusted days to 230 lb. of 155 days. Since the boar weighs 10 lb. over 230 pounds, dividing by 2 lb./day would give 5 days of age adjustment. Because the boar was heavier than 230 lb., the 5 days would be subtracted from 160 days to give 155 days to reach 230 lb. If the equation method of adjusting is used, the calculations are as follows:

$$\text{Days to 230 lb.} = 160 + (230–240) \left(\frac{(160-38)}{240} \right)$$

$$= 160 + (-10)(.51)$$
$$= 154.9 \text{ days}$$

Many of the very fast gaining boars to 220–230 lb. are fatter and mature earlier for their type, then they grow more slowly and less efficiently to heavier weights. Thus, it may be preferable to performance test boars to a given age, such as 180 or 200 days. This would test a boar to a weight heavier than normal market weight and would give a more accurate measure of a boar's genetic potential to sire fast-gaining market hogs.

Feed Efficiency

Feed costs make up 60% to 75% of the total production costs of a swine enterprise making it very important for a pig to be able to gain efficiently. Feed efficiency is generally measured as feed to gain ratio, or the amount of feed required to produce 100 lb. of gain. Barrows and gilts should require no more than 300 lb. of feed per 100 lb. of gain. Boars are generally more efficient and should require no more than 260 to 270 lb. of feed per 100 lb. of gain.

When measuring feed efficiency, it is ideal to feed the pigs individually and collect individual feed efficiency data. Since such a procedure is rather costly, it is acceptable to group feed pigs that are either fed with litter mates or grouped by sire. It is rather meaningless to measure feed efficiency on a group of pigs with more than one sire represented.

A producer should recognize that feed efficiency is affected by three factors: environment, feed intake above maintenance, and composition of gain. The first factor cannot be improved through selection. However, since it is more efficient to produce muscle than it is to produce fat, a producer can improve feed efficiency by selecting for leaner, later maturing breeding stock.

Carcass Merit

The swine carcass traits and their importance are discussed in Sections 5 and 6. When comparing these traits between animals, it is important to consider all of the pigs at a constant weight, since weight can greatly influence the amount of fat and muscle present in the carcass. Accordingly, adjustments similar to those for days to 230 lb. are necessary for backfat and loin eye area measurements.

Backfat can be adjusted to a 230 lb. liveweight basis by the following formula:

$$\text{Adjusted Backfat (BF)} = \text{actual BF} + (230 - \text{actual weight})\frac{\text{actual BF}}{(\text{actual weight} - 25)}$$

Thus, a pig that probed 1.1 in. of average backfat at 220 lb. would have an adjusted backfat of 1.156 in. calculated as follows:

$$\text{Adjusted BF} = 1.1 + (230-220)\frac{1.1}{(220-25)}$$
$$= 1.1 + (10)\,(.0056)$$
$$= 1.1 + .056$$
$$= 1.156$$

Loin eye area adjustments can be made by adding or subtracting .013 in.^{2} for each pound below or above 230 lb. A boar that sonorays a 5.0 in.^{2} loin eye at 220 lb. would have an adjusted loin eye area of 5.13 in.^{2}. Since the boar weighs 10 lb. less than 230 lb., an adjustment of .13 in.^{2} (10 lb. $\times$ .013 in.^{2}/lb.) is added to the actual measurement of 5.0 in.^{2} to give the adjusted loin eye area measurement of 5.13 in.^{2} at 230 lb.

Central Swine Test Programs

Central swine tests are utilized to compare the rate of gain, feed conversion, loin eye area, and backfat of individual pigs or groups of pigs (preferably littermates or half-sibs) from different farms. The pigs are tested at one location under uniform conditions in order to remove potential environmental differences in performance. In addition to their primary function, central tests serve to educate producers regarding performance records and to provide a supply of performance tested boars for both commercial and purebred producers. The 1987 NSIF guidelines recommend that pigs be weighed on test between 70 and 80 lb. and weighed off test between 230 and 240 lb. The NSIF recommends the following selection indexes be used to rank the boars at the end of a test:

    a. For test pens including only one animal and feed efficiency measured:
$$\text{Index} = 100 + 70(G - \bar{G}) - 75(B - \bar{B}) - 55(F - \bar{F})$$
    b. For test pens including two or more full and half-sibs and feed efficiency measured:
$$\text{Index} = 100 + 80(G - \bar{G}) - 85(B - \bar{B}) - 80(F - \bar{F})$$
    c. For tests where only gain and backfat are measured:
$$\text{Index} = 100 + 112(G - \bar{G}) - 120(B - \bar{B})$$

where: G = rate of gain; B = backfat and F = feed efficiency.

It is imperative that breeding animals be structurally correct and sound to carry out their functions. Therefore, most test stations score the boars for feet and leg soundness at the end of the test period, using the following 10-point scoring system.

- Unacceptable (1–3 points). Severe structure problems that restrict animal's ability to breed.
- Good (4–7 points). Animals with slight structural and/or movement problems.
- Excellent (8–10 points). No obvious structural or movement problems.

Most stations require a soundness score of 4 points or higher before allowing a boar into the test station sale, regardless of his performance index rank. Structural soundness will be discussed in more detail in Section 8.

Specification Based Selection Programs

When selecting swine it is important to realize that certain situations require different types of animals. All animals have traits that may make them superior under one set of circumstances; yet under different conditions, these same traits may be of little value and could even be liabilities. For example, an extremely lean, muscular boar is very desirable for a terminal sire (all progeny marketed). However, since research has shown extreme leanness and muscling to be negatively correlated to reproductive performance, these same traits are likely to make this boar undesirable for generating replacement gilts.

When selecting swine, one should ask the following questions.

1. How are the selected boars (gilts) going to be used (selection purpose)?
2. Under what conditions are the boars (gilts) expected to perform (selection situation)?
3. Based on the purpose and the situation, what traits are most important (selection priorities)?

The selection purpose and situation are collectively referred to as the *scenario*. Once you understand the scenario, you can accurately determine which traits are the priorities for selection. With that information, one can choose the correct boar (gilt) for that specific situation and purpose.

With boars, the selection purpose can generally be broken into paternal (terminal sire), maternal (generate replacement gilts), or combined maternal-paternal usage. If a boar is slated to be used as a paternal line sire, the growth and carcass traits should receive top priority, while traits such as adjusted 21-day litter weight and dam's SPI should be of little concern. If a boar is to be used as a maternal line sire, the dam and litter data (litter size, adjusted 21-day litter weight, SPI, SPBV) should receive high priority, while growth traits should receive a moderate priority, and carcass traits a low priority.

The primary concern regarding the selection situation is the degree of confinement housing in which the boars, gilts, sows, and market hogs must function. The higher the degree of confinement or concrete, the higher the selection priority must be for structural soundness.

As an example, consider the selection of Yorkshire boars for the following scenario:

- Three-breed rotational cross
- Used on high growth, low fat Duroc X Hampshire sows
- Gilts to be retained in herd, barrows fed to market
- Total confinement production system

The scenario indicates the need for a maternal line or possibly a maternal-paternal combination sire. Since the available sows are high in growth and cutability, the top priorities for boar selection should be structural soundness, because of the confinement and maternal traits, such as litter size and milking ability (21-day litter weight). Growth rate and carcass merit are still important to the overall production system; however, they should receive only moderate or low priority in this selection scenario.

Consider another example scenario for the selection of Hampshire boars:

- Terminal sire in farrow to finish operation
- Used on maternal line Landrace X Yorkshire gilts
- Gilts and barrows marketed on grade and yield basis
- Minimal confinement—primarily outside lots

The scenario calls for a paternal line sire; thus, growth rate, leanness and muscling should receive top selection priority. Since no replacements are kept and confinement is minimal, structural soundness should only receive moderate consideration. Other than litter size, the maternal traits should receive little or no consideration in this scenario.

Evaluation of Market Hog Performance

For many years, market hogs have been evaluated solely on their carcass merit. This type of evaluation obviously omits economically important production traits such as growth and feed efficiency. However, the evaluation of market hogs strictly on performance traits ignores important differences in composition of the gain. Therefore, the evaluation of market hog performance should combine an appraisal of both production records and carcass characteristics. The NPPC has published procedures to determine the pounds of acceptable quality lean pork gain per day of age. This measure of lean pork growth provides producers a valuable tool for combining the evaluation of the growth and carcass merits of market hogs into one measurable trait. The following equation can be used when the age of the market hog is known to calculate the pounds of acceptable quality lean pork gain per day of age.

$$\text{Pounds of acceptable quality lean pork gain per day of age} = .63 + .0029 \times \text{hot carcass wt. (lb.)} + .009 \times \text{loin eye area (in.}^2) - .09 \times \text{10th rib fat depth (in.)} - .0032 \times \text{age (days)}$$

This procedure essentially ranks pigs on their true growth capabilities. That is, the ability to produce the most lean product over a shorter period of time.

This lean gain-per-day concept can also be utilized to evaluate performance tested market hog contests. By combining this measure of performance with visual appraisals of structural soundness and carcass quality, these pigs can be evaluated and ranked from a total value standpoint. Discussions of the visual appraisals of structural soundness and carcass quality are found in Sections 8 and 6. Entries which meet the minimum qualifications for soundness and carcass quality can be ranked by the following equation:

Pounds of acceptable quality = .9 + .0047 × hot carcass wt. (lb.)
lean pork gain per day on test   + .018 × loin eye area (in.²)
     − .15 × 10th rib fat depth (in.)
     − .007 × days on test
     − .0044 × initial live wt. on test (lb.)

For example, a pig that weighed on test at 55 lb. and after 90 days on test yielded a 160 lb. carcass with a 10th rib fat depth of .8 in. and a loin eye area of 5.0 in.² would have a lean pork gain per day on test of .75 lb. calculated as follows:

Pounds of acceptable quality = .9 + .0047 × 160
lean pork gain per day on test   + .018 × 5.0
     − .15 × .8
     − .007 × 90
     − .0044 × 55
   = .75 lb. per day

Pounds of acceptable quality lean pork gain per day on test can also be computed by using the Table of Conversion Values found in Appendix K.

Visual Evaluation of Breeding Swine

Fortunately swine breeders can make rapid change through their selection programs due to the relatively short generation interval. They can more easily recover from selection mistakes and progress more rapidly toward their production goals than the cattleman or sheepman. Though swine types frequently change, a discussion of performance traits should indicate that the successful swine producer is selecting structurally sound breeding stock that will produce large litters of efficient, fast growing pigs. Swine producers must also produce a large quantity of muscle with acceptable quality and leanness.

Skeletal Correctness

As more and more swine are being raised in confinement production systems, skeletal structure has become increasingly more important to successful swine production. Any skeletal unsoundnesses are magnified when hogs are raised on concrete. Therefore, the seedstock producer must focus on producing durable, structurally sound hogs that are adaptable to these confinement conditions.

The boar in Figure 8.1 has a desirable skeletal structure as viewed from the side. Note the flatter top, more level rump, and higher tail setting as compared to the high topped, steep rumped boar in Figure 8.2. In hogs with a rump this steep, the hip, stifle, and hock joints have a tendency to lock in a straight line when the hog walks or the boar is in the breeding position. This causes a kicking action when the hog moves or could cause the boar to fall backwards when mounting the sow. In contrast, the rear legs on the more level rumped hogs have more angle and flex at the joints to more adequately cushion the walk and give support when in the breeding position.

The high arch of top (Figure 8.2) is associated with the shoulder blade being pushed forward on a straight line with the front legs. This straightness of shoulder causes abnormal pressure at the scapula-humerus joint and at the knee joint. This usually results in the hog being buckled over at the knees (Figure 8.3). These hogs are usually straight on their pasterns and walk with a short, choppy stride. On the other hand, the flatter-topped boar (Figure 8.1) has a more sloping shoulder blade. The front legs slope from the shoulder and prevent abnormal pressure on the knee joint. The pasterns are sloping and long as shown in Figure 8.4. This boar will walk with a long, well cushioned stride and should remain sound on concrete.

When viewed from the front, the hog should be straight legged (Figure 8.5) and have adequate substance of bone. The toes should be even in size because a short toe (generally the inside toe), as shown in Figure 8.6, will cause abnormal wear on the other toe which could cause lameness.

When viewed from the rear, the hog should stand squarely on its rear legs, yet toe out slightly from the pastern down. Though rugged bone is desirable, a large coarse, round bone is not. The bone should have a flat appearance with the widest part visible when viewed from the side.

Size and Scale

Production of fast gaining market hogs with the ability to gain efficiently up to heavy market weights is accomplished most readily through the selection of long bodied, large scaled breeding stock. These large framed hogs are lean and, thus, more efficient at a given weight. They should have the ability to be marketed at 240 to 280 lb., when economically feasible, without slowing down in growth rate or depositing excess body fat at these heavy weights.

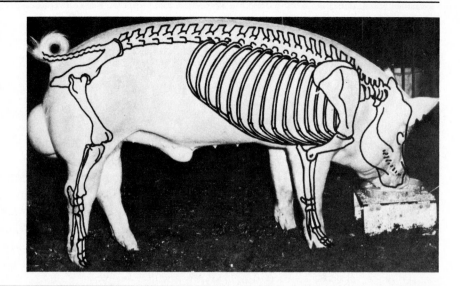

Figure 8.1. Illustration of a boar with a desirable skeletal structure. (Courtesy of American Yorkshire Club).

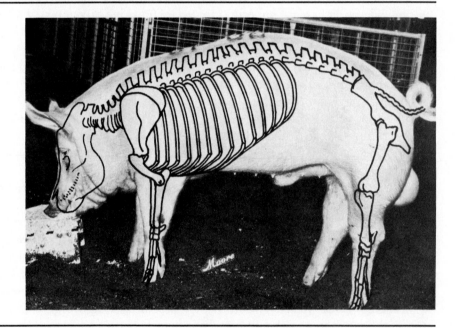

Figure 8.2. Illustration of a skeletally incorrect boar that is high topped, steep rumped and straight shouldered. (Courtesy of American Yorkshire Club).

Capacity

Hogs should exhibit volume and dimension through the rib and body cavity to allow for adequate breeding and feeding capacity. When viewed from the side, a broody, productive sow (Figure 8.7) is deep in both the fore and rear rib, long bodied, and has moderate depth in her rear flank. She is sprung wide, has a long, arching rib, and has a wide chest floor. In contrast, the gilt in Figure 8.8 is shallow and round in her rib structure, shallow in her rear flank, and base narrow when viewed from the front. The student should be aware that the areas of the rib and lower body cavity are highly predisposed to fat and waste. Therefore, what may appear to be a rather wide sprung, deep-sided hog may actually be a fat hog. Also, remember that capacity is a three dimensional measurement; thus, a high capacity hog must excel in the three dimensions of width, depth, and length of body.

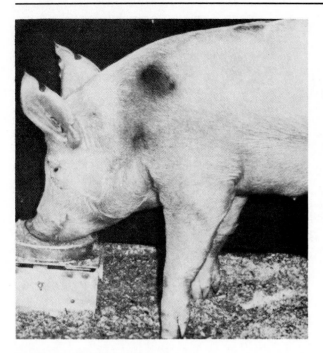

Figure 8.3. Illustration of buck knees. (Courtesy of American Yorkshire Club).

Figure 8.4. Illustration of long, sloping pasterns. (Courtesy of American Yorkshire Club).

Figure 8.5. Illustration of correct front leg structure and evenly sized toes.

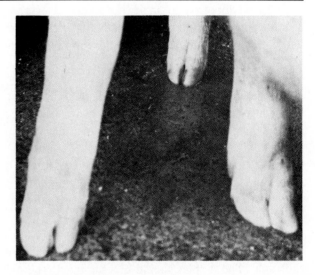

Figure 8.6. Illustration of a pig that is splay footed and also has short inside toes.

Figure 8.7. Illustration of a broody, deep bodied gilt. (Courtesy of American Hampshire Herdsman).

Figure 8.8. Illustration of a shallow bodied gilt that is shallow in her flank and narrow in her chest.

Muscle

In order to grow rapidly and efficiently, market hogs must be muscular. Since muscling is highly heritable and can be accurately observed in the live animal, selection for muscling can result in considerable improvement.

The boars pictured in Figure 8.9 are thick and expressively muscled. The boars in Figure 8.10 are light muscled. Note their narrow, flat muscle shape.

Remember that no single trait should be overemphasized. Some producers believe that extreme amounts of muscling may hinder reproduction efficiency (breeding or farrowing herd) of the breeding herd. Hence, while muscling of most herds could be improved, it may be wise to avoid extremes.

Leanness

The importance of producing lean hogs cannot be overemphasized. Fat is neither efficient to produce, nor economical to trim off to obtain consumer acceptance. Production of lean market hogs can be attained through selection of lean breeding stock because leanness is highly heritable. Hogs should be lean down their top and over the edge of the loin and should show adequate shoulder blade movement at the walk. Other areas that are highly predisposed to fat are the jowl, elbow pockets, fore and rear flanks, underline, and the seam and base of the ham.

Underlines

Since underline characteristics are highly heritable, they should be emphasized in the selection of both boars and gilts. An acceptable underline has a minimum of six functional, evenly-spaced nipples on each side. The nipples should be prominent (the nipple should be well-defined from the teat) and uniform in size. The gilt in Figure 8.11 has an excellent underline. The first teat is directly behind the front leg which will allow ample room for pigs to nurse. In contrast, the gilt's underline in Figure 8.12 shows that the teats start further back and are poorly spaced. There is less mammary tissue available for each teat; consequently, less milk will be produced. The underline should also be free of pin, inverted or blind nipples (Figure 8.13). The sow in Figure 8.14 has an excellent underline. She has evenly spaced nipples and well-defined udder sections with evidence of ample secretory tissue above each section to allow for high milk production.

Figure 8.9. Illustration of thick, expressively muscled boar. (Courtesy of American Hampshire Herdsman and American Yorkshire Club).

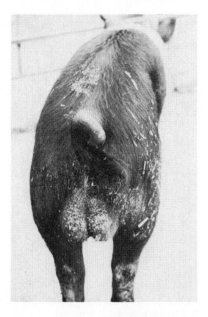

Figure 8.10. Illustration of a narrow topped, light muscled boar (left) and a light muscled unexpressive boar (right). (Courtesy of American Hampshire Herdsman and American Yorkshire Club).

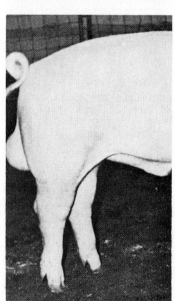

Figure 8.11. Illustration of an excellent underline. (Courtesy of American Yorkshire Club).

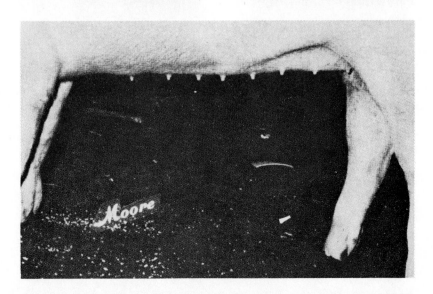

Figure 8.12. Illustration of a poorly spaced underline.

Figure 8.13. Illustrations showing a pin nipple (A) indicated by the arrow with a normal nipple on either side of it, inverted nipple (B) and blind nipple (C) indicated by the arrow compared to the normal nipple to the left of the photograph.

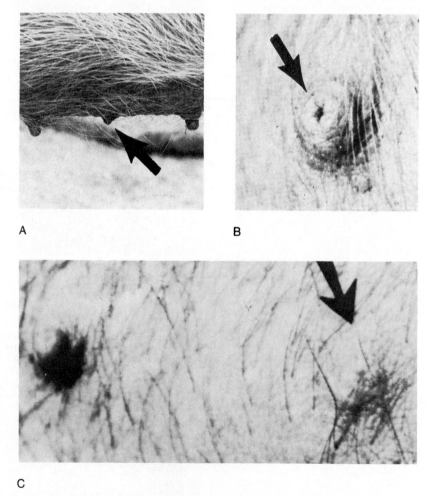

A

B

C

Figure 8.14. Illustration of a sow with an excellent underline. (Courtesy of American Hampshire Herdsman).

Figure 8.15. Illustration of an upturned vulva.

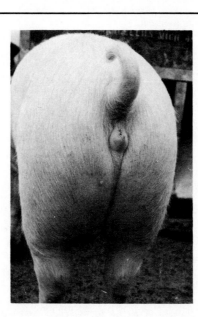

Figure 8.16. Illustration of an infantile vulva.

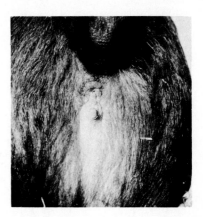

Sex Character

Even though measurement of sex character is very subjective, gilts and sows should have a feminine appearance, and boars should look masculine. These differences are most noticeable in the head and neck region. Boars should also show ample testicular development. Boars that develop their masculinity at a very early age should be discriminated against, however, because this is usually a sign of early maturity. A breeding gilt should have a fully developed vulva positioned to allow entrance of the boar during breeding. The gilt in Figure 8.15 has an upturned vulva which will prohibit breeding. An infantile vulva (Figure 8.16) indicates a poorly developed reproductive tract and thus poor fertility.

Breed Character

Breed character is a highly subjective trait that varies in importance from one producer to the next. For the purposes of this manual, sufficient breed character to qualify a gilt or boar for registry with the particular breed association will be considered acceptable.

Live Cattle Evaluation, Grading, and Pricing

Evaluation

Live market cattle evaluation is essentially an estimation of important carcass characteristics. The specific characteristics evaluated are those that provide an indication of amount of fat and/or muscle (cutability), as well as quality grade, which in turn determines carcass value. Carcass value is usually used to calculate live value. A definition, brief description, ranges, and the mechanics used in estimating each carcass characteristic will be presented in this section. The student should familiarize him or herself with the normal ranges and the mechanics involved for evaluating each characteristic.

Weight

Definition: Live weight is the actual weight of the cattle at the time of evaluation or immediately prior to slaughter.

Carcass weight may be either hot (wt. of dressed carcass just prior to chilling) or chilled (wt. after carcass chilling) weight, and both are used in the beef industry. In either case, hot and chilled carcass weights are actual weights. Generally, hot carcass weight is 1–2% (av. of 1½%) higher than or 101.5% of chilled carcass weight.

Live weight

Extreme Range:	800–1700 lb.
Normal Range:	950–1500 lb.
Average:	1150 lb.

These weight ranges represent steers and bullocks; the upper weight of each range would generally be 100 to 300 lb. less for heifers.

Weight is easily obtained, and it is the most commonly used characteristic for determining value, even though by itself it is not a very precise estimate of cutability. Producers use weight to calculate production efficiency (i.e., weight per day of age); and live cattle, carcasses, and beef cuts are bought and sold largely on a weight and grade basis today. However, weight is normally combined with one or several carcass characteristics to determine cutability and/or value.

Live and carcass weights usually are not estimated, but are actual weights. Carcass weight (either hot or chilled) can be calculated from live weight by multiplying by dressing percentage. The values presented in this section for each characteristic are representative of cattle of normal market weight (approximately 950 to 1250 lb.).

Hot carcass weight is one of the factors used to calculate yield grade. As hot carcass weight increases, yield grade also increases in numerical value (toward 5.0), but the percentage of boneless, closely trimmed retail cuts decreases. The reason is because as weight increases, carcass fat also usually increases. However, this relationship is most accurate for medium size steers of average muscling, thus, as body size and growthiness, and degree of muscling increase or decrease, the relationship becomes less accurate. Heifers generally are underestimated because they are fatter than steers of the same weight, and bullocks are overestimated because they are much leaner than steers of the same weight.

Dressing Percentage

Definition: (Chilled carcass weight ÷ live weight) × 100.

Extreme Range:	45–68%
Normal Range:	55–67% for steers, bullocks, and heifers
Average:	62% for Choice steers, bullocks and heifers

As indicated, dressing percentage varies with the grade, type, degree of muscling, and condition of the cattle being evaluated. For example, an extremely thin, dairy cow may dress below 45%, whereas a prime steer may dress over 65%. The factors that have the greatest effect on dressing percentage of cattle in order of relative importance are: (1) the amount of fill (contents of the stomach compartments and intestines) because dressing percentage decreases as fill increases; (2) degree of muscling because dressing percentage is higher among heavily muscled cattle compared to lighter muscled cattle; (3) weight of the hide, head, and feet—with hide weight being the most variable—because as hide weight increases, dressing percentage decreases; and (4) degree of fatness (finish). Fat has little effect on dressing percentage when compared among cattle of the same fill. For extreme degrees of fatness, very fat cattle may dress as much as 1% higher than lean cattle. Dressing percentage is lowest in young, light weight cattle and increases as they increase in age and weight. As cattle increase in age and weight, viscera becomes a progressively smaller proportion of the body; thus, dressing percentage increases.

When estimating dressing percentage of steers, heifers, and bullocks (bulls under 2 years of age) of the same live weight, chronological age, and fill, bullocks will have the lowest dressing percentage, steers will have the highest dressing percentage, and heifers will be intermediate. Even though bullocks are the heaviest muscled, they will have lower dressing percentages than steers or heifers of the same weight and age because they have heavier hides, heads, and feet. Heifers will dress about 2% less than steers of the same weight and chronological age because they are physiologically more mature and further into the fattening phase. Thus, they have more internal fat associated with their stomach and intestines, which is removed during visceration.

To approximate the stage of the growth curve at which bullocks, steers, and heifers would be similar in their amount of carcass fat, bullocks would average 130% of the weight of steers, and heifers would be about 85% of the steer weight. This "rule of thumb" comparison is valid only within a cattle type (i.e., large framed, growthy cattle, as compared to small framed, short bodied, small cattle, or those intermediate between these two extremes). To illustrate, within intermediate-body type cattle, for example, a steer weighing 1150 lb. would have approximately the same amount of carcass fat as a 975 lb. heifer or a 1500 lb. bullock. In cattle evaluation of different sexes, the live weight spread is usually much lsss than those in the above example, so that differences in fat or stage of the growth curve must be taken into account when estimating dressing percentage of steers, heifers, and bullocks.

Since quality grade is related to degree of fatness and dressing percentage varies with fat, the normal ranges as well as average dressing percentage for each quality grade are presented in Table 9.1.

Table 9.1 Dressing Percentage of Cattle by Quality Grade.

Quality Grade	Range, %	Average, %
Prime	62–66	64
Choice	59–64	62
Select	58–61	60
Standard	55–60	57
Commercial	54–62	57
Utility	49–57	53
Cutter*	45–54	49
Canner*	40–48	45

*Composed almost entirely of cows.

Fat Thickness

Definition: Depth of fat in tenths of inches over the ribeye muscle at the 12th rib. It consists of a single measurement or estimate at a point ¾ of the lateral length of the ribeye muscle from the split chine bone as shown in Figure 9.1

Extreme Range:	.05–1.4 in.
Normal Range:	.15–1.0 in. for steers and heifers. Bullocks would have a normal range of .05–.5 in.
Average:	.5 in. for Choice steers and heifers. Choice bullocks would average about .35 in.

The amount of external fat that can be tolerated on a beef animal is a matter of debate. Most experts agree that anything over .08 in./100 lb. of carcass weight is too much. This would be the equivalent of .55 in. on an 1150 lb. animal dressing 62%. While fat thicknesses less than .08 in./100 lb of carcass weight are most desirable, a minimum of .2 in. of fat at the 12th rib is considered necessary to protect the carcass against excessive shrink, discoloration, and loss of bloom during storage and handling.

Fat thickness at the 12th rib is one of the factors used to calculate yield grade. Fat thickness is an assessment of external fat on the carcass. Thus, as it increases, it lowers retail yield. As fat thickness increases, yield grade increases in numerical value (toward 5.0) but the percentage of boneless, closely trimmed retail cuts decreases.

The location of the 12th rib is indicated on the side view of the steer in Figure 9.1. The top view of the steer shows that the fat thickness measurement is estimated approximately 4½–5 in. from the dorsal midline (X's) because this location approximates the ¾ lateral length measurement of the longissimus muscle at the 12th rib where the actual measurement is made on the carcass as is shown in Figure 9.1(C).

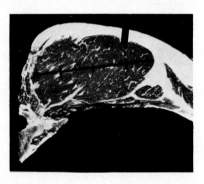

A   B   C

Figure 9.1. A side (A) and a top view (B) of a steer showing the approximate location of the 12th rib which is where fat thickness and ribeye area are estimated. In the side view (A) the location of the 12th rib is identified with a heavy white line and indicated by an arrow. In the top view (B) the dorsal midline is indicated by a dotted line. Fat thickness is estimated 4 1/2-5 in. laterally from the dorsal midline at the 12th rib. This location is indicated in the figure by an X on the right and left side of the dorsal midline. Illustration (C) shows the procedure for measuring or estimating fat thickness on the 12th ribeye interface of a beef carcass. Fat is estimated or measured at a point 3/4 the lateral length of the ribeye muscle perpendicular to the outer surface of the fat as shown in the figure.

Ribeye Area

Definition: Area of the longissimus muscle measured in square inches at the 12th rib interface on the beef forequarter as shown in Figure 9.2.

Extreme Range: 7.0–19.5 in.²
Normal Range: 10.0–17.0 in.²
Average: 12.6 in.² for 1150 lb. steers. Bullocks will average about 1 in.² larger than the average for steers, and heifers 1 in.² less than steers of the same weight.

A guideline for estimating the ribeye area on live steers of average muscling is to use 1.1 in.²/100 lb. of live weight between 900 to 1250 lb. Over 1251 lb., the ribeye area will not increase at the rate of 1.1 in.²/100 lb. Thus, an 1150 lb. steer of average muscling will have approximately 12.6 in.² of ribeye area. If the steer is heavier muscled than average, adjust the estimate upward commensurate with the degree of muscling in excess of average muscling. Likewise, if the steer is lighter muscled than average, adjust the estimate downward commensurate with the extent of muscling less than average. For estimating the ribeye area of bullocks and heifers, use the steer estimates for muscling and then adjust the estimates for either bullocks or heifers as described above.

The ribeye area is a fair to good indicator of total carcass muscle. However, the ribeye area is widely used as an indicator of beef carcass muscling because it can be accurately and easily measured on the ribbed carcass. It is the largest muscle in the carcass and the most valuable because it is the major muscle comprising the steaks and roasts of the wholesale loin and rib.

The ribeye area at the 12th rib is one of the factors used to calculate yield grade. As the ribeye area increases, yield grade decreases in numerical value (toward 1.0) but the percentage of boneless, closely trimmed retail cuts increases. The ribeye area is the only yield grade factor that assesses muscling. The other three factors are essentially assessments of fat.

The depth (dorsal-ventral dimension) and width (lateral dimension) of the muscling in the loin-rib junction at the 12th rib should be evaluated to assess ribeye area.

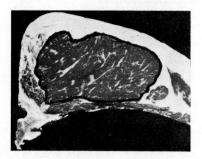

Figure 9.2. An illustration showing the ribeye muscle interface at the 12th rib. The perimeter of the ribeye muscle is outlined with a black line to distinguish it from the small muscles surrounding the eye muscle which are not included in the area measurement or estimate.

Kidney, Pelvic and Heart Fat

Definition: The internal carcass fat associated with the kidney, pelvic cavity, and heart expressed as a percentage of chilled carcass weight. The kidney is included in the estimate of kidney fat.

Extreme Range: .5–6 .0%
Normal Range: 1.0–4.5%
Average: 3.0% for steers weighing 1150 lb. alive or for a 700 lb. carcass with .5 in. of 12th rib fat thickness. At the same weight, heifers will average about 1.0% more than steers, and bullocks will average

about 1.0% less than steers. Large framed, growthy cattle will average about 1.0% less than intermediate size cattle while small framed short bodied small cattle will average about 1.0% more than intermediate size cattle. Dairy type cattle will average about 1.5% more kidney, pelvic, and heart fat than the same weight beef type cattle of corresponding sexes.

The percentage of kidney, pelvic, and heart fat (KPH) is one of the factors used to calculate yield grade. As the percentage of KPH fat increases, yield grade increases in numerical value (toward 5.0) but the percentage of boneless, closely trimmed retail cuts decreases. The percentage of KPH fat is an assessment of internal fat in the carcass; thus, as it increases, it lowers retail yield.

The percentage of kidney, pelvic, and heart fat may be estimated on live cattle using the estimated 12th rib fat thickness as a guideline as shown below in Table 9.2.

Table 9.2   Estimated Percentage Kidney, Pelvic, and Heart Fat *from Estimated 12th Rib Fat Thickness.*

Estimated 12th Rib Fat Thickness, In.	Estimated % Kidney, Pelvic, and Heart Fat
.1 .2 .3	1.5-2.5%
.4 .5 .6	2.5-3.5%
.7 .8 .9	3.5-4.5%
1.0 1.1 1.2	$\geq$ 4.5%

Marbling

Definition: The intermingling of fat within the muscle (intramuscular fat). Marbling is normally evaluated in the ribeye muscle at the 12th rib.

Extreme Range:	Devoid—Abundant
Normal Range:	Traces—Abundant
Average:	Small to Modest. This is the amount of marbling necessary to grade low to average Choice.

Photographs of ribeye muscles showing each of the degrees of marbling are presented in Section 10.

The above terms are used by the Federal Grading Service, and the extreme range includes the degrees for quality grades from Canner to Prime. The midpoint of the range in marbling is a Small to Modest amount which qualifies for the low to average Choice grade. Modest marbling is typical of intermediate type and size steers weighing 1000-1150 lb. Heifers of the same weight usually have 1 to 2 degrees more marbling than steers, and bullocks at the same weight or chronological age usually have 2 to 3 degrees less than steers. In addition, large framed, growthy cattle have less marbling than intermediate type and size cattle, which, in turn, has less marbling than early maturing, small framed, short-bodied cattle at the same chronological age or live weight.

Marbling is usually estimated from the amount of external fat on live cattle, and it is generally assumed that fatter cattle have the highest degrees of marbling and higher quality grades, whereas cattle with very little external fat have the lowest degrees of marbling and lowest quality grades. Length of time on full feed, if known, is highly related to degree of marbling. Long fed cattle will generally have higher degrees of marbling than short fed cattle, and the latter will have lower degrees of marbling. The lowest degrees of marbling are found in cattle off pasture, off low energy rations (high roughage), or young cattle that have not reached the fattening phase of the growth curve.

Marbling is the most important factor affecting quality grade; thus, fatness is an important factor in the estimation of both yield and quality grade.

Maturity

Definition: Maturity is an estimation of the chronological age of the animal or carcass and is accomplished by assessing the physiological stages of maturity of bone and muscle characteristics. The degree of ossification of the thoracic cartilages (buttons), as well as in the cartilage associated with the lumbar and sacral vertebrae; the shape and color of the ribs, and the color of lean in the longissimus muscle at the 12th rib are used to assess maturity.

Extreme Range:	A to E
Normal Range:	A to E

A maturity is the most youthful (9 to 30 months), while E maturity is the oldest group (96 months and older). Cattle eligible for the U.S. Prime, Choice, Select and Standard grades must be either A or B maturity. C, D, and E maturity cattle are only eligible for the U.S. Commercial, Utility, Cutter, or Canner quality grades. Bullocks must be A maturity; therefore, intact males older than 24 months of age are classified as bulls and are not eligible for quality grading. At the same weight or chronological age, heifers physiologically (assessed by bone and muscle characteristics) more mature than steers, and bullocks physiologically less mature than steers. Large framed, growthy cattle are physiologically less mature at any given chronological age than small framed, short-bodied cattle.

Live Cattle Grading

Beef grading involves two separate and distinct procedures. These grade procedures include the quality grade (U.S. Prime, U.S. Choice, U.S. Select, etc.) and Yield grade (1, 2, 3, 4 and 5). Each of these grading systems will be discussed in more detail in Section 10 in the discussion of beef carcass grading.

Quality Grade

Carcass quality grade is based upon an evaluation of the degree of marbling and the degree of maturity. Since marbling and maturity factors cannot be accurately determined on live cattle, live quality grade is largely based on an evaluation of fatness. Even though finish is only slightly correlated with degree of marbling, for lack of a better criterion, the amount of finish is evaluated in order to predict marbling in everyday practice. Thus, it might be concluded that high grading cattle have to be very fat, but fortunately this is usually not the case and only a moderate amount of external fat is needed to ensure Choice or Prime grading cattle. Actual maturity is seldom known under normal marketing conditions, but some characteristics such as length of switch, refinement of head, and bone are associated with maturity. Grade is estimated to the nearest ⅓ (i.e., U.S. Prime+, U.S. Prime 0, U.S. Prime − U.S. Choice +, etc.). Photographs of steers representing each of the five quality grades appear in Figure 9.3.

Yield Grade

Yield grade identifies cattle for differences in yields of boneless, closely trimmed retail cuts from the round, loin, rib and chuck. Yield grade is often used synonomously with cutability. The yield of boneless, closely trimmed, retail cuts (cutability) is usually expressed as a percentage of carcass weight (i.e., 51.0%,

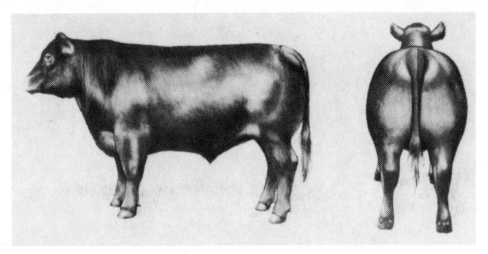

Prime

Choice

Select

Figure 9.3. Illustrations reprsentative of five of the quality grades of steers.

Standard

Utility

Figure 9.3. *(continued)*

etc). However, the percentage figure is converted to a yield grade designation between 1.0 and 5.9. A yield grade of 1.0 is equivalent to 54.6%, whereas a 5.9 yield grade is equivalent to 43.3% boneless, closely trimmed, retail cuts from the round, loin, rib, and chuck.

The factors used to determine yield grade are: (1) fat thickness at the 12th rib which is adjusted up or down depending upon the distribution of fat over the external surface of the animal; (2) ribeye area; (3) hot carcass weight; and (4) percentage kidney, pelvic, and heart fat. Fat thickness, ribeye area, hot carcass weight, and percentage kidney, pelvic and heart fat (KPH) are estimated; and yield grade is determined as described below.

In order to establish a base to estimate yield grade on live cattle, a yield grade of 3.5 is used as the base yield grade. The 3.5 yield grade is equivalent to a 600 lb. carcass with .6 in. of fat (12th rib), a 11.0 in.² ribeye area, and 3.5% KPH. Since most cattle differ from these base values, the yield grade of each cattle is determined by adjusting the base yield grade as follows:

1. Fat thickness at the 12th rib—for each .1 in. of fat thickness over .6 in., add .25 of a yield grade; and for each .1 in. under .6 in., subtract .25 of a yield grade from the base of 3.5. This adjustment of yield grade for fat thickness is used to determine what is known as the preliminary yield grade

(PYG). The PYG in increments of .1 in. of fat thickness is shown in Table 9.3. The estimate of fat thickness at the 12th rib is adjusted, if necessary, for lack of uniformity of distribution, and the adjusted fat thickness is used to determine PYG. PYG is then adjusted for ribeye area, hot carcass weight; and percentage kidney, pelvic, and heart fat as described below in 2, 3, and 4.

2. Ribeye area—for each square inch of ribeye area in excess of 11.0 in.^{2}, subtract .3 of a yield grade; and for each square inch less than 11.0 in.^{2}, add .3 of a yield grade.

3. Hot carcass weight—for each 25 lb. of hot carcass weight in excess of 600 lb., add .1 of a yield grade; and for each 25 lb. of hot carcass weight less than 600 lb., subtract .1 of a yield grade. Hot carcass weight is estimated by multiplying live weight by the estimated dressing % = chilled carcass weight $\times$ 1.015 (101.5%) = hot carcass weight.

4. % KPH—for each .5% KPH in excess of 3.5%, add .1 of a yield grade; and for each .5% KPH less than 3.5%, subtract .1 of a yield grade.

Table 9.3 Preliminary Yield Grade Equivalent to Adjusted Fat Thickness Estimate.

	Adjusted Fat Thickness Estimate, In.	PYG
	.1	2.25
	.2	2.5
	.3	2.75
	.4	3.0
	.5	3.25
Base	.6	3.5
	.7	3.75
	.8	4.0
	.9	4.25
	1.0	4.5
	1.1	4.75
	1.2	5.0

In order to intelligently estimate yield grade, it is absolutely necessary to know the magnitude of adjustment in yield grade that is contributed by each factor. It should be emphasized that as fat thickness, KPH, and hot carcass weight increase, yield grade increases, whereas when ribeye area increases, yield grade decreases. Also, remember that a yield grade of 1 means the highest cutability (yield of boneless, closely trimmed retail cuts from the round, loin, rib, and chuck); and a yield grade of 5.9 means the lowest cutability. Thus, a carcass with a yield grade of 5.9 has considerable fat and a relatively small ribeye area. It is also important to remember that the base carcass is one with a yield grade of 3.5. The following two examples should help to illustrate the procedure for estimating yield grade.

Your estimates of adjusted fat thickness, dressing percentage (for arriving at hot carcass weight), and ribeye area will be used in the evaluation of yield grade. Kidney, pelvic, and heart fat is determined from adjusted 12th rib fat thickness as illustrated in Table 9.2.

Examples:

	Steer A	Steer B
Live wt., lb.	1270	1050
Dressing %	61.0	63.0
Fat thickness, in.	.3	.7
Ribeye area, in.^{2}	14.3	10.6

Steer A has .3 in. less estimated 12th rib fat thickness (.3 in.) than the base of .6 in. and the PYG for .3 in. = 2.75. Steer A was estimated to have 14.3 in.^{2} of ribeye area which is 3.3 in.^{2} above the base of 11.0 in.^{2}. Each 1.0 in.^{2} is equivalent to .3 yield grade or 1.0 yield grade adjustment for ribeye area (3.3

in.² × .3 yield grade= 1.0 yield grade). The ribeye area adjustment of 1.0 is subtracted from the above PYG (2.75) which was adjusted for fat thickness; therefore, 2.75 − 1.0 = 1.75 which is the yield grade after adjusting for both fat thickness and ribeye area. Next, the yield grade is adjusted for hot carcass weight. Steer A has a 786 lb. hot carcass weight, (1270 lb. × .61 [61% estimated dressing % = 775 chilled carcass wt. × 1.015 to convert chilled carcass wt. to hot carcass wt.] = 786 lb.) which is 186 lb. above the base of 600 lb. Since each 25 lb. of hot carcass weight is equivalent to .1 yield grade, the hot carcass weight of steer A differs from the base by approximately 7.4, 25 lb. increments. Thus, 7.4 × .1 yield grade = .74 yield grade is the adjustment for hot carcass weight. Because the hot carcass weight of steer A is above the base, the adjustment is added to the 1.75 yield grade which was adjusted for fat thickness and ribeye area. Therefore, 1.75 + .74 = 2.49 which is the yield grade after adjusting for fat thickness, ribeye area, and hot carcass weight. The adjustment for KPH must now be made. Since percent of KPH is estimated from the estimated 12th rib fat thickness as explained previously, the estimated .3 in. of fat is equivalent to 2.5% kidney, pelvic, and heart fat (Table 9.2). Since each .5% of kidney, pelvic, and heart fat is equivalent to .1 yield grade, the adjustment is .1 yield grade (2, .5%'s × .1 yield grade = .2 yield grade). Therefore, the .2 yield grade adjustment for KPH is subtracted from the yield grade (2.49) adjusted for fat thickness, ribeye area, and hot carcass weight, 2.49 − .2 = 2.29 yield grade. Thus, the final yield grade of steer A is 2.2 after adjusting for all four factors. Final yield grade is never rounded up.

For steer B the base yield grade of 3.5 is adjusted to a PYG of 3.75 because this steer has .1 in. of fat thickness above the base of .6 in., and each .1 in. is equivalent to .25 yield grade. Ribeye area adjustment is .15 yield grade because the area is .5 in.² (.5 in.² × .3 = .15) below the base; therefore, 3.75 + .15 = 3.90 yield grade. Hot carcass weight of steer B is 671 lb. (1050 lb. × .63% = 662 lb. × 1.015 = 671 lb.). The adjustment is approximately .3 yield grade; therefore, 3.90 + .3 = 4.20 yield grade. No adjustment for KPH is made for steer B since it has the base KPH of 3.5% based on the estimated .7 in. of 12th rib fat thickness (Table 9.2). Therefore, the final yield grade yield grade for steer B is 4.2.

Weight-Eye Method of Calculating Yield Grade of Live Cattle

1. Calculate the PYG using the method previously described (Table 9.3).
2. Adjust the PYG using estimates of hot carcass weight and the ribeye area. The student is reminded to calculate hot carcass weight by multiplying live weight by the estimated dressing percentage to obtain an estimate of cold carcass weight and then multiplying cold carcass weight by 1.015 (101.5%) to obtain the estimate of hot carcass weight. The ribeye area is influenced by carcass weight. Animals with typical muscling would have ribeyes of the following size.

	Approximate Live Wt. (Lb.)	Hot Carcass Wt. (Lb.)	REA (In.²)	Approximate Live Wt. (Lb.)	Hot Carcass Wt. (Lb.)	REA (In.²)
	790	500	9.8	1150	725	12.5
	830	525	10.1	1190	750	12.8
	870	550	10.4	1230	775	13.1
	910	575	10.7	1270	800	13.4
				1310	825	13.7
Base	950	600	11.0	1350	850	14.0
				1390	875	14.3
	990	625	11.3	1430	900	14.6
	1030	650	11.6			
	1070	675	11.9			
	1110	700	12.2			

In other words, a 600 lb. carcass (950 lb. steer with a 62% dressing percentage would have a 600 lb. hot carcass weight or 591 lb. chilled carcass weight) would have an 11.0 in.² ribeye. For every 25 lb. over 600 lb., add .3 in.² to the 11.0 in.² required ribeye (RREA); and for every 25 lb. under 600 lb., subtract

.3 in.² from the 11.0 in.² RREA. Then for each 1 in.² of estimated ribeye in excess of the calculated RREA, subtract .3 of a yield grade from the PYG; and for each 1 in.² of ribeye area less than the calculated RREA, add .3 of a yield grade to the PYG.

3. Percentage KPH—Adjust for percentage KPH using the method previously described.

The use of the weight-eye method is illustrated with the following example:

	Steer C
Live wt., lb.	1100
Dressing %	62.5
Cold carcass wt., lb.	690
Hot carcass wt., lb.	700
Fat thickness, in.	.6
Ribeye area, in.²	13.2

Steer C has an estimated 12th rib fat thickness equal to the base of .6 in. and has a PYG of 3.5. Steer C was estimated to have a carcass weight of 700 lb. which is 100 lb. greater than the base of 600 lb. (100 lb. = 4, 25 lb. increments). Twenty-five lb. is equivalent to .3 in.² of ribeye. So add 4 × .3 in.² = 1.2 in.² to the base RREA of 11.0 in.². Therefore, the RREA equals 12.2 in.² (11.0 in.² + 1.2 in.² = 12.2 in.²). Steer C was estimated to have 13.2 in.² of ribeye area which is 1.0 in.² above the RREA of 12.2 in.². Each 1.0 in.² is equivalent to .3 yield grade or .3 yield grade adjustment for ribeye area (1.0 in.² × .3 yield grade = .3 yield grade). The ribeye area adjustment of .3 is subtracted from the PYG (3.5); therefore 3.5 − .3 = 3.2 yield grade after adjusting for fat thickness, carcass weight, and ribeye area. The adjustment for KPH must now be made. The estimated .6 in. of fat is equivalent to 3.0% kidney, pelvic, and heart fat (Table 9.2). Since 3.0% is .5% less than the base of 3.5%, a .1 yield grade adjustment is made by subtracting the .1 from 3.2 = 3.1. The final yield grade of steer C is 3.1.

Use of the weight-eye method is further illustrated in the following two examples:

	Adj. Fat Thickness	HCW	REA	% KPH	
Steer D (870 live wt.)					
Estimated values	.2 in.	550 lb.	10.4 in.²	2.0%	
Adjustment factors	−1.0 or	−.6 in.² or	—	−.3	= 2.2 FYG
	PYG = 2.5	RREA = 10.4			
Steer E (1270 live wt.)					
Estimated values	.8 in.	800 lb.	11.1 in.²	4.0%	
Adjustment factors	+ .5 or	+2.4 in.² or	+.7	+.1	= 4.8 FYG
	PYG = 4.0	RREA = 13.4			

Photographs of steers representative of the five yield grades are shown in Figure 9.4.

Live Cattle Pricing

Calculating the Live Price of Cattle

In order to price live cattle, the student must determine class (sex) and estimate dressing percentage, carcass quality grade, and yield grade. The class is determined, and quality grade is estimated in order to select the correct carcass value per hundred weight. The carcass price/cwt varies with daily market fluctuations, but the following carcass prices/cwt are presented to illustrate the live pricing procedure.

Yield Grade 1

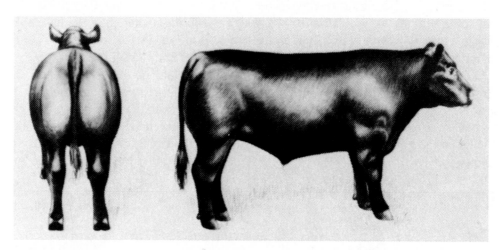

Yield Grade 2

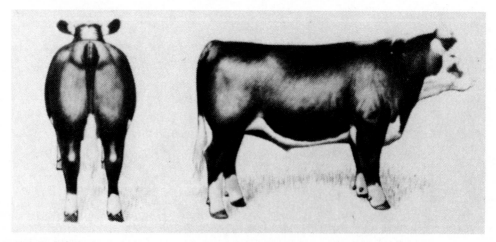

Yield Grade 3

Figure 9.4. An illustration representative of each of the yield grades of cattle.

Yield Grade 4

Yield Grade 5

Figure 9.4. *(continued)*

Example Carcass Prices/cwt

	Steer	Bullock	Heifer
U.S. Prime	$115	$111	$110
U.S. Choice	$112	$108	$107
U.S. Select	$107	$103	$102
U.S. Standard	$100	$ 96	$ 94

The base yield grade used for determining live price may vary from time to time and from one establishment to another; but to illustrate the calculation of live price/cwt, a base yield grade of 3.2 will be selected for use in the examples presented below. The above prices for each quality grade and class are those for carcasses with a yield grade of 3.2. For every .1 yield grade below 3.2, add $.25/cwt to the carcass price; and for each .1 yield grade above 3.2, subtract $.25/cwt from the carcass price.

To illustrate how live price per hundred is determined, you are again referred to the estimates of steer A and B presented earlier in this section. Also, let's assume that the estimated carcass quality grade of steer A is U.S. Choice and that of steer B is U.S. Select.

Steer A had a final yield grade of 2.2 which is 1.0 yield grade less than the base of 3.2 for calculating live price. The carcass price/cwt of U.S. Choice steers with a yield grade of 3.2 is $112.00/cwt. Since the yield grade was 1.0 less than the base and each .1 yield grade is equivalent to $.25/cwt, the carcass price/cwt of steer A is $114.50 [112.00 + (10 × $.25) = $114.50]. The carcass price/cwt ($114.50) is then multiplied by the estimated dressing percentage (61% for steer A). The live price/cwt for steer A is $69.84 ($114.50/cwt × .61 = $69.84). The live price is rounded to the nearest $.10; thus, the live price of steer A is $69.80/cwt.

Steer B had a final yield grade of 4.2 which is 1.0 yield grade higher than the base of 3.2. The carcass price of U.S. Select steers with a yield grade of 3.2 is $107.00/cwt. Since the deviation of steer B is 1.0 yield grade above the base of 3.2, $2.50 (10 × $.25 = $2.50) is subtracted from the base carcass price of $107.00 ($107.00 − $2.50 = $104.50) to obtain the carcass price/cwt for a U.S. Select grade steer with a yield grade of 4.2. The carcass price/cwt of $104.50 × .63 (dressing % of steer B) = $65.84 or $65.80/cwt which is the live price of steer B after rounding.

The mechanics of determining the live price/cwt for bullocks and heifers are identical to those for steers. Be sure to use the correct base carcass price/cwt for the estimated quality grade and the correct class price/cwt. Also, remember the base yield grade for calculating yield grade is always 3.5; however, the base yield grade for calculating live price/cwt is 3.2 in the above examples, but it may be any other value, such as 3.0, 3.5, etc.

Estimating Carcass Traits of Live Market Cattle

The major carcass traits evaluated in market cattle are fat thickness at the 12th rib (BF), ribeye area (REA), yield grade (YG), and quaity grade (QG). As was discussed earlier, BF and REA are the major factors that effect YG. BF is used to determine the preliminary yield grade (PYG), to estimate percentage kidney, heart, and pelvic fat (% KPH), and to estimate the dressing percentage needed to calculate carcass weight. BF can be estimated by the same relationships of weight to frame and thickness that were discussed in the market hog section. REA can be estimated by using the carcass weight-REA relationship discussed earlier in this section to determine the normal REA for an average muscled carcass (steer) and then adjusting 1.0–2.0 in.^{2} for cattle that are either light or heavy muscled.

An increase in the external fat of a steer, heifer, or bullock should be accompanied by an increase in the amount of intramuscular fat. Therefore, QG is best estimated in the live animal from BF. However, other factors, such as breed, energy level, and days on feed, result in a great deal of individual variation among cattle. Therefore, QG is one of the most difficult traits to estimate accurately. The information in Table 9.4 can be used as a guideline for the amount of fat usually associated with each QG.

Steer D (Figure 9.5, upper two photographs) weighs 1150 lb. and appears to be very muscular and correctly finished. Steer D has some fat in the brisket, flank, and cod and appears to have adequate fat cover over his rib. He will have about .45 in. of fat at the 12th rib and, therefore, will have about 3.0% KPH and a dressing % of about 63 on a hot carcass basis. This would give D a hot carcass weight of approximately 725 lb. Using the carcass weight-REA relationship, D should have a REA of 12.5 in.^{2}. However, D appears much heavier muscled than average. He stands wide, is very expressively muscled through the round, and appears thick and muscular through the rump and loin. From the side, one can see

Table 9.4.	Fat Thickness—Quality Grade Interrelationship.		
	Fat Thickness	**Quality Grade**	
	.1–.2	Standard$^+$	– Select$^-$
	.2–.3	Select$^-$	– Select$^+$
	.30–.45	Select$^+$	– Choice$^-$
	.45–.60	Choice$^-$	– Choice^o
	.60–.80	Choice^o	– Choice$^+$
	>.80	Choice$^+$	– Prime^o

that D has a muscular forearm and a long bulging stifle. Therefore, add about 2.0 in.^{2} to the carcass weight-REA relationship and estimate D to have 14.5 in.^{2} of REA. These estimates would give steer D a yield grade of 2.4 and a quality grade of low Choice.

Steer E (Figure 9.5, middle two photographs) weighs 1100 lb. and appears lean with average muscling. E is large framed, very trim through the brisket, flanks and cod, and does not appear to have much fat cover over the rib. E will have about .3 in. of BF and, therefore, will have about 2.5% KPH and a dressing percentage of about 61 on a hot carcass basis or approximately 675 lb. of hot carcass weight. Using the carcass weight-REA relationship, E should have a REA of 11.9 in.^{2}. Since E appears to be average in his muscling, 11.9 in.^{2} would be his REA estimate. These factors would give E a yield grade of 2.55. Since it appears that E may be leaner than .3 in., the final yield grade should be rounded to 2.5. Steer E would be expected to have a quality grade estimate of high Select.

Steer F (Figure 9.5, lower two photographs) weighs 1050 lb. and appears small framed, light muscled, and fatter than steers D or E. F is weak topped and appears fat over the rib and loin edge. He is also heavy fronted, full in the flank, and patchy about the tail head. F is flat and short in the stifle and is narrow through the rump and round. He will have approximately .6 in. of BF, about 3.5% KPH, and a dressing percentage of 64 on a hot carcass basis or about 675 lb. of hot carcass weight. Thus F should have 11.9 in.^{2} of REA. However, since F is light muscled, subtract about 1.7 in.^{2} from the carcass weight-REA relationship and estimate his REA at 10.2 in.^{2}. These estimates would give steer F a yield grade of 4.0 and a quality grade of average Choice.

Steer D

Steer E

Steer F

Figure 9.5. Photographs showing rear and side views of three market steers illustrating differences in muscle, fat, frame and thickness. These photographs are intended to aid the student in his/her initial attempt at estimation of carcass characteristics in live cattle.

Beef Carcass Evaluation, Grading, and Pricing

Beef Carcass Evaluation

The first step in beef carcass evaluation is the determination of class or sex group. Class determination of beef carcasses is based on evidences of maturity and sex condition at the time of slaughter. The classes of beef carcasses are steer, bullock, heifer, cow, and bull (Table 10.1). The class of beef carcasses formerly known as stag was redesignated in the 1973 beef grade standards as either bullock or bull depending on their skeletal maturity (i.e., the young carcasses are designated bullocks and the more mature carcasses are designated bulls). In addition to class, the bovine species is subdivided into kind (i.e., beef, calves and veal).

Determination of Kind

The differentiation between veal, calf, and beef carcasses is made primarily on the basis of the color of lean, although such factors as texture of lean, character of the fat; color, size and ossification of the bone and cartilages, and the general contour of the carcass are also given consideration.

Table 10.1 Market Kinds, Classes and Grades of Cattle.

| Market Kind and Class* | Market Grade** | |
	Quality Grade	Yield Grade
Slaughter cattle		
Steer	Prime, Choice, Select, Standard, Commercial, Utility, Cutter, Canner	1 to 5
Bullock	Prime, Choice, Select, Standard, Utility	1 to 5
Heifer	Prime, Choice, Select, Standard, Commercial, Utility, Cutter, Canner	1 to 5
Cow	Choice, Select, Standard, Commercial, Utility, Cutter, Canner	1 to 5
Bull	Not eligible for quality grade	1 to 5
Slaughter veal		
Steer, heifer and bull	Prime, Choice, Good, Standard, Utility	none
Slaughter calves		
Steer, heifer and bull	Prime, Choice, Good, Standard, Utility	none

| | Market Grade | |
	Frame Size	Thickness of Muscling
Feeder cattle and calves		
Steer***	Large, Medium, Small	1, 2, 3
Heifer***	Large, Medium, Small	1, 2, 3
Cow***	Large, Medium, Small	1, 2, 3
Bull	Ungraded	
Stag	Ungraded	

*Difference between bullock and bull carcasses is based solely on evidences of skeletal maturity. Bullock carcasses must have A skeletal maturity; evidence of B or older maturity classifies male carcasses as bull. When officially graded, bull or bullock carcasses are identified for its class; i.e., bull or bullock.

**Quality grades are shown for each market kind and class. Yield grades 1 through 5 are applicable to all slaughter cattle only. Difference between Commercial and Standard, based on maturity of animals. Commercial—more mature; Standard—younger animals.

***Unthrifty animals are graded inferior regardless of frame size and muscle thickness.

Veal

Veal carcasses have a grayish pink to a dark grayish pink color of lean that is smooth and velvety in texture. They also have a slightly soft, pliable character of fat, and narrow and very red ribs.

Calf

Compared to veal, calf carcasses have a grayish red to moderately red color of lean, a flakier type of fat, and somewhat wider ribs with less pronounced evidences of red color.

Beef

Beef carcasses, on the other hand, have evidences of more advanced maturity. Color of lean is moderately red in young beef carcasses and may be very dark red in mature beef carcasses. Fat is flaky and ribs show evidence of flatness and are slightly red in color in young beef carcasses. Cartilage shows some evidence of ossification in the sacral and lumbar regions compared to calf carcasses.

Determination of Class

Since the quality grade standards and some of the qualitative properties (i.e., color, texture, etc.) of beef carcasses vary by class, identification of class is necessary in carcass evaluation. The following characteristics are used to identify and categorize beef carcasses into their respective classes.

Steers

Steer carcasses are identified by the typically rough and irregular shaped fat deposit in the cod region, the presence of a relatively small pizzle eye (white disc caudal to the aitch bone; it is the severed proximal portion of the penis), a relatively small pelvic cavity, a curved aitch bone, and the typical bald spot or small lean area on the inside of the round ventral to the aitch bone (Figure 10.1). The bald spot is the exposed portion of the gracilis muscle, and it is sometimes referred to as being diamond shaped in steer, bullock, and bull carcasses. The first two characteristics are superior to the others, and they are most frequently used for identifying steer carcasses.

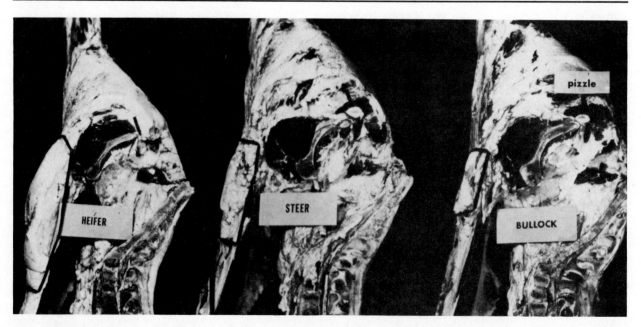

Figure 10.1. Illustration on a heifer, steer and bullock carcass showing presence or absence of the pizzle eye, udder (U), cod (C) and scrotal (S) fat, shape of aitch bone, gracilis muscle and width of pelvic cavity.

Bullocks

Bullock carcasses, in contrast to steers, are identified by their disproportionately heavy development of rounds, noticeable crests, thickly fleshed chucks as shown in Figure 10.2, and large prominent pizzle eyes. Bullock carcasses usually have a noticeably developed small, round muscle adjacent to the hip bone commonly referred to as the jump muscle. In carcasses with considerable external fat, the development of this muscle may be obscured. The scrotal fat of bullocks is typically rough and irregular in shape like that of steers and bulls. The appearance of this fat deposit of steers, bullocks, and bulls contrasts the smooth fat deposit of the udder in heifers (Figure 10.1). The lean of bullocks is usually darker and coarser in texture than that of steers, but usually it is not as dark or as coarse as that from bulls. The distinction between bullock and bull carcasses is based solely on their evidences of skeletal (bone and cartilage) maturity with bullocks being the younger of these two classes.

Bulls

Bull carcasses are identified by their disproportionately heavy development of rounds, noticeable crests, thickly fleshed chucks, and large prominent pizzle eyes. Bull carcasses also have a noticeably developed jump muscle. In carcasses with considerable external fat, the development of this muscle may be obscured. The scrotal fat is typically rough and irregular in shape like the fat found in steers and bullocks, which contrasts the smooth udder fat of heifers. The lean is usually dark red and coarse textured. In contrast to bullocks, the bone characteristics of bulls show evidence of advancing skeletal maturity.

Heifers

Heifer carcasses are identified by the smooth, uniform fat deposit in the udder region, the absence of the pizzle eye, a slightly larger pelvic cavity, and a straighter aitch bone than steers (Figure 10.1). Heifer carcasses have a larger bald spot (gracilis muscle) because the muscle has less fat covering it than steers. The bald spot is bean-shaped. Heifer carcasses also tend to be more angular than steers and they are usually less heavily muscled, especially in the round, loin, rib, and chuck regions (Figure 10.2). In fact, the round in heifer carcasses is frequently tapering and concave in its contour. However, udder fat and absence of a pizzle eye are most frequently used to classify carcasses as heifers.

Cows

Cow carcasses are identified by their relatively large pelvic cavity and nearly straight aitch bone. These characteristics represent the anatomical adjustment of the pelvis to accommodate parturition (calving). The cow udder that has had many years of lactation is rather large and unattractive; consequently, it is usually removed during the slaughter process. However, when the udder is present it may be "wet" (i.e., showing evidence of lactation). The hips of cow carcasses usually range from slightly prominent to very prominent. Most cows are old when marketed, and in such carcasses the sacral vertebrae are fused and appear as essentially one bone. All bones are usually hard, white, and the cartilage associated with the vertebrae and aitch bone are completely ossified, except for the buttons which may not be completely ossified. In heifer carcasses the udder usually is present, while in most cow carcasses it is removed. However, neither condition is an absolute requirement for class designation.

Calves and Veal

Calves and veal carcasses are also classified as steers, heifers, and bulls; however, since these animals have not attained sexual maturity, the effects upon qualitative properties are negligible and are not considered in the evaluation and grading of their carcasses. The classes and kinds of bovine animals described in this section include only those of slaughter animals, even though stocker and feeder cattle are shown in Table 10.1.

In addition to determination of kind and class, beef carcass evaluation includes an estimation of degree of marbling and maturity. These two factors are used to determine quality grade, and they will be described in detail in the discussion of beef quality grade. Evaluation also includes an estimation or measurement of ribeye area, 12th rib fat thickness; and percentage kidney, heart, and pelvic fat. These three factors and hot carcass weight are used to determine yield grade, and their measurement or estimation will be described in the discussion of the yield grading procedure.

Figure 10.2. Illustrations showing the contour and conformation of a heifer, steer and bullock carcass.

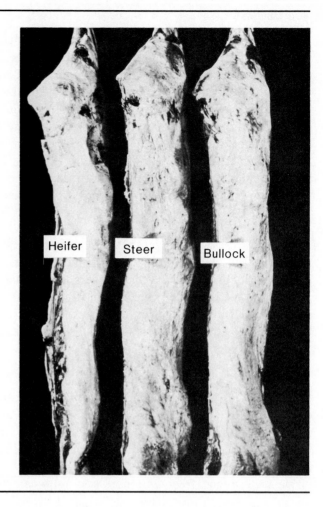

Weight

Hot carcass weight is almost always obtained on beef carcasses just before chilling, and chilled carcass weight is usually calculated from hot carcass weight because the chilled carcass is not always weighed. Hot carcass weight is 1 to 2% (average 1 1/2%) higher than chilled carcass weight. To calculate chilled carcass weight from actual hot carcass weight, multiply hot carcass weight by .985. If only chilled carcass weight is available and hot carcass weight is needed, multiply chilled carcass weight by 1.015.

Dressing Percentage

Chilled carcass weight (actual or calculated) is divided by live weight and multiplied by 100 to obtain dressing percentage.

Beef Carcass Grading

The importance of a uniform method or system of grading slaughter beef has been apparent to the U.S. Department of Agriculture (U.S.D.A.) for many years. This standardization facilitates the industry's marketing system from producer to the retailer and consumer. The consumer has played an important role in the development of the grade standards. Consumers demand high quality lean beef with a minimum amount of waste fat and bone. A working knowledge of the factors that affect this type of product is essential for an understanding of the standardization and grading systems.

History

Since the first standards were formulated in 1916, many amendments and changes have been adopted to meet the demands of the time. In 1925, tentative standards for the market classes of cattle were published. Two years later, official grading began on a voluntary basis. The official standards were amended in 1939 to allow a single standard for the grading and labeling of steer, heifer, and cow beef. Changes in terminology also resulted in reference to Commercial, Utility, and Canner beef. Late in 1950, another amendment combined the standards for grades of slaughter steers, heifers, and cows into a single standard and set up minimum requirements for each grade. The grade standards applicable to slaughter steers and heifers were changed, and the Prime and Choice grades were combined under the designation of Prime. The Good grade was changed to Choice. The Commercial grade was divided into two grades (Good and Commercial). In 1956, the Commercial grade was changed and divided into two grades: Standard and Commercial. The Standard grade was applied to carcasses from the younger portion of the Commercial grade. In 1966, another change resulted in the reduction of marbling requirements one and one-half degrees for Prime, one degree for Choice, and three quarters of a degree for Good and Standard. In addition, a second grading system was adopted to identify carcasses on the basis of their cutability (yield grades). The yield grades were numbered 1 through 5 with 1 representing the highest yield of boneless, closely trimmed retail cuts from the round, loin, rib, and chuck; and 5 the lowest yield. In 1973, a special grade for young bulls was established, and they have since been referred to as Bullocks. As of February 23, 1976, four major changes were implemented as part of the Beef Grading Standards. (1) All beef graded must be graded for both quality and yield. Previously, a packer could have carcasses graded for one or the other or both. (2) Marbling requirements were reduced slightly for the Choice and Prime grades. (3) The minimum amounts of marbling specified for carcasses of cattle approximately 9 months of age remained unchanged through approximately 30 months of age. Previously, the standards required increased marbling to compensate for increased maturity of all carcasses. For the Good grade, the minimum marbling requirement would be increased for the youngest carcasses. (4) Conformation was eliminated as a factor in the quality grading system, since research had indicated that carcass shape has very little influence on the palatability characteristics of meat. On November 23, 1987, the name of the Good grade was changed to the Select grade. Effective April 9, 1989, beef carcasses no longer are required to be graded for both yield and quality when graded. For further study of the standards, see the "Official United States Standards For Grades of Carcass Beef," U.S.D.A. Agriculture Marketing Service.

Beef Carcass Grades

A summarization of market kinds, classes, and grades of the bovine species is presented in Table 10.1. Slaughter veal and calf carcasses are graded for quality only. Beef carcasses when graded are graded for both yield and quality, except bull carcasses are yield graded only. Quality grade is a composite evaluation of factors that affect the palatability of meat (i.e., tenderness, juiciness and flavor). The quality factors evaluated and their relative importance are different for specific classes of carcasses, and they will be emphasized in the subsequent discussion. Yield grade is an estimation of the expected yield of boneless, closely trimmed (approximately .3 in. of fat left on the cuts), retail cuts from the round, loin, rib, and chuck.

Ribbing

Beef carcasses must be "ribbed" before they can be graded. Ribbing is the process of cutting one or both sides of the carcass between the 12th and 13th rib to expose the ribeye (longissimus) muscle, marbling, and fat thickness. Usually, ribbing is done by counting down the backbone 7½ vertebrae from the lumbar-sacral junction and sawing across the midpoint of the 8th vertebra at right angles to the backbone as shown in Figure 10.3. After sawing through the vertebra, a knife is used to follow the curvature of the 12th rib to complete the exposure of the ribeye muscle so that marbling, ribeye area, lean firmness, color and texture, and fat thickness can be determined.

The typical purplish red color of the freshly cut ribeye muscle is due to unoxygenated myoglobin—the muscle pigment. With increased time of exposure, the muscle surface picks up oxygen from the air and becomes oxygenated to form a bright red color. All of us are familiar with the oxygenated form of myoglobin in fresh meat in the retail display case. This brightened condition is called "bloom". The fresh cut

Figure 10.3. Illustration showing the site for ribbing located 7 1/2 vertebrae cranial from the lumbar-sacral junction (left photograph) and a saw cut through the vertebrae as indicated by the arrow in the right photograph.

surface requires ½ to ¾ hour to reach optimum brightness. Beef quality grades are usually not determined prior to maximum bloom conditions. In some beef carcasses the ribbed muscle does not brighten, and the color remains dark red to almost black. These carcasses are called "dark cutters." Also, the uncovered ribeye tends to dehydrate as well as increase in darkness under warm conditions. In commercial practice, the ribeye is often covered with a plastic film to protect the color and maintain bloom during storage and shipping.

Beef Quality Grading

Beef carcass quality grade is based upon two major factors: (1) degree of marbling and (2) degree of maturity. In addition to these factors, color, texture, and firmness of lean in the ribeye muscle are considered in determining final quality grade. The beef quality grades are U.S.D.A. Prime, Choice, Select, Standard, Commercial, Utility, Cutter, and Canner.

Marbling is the intermingling or dispersion of fat within the lean (intramuscular fat). Marbling is estimated on the lean cut surface of the ribeye muscle at the 12th rib interface. The grade standards specify more marbling for the high grades (i.e., U.S.D.A. Prime and Choice) than in the lower grades (i.e., U.S.D.A. Select and Standard). Amount of marbling in the eye muscle is divided into ten degrees. These 10 degrees from lowest to highest are: (1) devoid, (2) practically devoid, (3) traces, (4) slight, (5) small, (6) modest, (7) moderate, (8) slightly abundant, (9) moderately abundant, and (10) abundant. The degrees of marbling are shown in Figure 10.4.

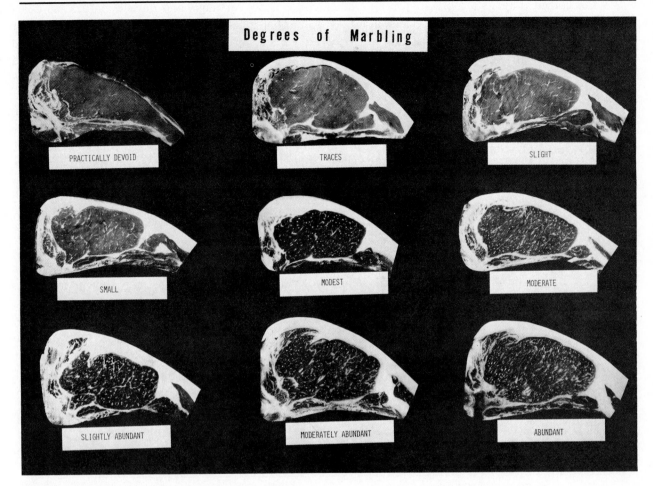

Figure 10.4. Illustrations of each of nine degrees of marbling.

In actual practice, Federal Meat Graders subdivide each degree of marbling into percentages in increments of 10% from 0 to 100% and the percentages are written as superscripts following the degree of marbling. Thus, small marbling would be identified as small[0], small[10], small[20], small[30], etc. through small[100]. The same procedure is followed for the other marbling degrees, with devoid naturally being an exception. The lowest amount of marbling within each of the other nine degrees is designated[0], the highest[100], and the middle of the range for the degree is designated[50].

Marbling is an indicator of eating quality, however, as it increases, it also increases the caloric content which may be considered a demerit. Marbling is associated with increased length of time on feed; hence, more feed is required to attain the higher degrees of marbling. Also, marbling is highly related to the type of feed fed (concentrate vs. roughage) as well as the animal's genetic capacity for laying down this fat deposit.

Maturity is the second factor used in determining quality grade, and it is included in the standards because the eating quality characteristics (i.e., tenderness, juiciness, and flavor) are related to animal age. Maturity refers to the physiological age of the animal rather than to the chronological age. The chronological age of most cattle is unknown; hence, physiological indicators of maturity are evaluated in the carcass to estimate chronological age, and they include bone characteristics, ossification of cartilage at various carcass locations, and color and texture of the ribeye muscle. Cartilage ossifies (becomes bone) and bone whitens (becomes harder, flinty-like and white) with increasing age. Additionally, color of lean becomes darker due to accumulation of myoglobin and texture becomes coarser (muscle fibers increase in size) with age. The cartilage and bone characteristics receive greater emphasis in determining maturity than color and texture because the latter characteristics are affected to a greater extent by factors other than physiological age.

Physiological age is a more appropriate indication of bone, cartilage, and muscle maturation characteristics than chronological age, because at any given chronological age steers, heifers and bullocks differ in their stage of physiological maturity. Physiological age represents the point on the growth curve attained by the animal at the time of slaughter. Consequently, bullocks at 18 months of age, for instance, would exhibit the most youthful bones, cartilage, and muscle characteristics; heifers the oldest bones, cartilage, and muscle characteristics; and steers would be intermediate.

As seen from Table 10.2, there are five maturity groups and they are designated by the letters A, B, C, D, and E. The A and B maturities are from young carcasses. The carcasses from mature cattle are designated C, D, and E. Because of the ossification that has occurred in the bones and cartilage, these C, D, and E maturity carcasses are called "hard boned." In actual practice, Federal Meat Graders subdivide the maturity groups into percentages in increments of 10% from 0 to 100% and the percentages are written as superscripts following the maturity letter designation. Thus, A maturity would be identified as A^0, A^{10}, A^{20}, A^{30}, etc. through A^{100} and the same for maturity groups B, C, D, and E. The youngest carcasses in each maturity group are designated ^{0} and the oldest ^{100} and the middle of each maturity is designated ^{50}.

The approximate chronological age in months for each beef carcass maturity group is presented in Figure 10.5. It should also be emphasized that an overlap may exist among adjacent maturity groups for carcasses from cattle of the same approximate chronological age. That is, carcasses may show more or less ossification for their chronological age; consequently, they may fall into older or younger maturity groups. Normally steers and heifers are A or B maturity, while most cows and bulls are C, D, and E maturity. However, some cows can qualify for B maturity; similarly, some steers and heifers may be C, D, or E in maturity. Bullock carcasses (by definition) must be in the A maturity group. Male carcasses showing evidence of sexual maturity that are B maturity and older are designated as bulls. Remember, bull carcasses are *not* quality graded, but may be yield graded. Bullock and bull carcasses are identified as such because the Federal Grader applies a stamp with the word "bullock" or "bull" on them. The maturity of each class of slaughter cattle eligible for each quality grade is presented in Table 10.2.

Table 10.2   Maturity of Each Class of Slaughter Cattle Eligible for Each Quality Grade.

U.S. Grade	Class and Maturity*			
	Bullock	**Steer**	**Heifer**	**Cow**
Prime	A	A,B	A,B	—
Choice	A	A,B	A,B	B
Select	A	A,B	A,B	B
Standard	A	A,B	A,B	B
Commercial	—	C,D,E	C,D,E	C,D,E
Utility	A	A,B,C,D,E,	A,B,C,D,E	B,C,D,E
Cutter	—	A,B,C,D,E	A,B,C,D,E	B,C,D,E
Canner	—	A,B,C,D,E	A,B,C,D,E	B,C,D,E

*Cows are not eligible for the Prime grade; bullocks must be in the A maturity group and if they exceed it they are classed as bulls and are not quality graded.

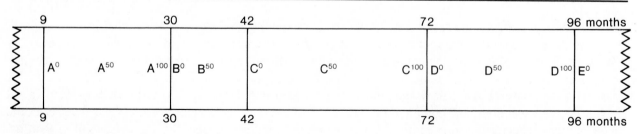

Figure 10.5. Illustration showing the range in months of age for each maturity. The ages in months from 9-96 months is drawn to scale for each maturity.

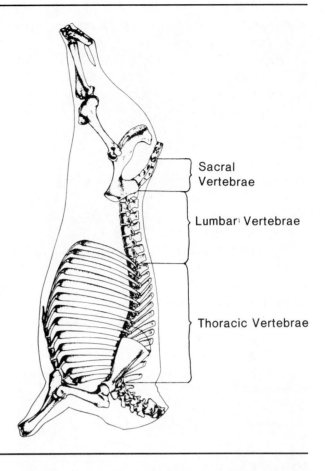

Figure 10.6. A skeletal diagram of beef carcass showing the location of the bones of the split backbone, namely, the sacral vertebrae, lumbar vertebrae and the thoracic vertebrae. Buttons, although not shown in this figure, are located on the dorsal tip of each spinous process of the thoracic vertebrae.

Sacral Vertebrae

Lumbar Vertebrae

Thoracic Vertebrae

The cartilages evaluated in determining beef carcass physiological maturity are associated with the vertebrae of the backbone, except the cervical vertebrae are not considered (Figure 10.6). Thus, the cartilage between and on the dorsal edges of the individual sacral (Figure 10.7) and lumbar vertebrae (Figure 10.8), as well as the cartilages located on the dorsal surface of the spinous processes of the thoracic vertebrae, or more commonly referred to as "buttons" (Figures 10.9 and 10.10), are evaluated. In the beef industry, all of these cartilage areas are considered in arriving at the maturity group. The sacral and lumbar cartilages are least ossified in the youngest or A maturity carcasses (Figures 10.7 and 10.8). Likewise, the buttons are most prominent, softest, and least ossified in the youngest carcasses (Figure 10.10). As maturity proceeds from A toward E, progressively more and more ossification becomes evident (Figures 10.7, 10.8, 10.9 and 10.10). The ribs in carcasses from A maturity cattle are quite round and narrow in cross-section with only a slight tendency toward flatness, whereas E maturity carcasses have wide and flat ribs (Figure 10.11). In addition, the ribs of A maturity carcasses show evidence of redness because they are involved in red blood cell manufacture in their marrow. Redness of the ribs gradually decreases with advancing age, and in C maturity they generally become white in color because they no longer manufacture red blood cells (Figure 10.11). Color and texture of the longissimus muscle are used to determine carcass maturity when these characteristics differ sufficiently from normal. Shades of light, intermediate, and dark color of lean are shown in Figure 10.12.

It should be emphasized that ossification of the cartilage in the sacral, lumbar, and thoracic (buttons) regions of the carcass does not occur simultaneously. In fact, there is a posterior-anterior progression. Thus, ossification begins in the sacral region. With advancing age, ossification proceeds to the lumbar region, and then even later, it begins in the thoracic region (buttons) of the carcass (Figure 10.13). Therefore, the sacral vertebrae ossify first and the most cranial thoracic vertebra button (1st thoracic) ossifies last. Because of this posterior-anterior progression of ossification, even the youngest A maturity carcasses will have some ossification in the sacral cartilage, less in the lumbar cartilage, and none in the buttons. These ossification

Figure 10.7. The left illustration is the sacral vertebrae of an A^{40}-A^{50} maturity and is indicated by a large black A. The outline and a small amount of cartilage is present on each vertebra. The right illustration is the sacral vertebrae of an E^{100} maturity. The individual bones have fused and no cartilage is present.

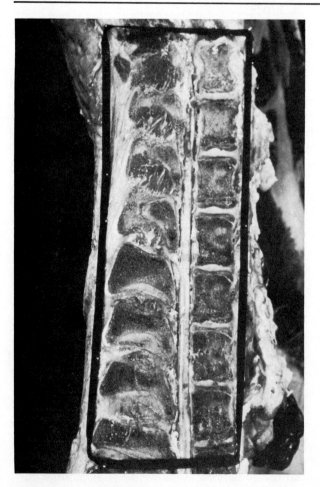
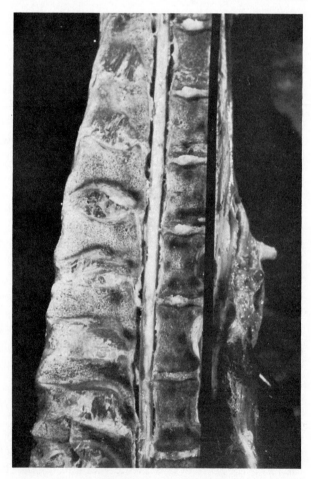

Figure 10.8. The left illustration of the lumbar vertebra (outlined in black) of a A^{30}-A^{50} maturity. The red color and cartilage are present on each vertebra. The right illustration of the lumbar vertebrae (outlined in black) of E^{100} maturity. The color is much whiter and no cartilage is present.

Figure 10.9. An illustration of a few thoracic vertebrae showing the cartliage or "buttons" on each vertebra. The heavy black arrow points to a button of approximately A^{40} maturity.

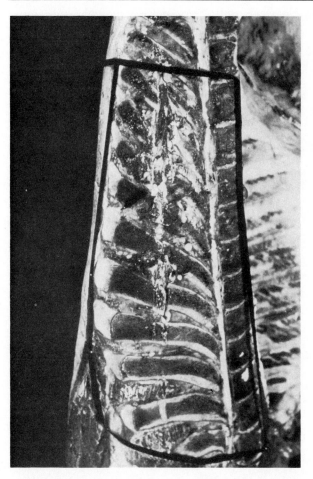

Figure 10.10. The left illustration of the thoracic vertebrae (outlined in black) of an A^{50} maturity. The bones have a red color and the buttons show no ossification. The right illustration is the thoracic vertebrae of an E^{50} maturity. The bones are whiter and remnants of button indicated by black arrows are nearly completely ossified.

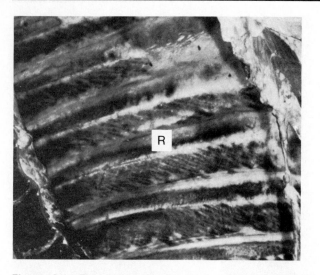

Figure 10.11. The left illustration are ribs from an A maturity carcass. One rib is labeled with an ''R'' and the ribs are quite rounded and red. The right illustration are ribs from C, D, or E maturity carcasses. One rib is labeled with an ''R'' and the ribs are quite flat and white.

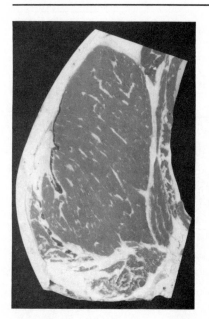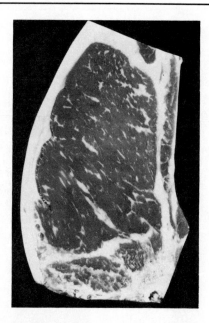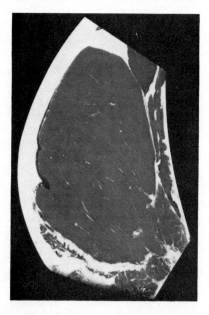

Normal   Slightly Dark   Dark

Figure 10.12. An illustration of ribeye muscle interfaces showing normal, slightly dark and dark color of lean represented by increasing darkness from left to right. Additionally, texture of lean is finest in the rib on the left, coarsest in the rib on the right and intermediate in the rib in the center.

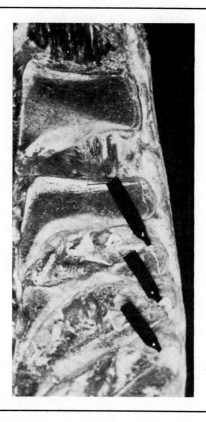

Figure 10.13. An illustration of a carcass at the lumbar-thoracic vertebrae junction. It shows nearly complete ossification of the lumbar cartilage but the buttons of the thoracic vertebrae are just beginning ossification. This is approximately B^{70} maturity.

differences in the various regions can be used to identify the physiological maturity of beef carcasses. The description of the sacral, lumbar, and thoracic ossification and rib shape characteristic of each of the maturity groups A through E is presented in Table 10.3. Some are also illustrated in Figures 10.7 through 10.13.

As seen in Table 10.3 the sacral vertebrae (sacrum) in mature carcasses are usually completely ossified and fused so that the sacrum appears as one bone (Figure 10.7). The sacrum may have visible delineations between the ossified sacral vertebrae in the C, D, and young E maturities; but in the most mature group of E maturity carcasses, it appears as one bone and the individual vertebrae cannot be identified. In addition, the cartilages of the lumbar and thoracic vertebrae progressively ossify with age (Figures 10.8 through 10.10) and the amount of ossification determines the maturity group. Also, the split backbones and the ribs (Figure 10.11) lose their redness and become white, hard, and flinty with advancing age. The ribs flatten and become less rounded in cross section (Figure 10.11). Once a tentative maturity group of a carcass has been established, an evaluation of the color and texture of the ribeye muscle (Figure 10.12) is made. Normally these two characteristics are used to finalize the maturity group tentatively established by inspection of the bone and cartilage characteristics in borderline and extreme cases.

In terms of chronological age, the buttons begin to ossify when the animal approaches 30 months of age. Beef at this age or younger (i.e., 9–30 months) is usually acceptably tender and is called the A maturity group (Figure 10.5). As the animal increases in age from 30 months to about 42 months, ossification of cartilage increases and there generally is a decrease in tenderness. The cattle with bone cartilage and muscle quality characteristics of this maturity group are called B maturity (Figure 10.5). While they are more mature than the A group, they are still acceptably tender; consequently, they may qualify for the U.S.D.A. Prime, Choice, Select and Standard grades (Table 10.2). In addition to the buttons, the cartilage between—and especially the dorsal edge of the vertebrae—is used to further subdivide the A and B maturity groups. At approximately 42 months of age, because ossification of cartilage in the sacral region has long since been completed and that in the lumbar region has also been completed within the preceding 6 months, the buttons of the thoracic region then begin to ossify extensively (Table 10.3, Figure 10.13). In addition, the

Table 10.3   Description of Some Beef Carcass Skeletal Characteristics for Various Maturities.[1,2,3,4]

| Maturity | Vertebrae | | | Ribs |
	Sacral	Lumbar	Thoracic	
A[0] to A[30]	Distinct separation. Cartilage very evident.	Cartilage evident on all vertebrae.	Cartilages evident on all vertebrae: soft porous, and very red chine bones pearly white cartilages.	Red and rounded, only slight tendency toward flatness.
A[90] to B[30]	Completely fused.	Nearly completely ossified, may be some cartilage.	Slightly red and slightly soft chine bones—cartilage have some evidence of ossification.	Slightly wide and slightly flat. Loss of some redness.
B[70] to B[100]	Completely fused.	Completely ossified.	Chine bones tinged w/ red—cartilages are partially ossified; lower thoracic buttons show roughness.	Slightly wide and flat. Slight flinty appearance.
(maximum maturity for Prime, Choice, Select, and Standard grades)				
C[0] to C[30]	Completely fused.	Completely ossified.	Chine bones tinged w/ red—cartilages are partially to moderately ossified.	Slightly wide and slightly flat. Somewhat bleached and slight flinty appearance.
C[70] to D[40]	Completely fused.	Completely ossified.	Moderately hard, rather white chine bones—cartilages show considerable ossification but outlines are plainly visible.	Moderately wide flat, bleached and flinty.
D[50] to D[100]	Completely fused.	Completely ossified.	Cartilages nearly completely ossified (70-100%). Fine outline still visible at the tips.	Wide and flat.
E[0] to E[30]	Completely fused.	Completely ossified.	Hard white chine bones; cartilages entirely ossified, outline barely visible	Wide and flat.
E[100]	Completely fused.	Completely ossified.	No visible outline of cartilage.	Wide and flat.

1. Youthful lean—fine texture, cherry red color.
2. With increasing age—texture may be coarser and lean tends to become darker.
3. Never change maturity based on bone and cartilage characteristics more than one full maturity group, i.e., A to B or vice versa because of inferior or superior color or texture.
4. These are written only as guidelines since variation and overlap does occur when applying percentages to maturities.

collagenous connective tissue associated with the muscles also undergoes extensive cross-linkages beginning at about 42 months of age which results in dramatic increases in toughness. Thus, carcasses from cattle over 42 months of age (C, D, and E maturity) are generally much tougher than those of either A or B maturity. Hence, this is the age break in the beef quality grading standards between young and old cattle. Only cattle less than 42 months of age (A and B maturity) qualify for the U.S.D.A. Prime, Choice, Select and Standard quality grades (Table 10.2). Because beef from these four grades is acceptably tender, they are merchandized as "block" beef (i.e., roasts and steaks). Carcasses over 42 months of age are only eligible to be graded U.S.D.A. Commercial, Utility, Cutter, and Canner as shown in Table 10.2. Because C, D, and E maturity carcasses lack acceptable tenderness, they are usually not merchandized as block beef. Instead, they are boned and used in processed meat products.

Table 10.2 shows that the U.S.D.A. Commercial and Standard grades differ in maturity. Thus, carcasses are eligible for one or the other. Young maturity (A and B) carcasses grade U.S. Standard and mature (C, D and E) carcasses grade U.S. Commercial. Carcasses not meeting the requirements of either Standard or Commercial are grade U.S. Utility. Hence, the Utility grade encompasses all of the maturity groups (A through E) because A and B maturity carcasses with deficient quality for the U.S. Standard grade, as well as mature carcasses (C, D and E maturity) with deficient quality for the Commercial grade,

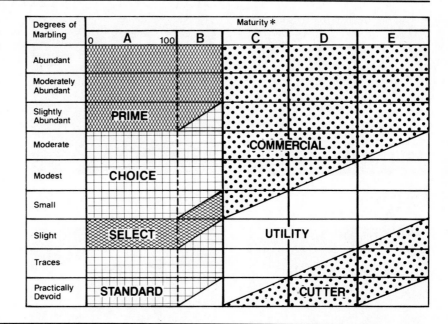

Figure 10.14. Relationship of marbling and maturity as used in determining final beef carcass quality grade. The range from 0 to 100 is shown in the figure for A maturity only, but B, C, D, and E maturities each range from 0 on the left to 100 on the right as illustrated for A maturity.

fall into the next lower grade which is U.S. Utility in both instances. The same point is true for the Cutter and Canner grades. However, it should be emphasized that by far the bulk of the carcasses in the Utility, Cutter, and Canner grades are from mature cattle and may have color, texture, and firmness of lean entering into the determination of the final grade.

Determination of Final Quality Grade

After the degree of maturity and marbling has been estimated on a carcass, these two factors are combined to arrive at a final quality grade (FQG) from the chart shown in Figure 10.14. Proficiency in quality grading requires many weeks of practice, but the principles of determining the FQG from Figure 10.14 can be easily acquired by learning a few basic fundamentals. These fundamentals involve learning the degrees of marbling in order from lowest to highest, the minimum marbling degree for each maturity group, and understanding the relationships between marbling and maturity in each quality grade. For example, a small degree of marbling is required to grade low Choice within A maturity regardless if the carcass is A^0 or A^{100}. However, for B maturity carcasses an increasing amount of marbling is required from B^0 to B^{100}. In the old maturities (C, D and E), the same relationship exists so that it takes a small ^{0} amount of marbling to grade low commercial for C^0 maturity, modest ^{0} for D^0 maturity, and moderate^0 for E^0 maturity. Each full degree of marbling (i.e., small^0 to modest^0), for instance, raises or lowers the FQG by one third grade. Except for A maturity, each degree of maturity C vs. D requires an additional degree of marbling to qualify for the same minimum grade. Within each maturity group (i.e., B, C, D and E) each 10% increment increase or decrease requires a corresponding 10% increase or decrease in degree of marbling. For example, B^{20} requires small^{20} for minimum Choice, while B^{70} requires small^{70} for low Choice. The Federal Grader uses the 10% increments to refine his calls and be more precise in determining FQG.

The quality factors that have been previously mentioned several times (i.e., muscle texture, color, and firmness) may enter into the determination of the FQG. For example, a dark colored lean (dark cutter) may lower the FQG by as much as one full grade depending upon the severity of darkness, "coarseness" of texture, and extent of firmness. In the older maturities, the FQG may be lowered as much as ½ grade except for Utility, Cutter, or Canner as this procedure is not used for them.

It should be pointed out that the discussion in this section does not cover all the details of beef quality grading, but it does serve to illustrate the principles involved and how the factors (marbling and maturity) are evaluated and combined to determine FQG. Examples representative of six of the quality grades are illustrated in Figure 10.15.

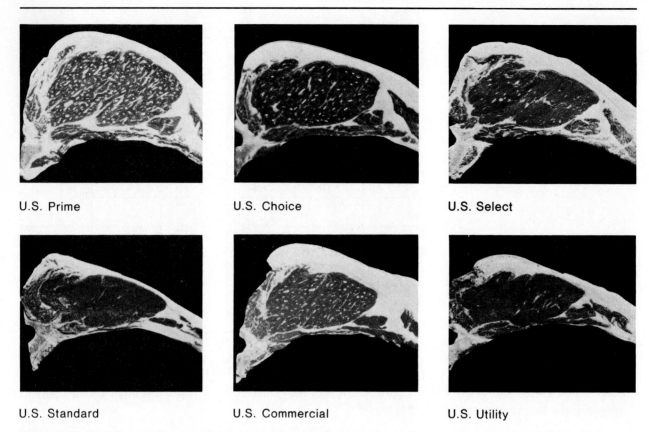

| U.S. Prime | U.S. Choice | U.S. Select |
| U.S. Standard | U.S. Commercial | U.S. Utility |

Figure 10.15. Illustrations of ribeye muscle interfaces at the 12th rib showing the marbling necessary to grade U.S. Prime, Choice, Select, Standard, Commercial and Utility.

Beef Yield Grading

Yield grade is a numerical value from 1 to 5 based upon the yield of boneless, closely trimmed (approximately .3 in.), retail cuts from the round, loin, rib, and chuck. These 4 wholesale cuts (Figure 10.16) make up approximately 75% of the weight, but about 90% of carcass value. Individually the round comprises about 23% of the weight and 29% of carcass value; the loin comprises 17% of the weight and 29% of the value; the rib 9% of the weight and 11% of the value; and the chuck comprises 26% of carcass weight and 21% of carcass value. Thus, the brisket, foreshank, plate, flank (thin meat), and kidney knob comprise the remaining 25% of carcass weight, but only about 10% of carcass value. Since the round, loin, rib, and chuck account for such a large proportion of total carcass weight (75%) and value (90%), the retail yield from them is used rather than the entire carcass. Additionally, the thin meat cuts are much more difficult to uniformly cut into retail cuts than the round, loin, rib, and chuck (RLRC) because they contain considerable quantities of seam fat which is time-consuming and difficult to remove.

In the official U.S.D.A. grading standards, yield grades range from 1.0 to 5.9, but only the whole number yield grade is "rolled" on the carcass by the grader. Thus, carcasses with yield grades of 3.0 to 3.9 are rolled yield grade 3; those with yield grades of 4.0 to 4.9 are rolled yield grade 4, etc. Yield grades close to next higher yield (i.e., 3.7, 3.8, 3.9), for instance, are not rounded topward but are rolled yield grade 3. The tenths of a yield grade are used to arrive at the whole number yield grade. Yield grades below 1.0 and above 5.9 are designated yield grade 1 and 5, respectively.

Cutting retail cuts from the carcass is the ultimate measure of value, but this is impossible to obtain on all carcasses. After studying a representative number of cattle, the U.S. Department of Agriculture found the following factors to have the greatest influence on carcass cutability: (1) fat thickness at the 12th rib; (2) ribeye area; (3) hot carcass weight; and (4) percentage kidney, pelvic, and heart fat (KPH). Using

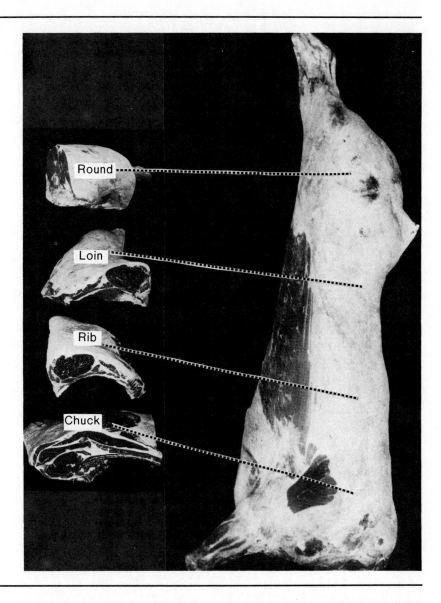

Figure 10.16. Illustration of a side of beef and the major primal cuts, i.e., round, loin, rib and chuck.

these factors, regression equations were developed that can be used to predict either the yield grade itself or the percentage of boneless, closely trimmed, retail cuts from the round, loin, rib, and chuck. The two equations follow:

$$\text{Yield grade} = 2.5 + (2.5 \times \text{adjusted fat thickness, 12th rib})$$
$$+ (.0038 \times \text{hot carcass wt.})$$
$$+ (.2 \times \text{percentage kidney, pelvic and heart fat})$$
$$- (.32 \times \text{ribeye area})$$

$$\% \text{ retail cuts} = 51.34 - (5.78 \times \text{adjusted fat thickness, 12th rib})$$
$$- (.0093 \times \text{hot carcass wt.})$$
$$- (.462 \times \text{percentage kidney, pelvic and heart fat})$$
$$+ (.740 \times \text{ribeye area})$$

The interconversion of yield grade and percentage retail cuts from the round, loin, rib, and chuck is presented in Table 10.4.

Table 10.4 Interconversion of Yield Grade and Percentage Boneless, Closely Trimmed Retail Cuts.

Yield Grade	% Retail Cuts	Yield Grade	% Retail Cuts	Yield Grade	% Retail Cuts	Yield Grade	% Retail Cuts	Yield Grade	% Retail Cuts
1.0	54.6	2.0	52.3	3.0	50.0	4.0	47.7	5.0	45.4
1.1	54.4	2.1	52.1	3.1	49.8	4.1	47.5	5.1	45.2
1.2	54.2	2.2	51.9	3.2	49.6	4.2	47.3	5.2	45.0
1.3	53.9	2.3	51.6	3.3	49.3	4.3	47.0	5.3	44.7
1.4	53.7	2.4	51.4	3.4	49.1	4.4	46.8	5.4	44.5
1.5	53.5	2.5	51.2	3.5	48.9	4.5	46.6	5.5	44.3
1.6	53.3	2.6	51.0	3.6	48.7	4.6	46.4	5.6	44.1
1.7	53.0	2.7	50.7	3.7	48.4	4.7	46.1	5.7	43.8
1.8	52.8	2.8	50.5	3.8	48.2	4.8	45.9	5.8	43.6
1.9	52.6	2.9	50.3	3.9	48.0	4.9	45.7	5.9	43.3

In actual everyday grading of beef carcasses, the regression equation is not used, but a working formula has been developed to simplify the procedure. The working formula involves the same four factors as the regression equation. The procedure for measurement or estimation of each of the four factors is described on page 100.

1. *Fat thickness at the 12th rib* can be an average of three fat measurements or a single fat measurement. The single fat measurement is used almost exclusively today, since it is less time-consuming and essentially as accurate as the average of three measurements. The measurement or estimate is made at right angles to the outer surface of the subcutaneous fat over the eye muscle and ¾ the lateral length of the eye muscle from the backbone as shown in Figure 10.17. If three fat measurements are made, they would correspond to ¼, ½, and ¾ the lateral length of the eye, and they would be obtained exactly like the single measurement (i.e., perpendicular to the outer surface of fat). The three measurements would then be averaged to obtain fat thickness. The 12th rib fat thickness measurement or estimate may be adjusted, as necessary, to reflect unusual amounts of fat on other parts of the carcass. In determining the amount of this adjustment, if any, particular attention is given to the amount of fat in such areas as the brisket, plate, flank, cod, scrotum or udder, inside round, rump and hip in relation to actual thickness of fat over the ribeye. Thus, in a carcass that is fatter over other areas than that indicated by the fat measurement over the ribeye, the measurement is adjusted upward. Conversely, in a carcass that has less fat over other areas than indicated by the fat measurement over the ribeye, the measurement is adjusted downward. In many carcasses no adjustment is necessary; however, an adjustment of .1 or .2 in. is not uncommon. Occasionally as much as .3 in. adjustment may be made to compensate for total external fat on the carcass because the fat measurement over the ribeye underestimates or overestimates total carcass fat. It should be emphasized that adjustments upward are much more frequently necessary than adjustments downward.

2. *Ribeye area* is determined either by a direct grid reading of the eye muscle or by a planimeter reading from a tracing of the eye muscle. The grid reading is faster and is used much more frequently than the planimeter method. Ribeye area is illustrated in Figure 10.18. Most Federal meat graders are familiar enough with estimating area so that they can accurately estimate area without the use of a grid.

When using the plastic grid, place it on the eye muscle with either the 8, 9 or 10 in.^{2} circumscribed area within the perimeter of the eye, depending on the largest circumscribed area that lies entirely within the eye (Figure 10.18B). Then count all the dots outside the 8, 9 or 10 in.^{2} circumscribed area but within the perimeter of the eye muscle. Count only the dots within the perimeter of the eye muscle while being careful not to include adjacent muscles. In the case of that lie directly on the perimeter of the muscle, count only every other dot so that area will not be overestimated. After all dots have been counted, divide the total counted by 10 (because there are 10 dots per in.^{2}). Then add this figure to the circumscribed area that was entirely within the perimeter of the eye muscle to obtain the area. The following example will illustrate the procedure involved. In the example carcass shown in Figure 10.18, the 8 in.^{2} area entirely fits within the perimeter of the eye, but the 9 in.^{2} area does not. A count of all dots outside the 8 in.^{2} circumscribed area but within the perimeter of the eye muscle totals 45. The 45 dots divided by 10 = 4.5 in.^{2}. The 4.5 added to the original 8 in.^{2} = 12.5 in.^{2} which is the ribeye area of the example carcass.

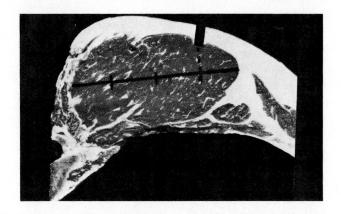

Figure 10.17. Illustration showing the site of the 12th rib fat thickness measurement or estimate.

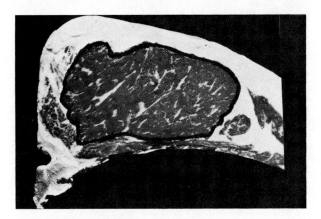

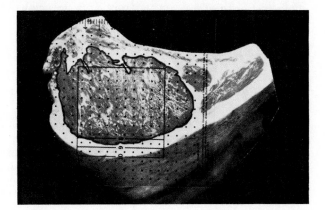

Figure 10.18. Illustration (left) showing the perimeter of the ribeye muscle outlined in black. The grid procedure for determining ribeye area is shown in the illustration on the right.

3. *Hot carcass weight* is usually obtained in beef slaughter plants, but the cold carcass is seldom weighed prior to shipping. Hot carcass weight should be obtained before the shroud is applied.

4. *Kidney, pelvic, and heart fat (KPH)* is estimated in pounds for each side. The two sides are totaled and divided by carcass weight to arrive at percentage. KPH will range from .5% to 6% and averages about 3.0%. Thus, a 700 lb. carcass will have 21 lb. of KPH or 10.5 lb. per side. Examples of two carcasses differing in % KPH are shown in Figure 10.19.

Application of Working Formula to Yield Grade Beef Carcasses

The same base is used for yield grading beef carcasses as for live cattle (i.e., 3.5). The 3.5 yield grade corresponds to a 600 lb. carcass with .6 in. of adjusted fat thickness, 3.5% KPH, and an 11.0 in.² ribeye area (REA). The working formula is generally used to yield grade carcasses in everday practice. The working formula is identical to the procedure described for live cattle.

1. Estimate the fat thickness at the 12th rib and adjust, if necessary. From this estimate determine a preliminary yield grade (PYG).

Figure 10.19. An illustration of two beef carcasses showing the outline (in black) of the kidney, pelvic, and heart fat. The kidney fat is labeled with a "K," the pelvic fat is labeled "P" and heart fat is labeled "H." The carcass on the left has 5% kidney, pelvic, and heart fat. The carcass on the right has 2.5% kidney, pelvic and heart fat.

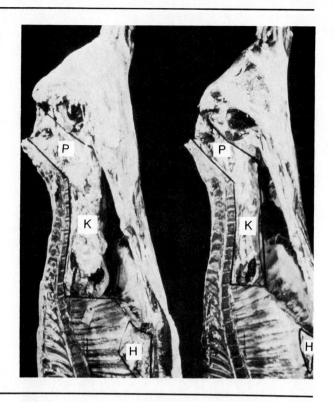

Adjusted Fat Thickness Estimate (In.)	PYG	Adjusted Fat Thickness Estimate (In.)	PYG
.1	= 2.25	.7	= 3.75
.2	= 2.5	.8	= 4.0
.3	= 2.75	.9	= 4.25
.4	= 3.0	1.0	= 4.5
.5	=3.25	1 .1	= 4.75
.6	= 3.5	1.2	= 5.0

For each .1 in. of adjusted 12th rib fat thickness in excess of .6 in., add .25 yield grade; and for each .1 in. of adjusted 12th rib fat thickness under .6 in., subtract .25 yield grade.

2. For each 1 in.² REA in excess of 11.0 in.², subtract .3 yield grade; and for each 1 in.² less than 11.0 in.², add .3 yield grade to the PYG.

3. For each 25 lb. of hot carcass weight (HCW) in excess of 600 lb., add .1 yield grade to the PYG; and for each 25 lb. HCW less than 600 lb., subtract .1 yield grade from the PYG. When HCW is not obtained, it can be calculated from chilled carcass weight. To obtain HCW from chilled carcass weight, multiply chilled carcass weight by 101.5% (1.015). This is the procedure used by the U.S.D.A., when HCW is not available. One of these weights is always obtained and usually it is HCW.

4. For each .5% KPH in excess of 3.5%, add .1 yield grade to the PYG; and for each .5% below 3.5%, subtract .1 yield grade from the PYG.

Use of the working formula to obtain final yield grade (FYG) is illustrated in the following example:

	Adj. Fat Thickness		REA	HCW	% KPH	
Estimated values	.4 in.		12.0 in.^{2}	650 lb.	3.0%	
Adjustment factors	− .5 or PYG = 3.0		− .3	+ .2	− .1	= 2.8 FYG

Weight-Eye Method of Calculating Yield Grade of Beef Carcasses

1. Calculate the PYG using the method previously described for the working formula.
2. Adjust the PYG using hot carcass weight and ribeye area. Ribeye area is influenced by carcass weight. Carcasses with typical muscling would have ribeyes of the following sizes:

Hot Carcass Wt. (Lb.)	Ribeye Area (In.^{2})	Hot Carcass Wt. (Lb.)	Ribeye Area (In.^{2})
500	9.8	700	12.2
525	10.1	725	12.5
550	10.4	750	12.8
575	10.7	775	13.1
		800	13.4
Base 600	11.0	825	13.7
		850	14.0
		875	14.3
625	11.3		
650	11.6		
675	11.9		

In other words, a typical 600 lb. carcass would have an 11.0 in.^{2} ribeye. For every 25 lb. over 600, add .3 in.^{2} to the 11.0 in.^{2} required ribeye (RREA); and for every 25 lb. under 600 lb., subtract .3 in.^{2} from the 11.0 in.^{2} RREA. Then for each 1 in.^{2} of estimated ribeye in excess of the calculated RREA, subtract .3 of a yield grade from the PYG; and for each 1 in.^{2} of ribeye area less than the calculated RREA, add .3 of a yield grade to the PYG.

3. % KPH—Adjust for % KPH using the method previously described for the working formula.

The use of the weight-eye method is illustrated by the following example:

	Adj. Fat Thickness	HCW	REA	% KPH	
Estimated values	.4 in.	650 lb.	12.0 in.^{2}	3.0%	
Adjustment factors	−.5 or PYG = 3.0	+.6 in.^{2} or RREA = 11.6	−.1	−.1	= 2.8 FYG

Illustrations of carcasses representative of each of the five yield grades are shown in Figures 10.20 through 10.24.

Figure 10.20. A carcass representative of yield grade 1. The carcass has .2 in. 12th rib fat thickness, 13.9 in.² ribeye area, 2.5% KPH and 645 lb. hot carcass weight.

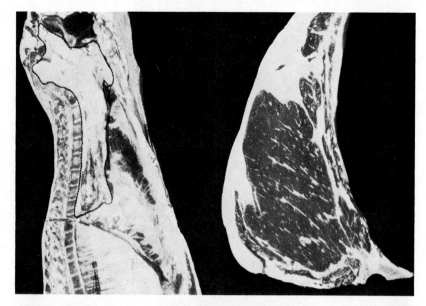

Figure 10.21. A carcass representative of yield grade 2. The carcass has .4 in. 12th rib fat thickness, 12.3 in.² ribeye area, 2.5% KPH and 605 lb. hot carcass weight.

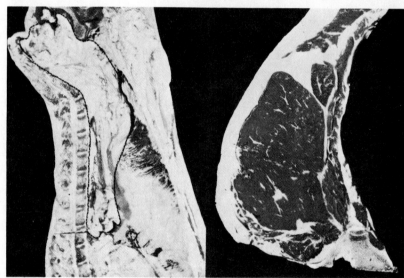

Figure 10.22. A carcass representative of yield grade 3. The carcass has .6 in. 12th rib fat thickness, 11.8 in.² ribeye area, 3.5% KPH and 700 lb. hot carcass weight.

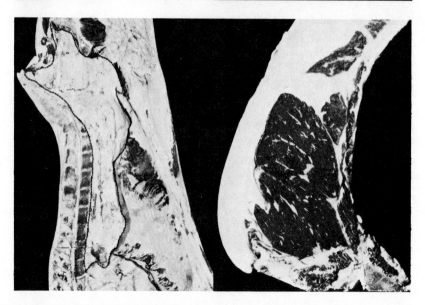

Figure 10.23. A carcass representative of yield grade 4. The carcass has .9 in. 12th rib fat thickness, 10.5 in.² ribeye area, 3.5 KPH and 665 lb. hot carcass weight.

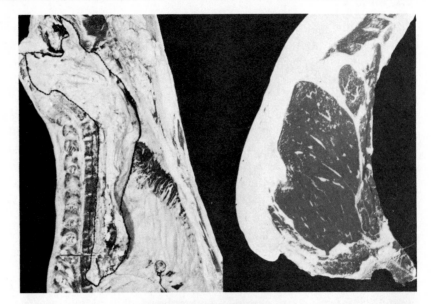

Figure 10.24. A carcass representative of yield grade 5. The carcass has 1.1 in. 12th rib fat thickness, 10.9 in.² ribeye area, 5.0% KPH and 750 lb. hot carcass weight.

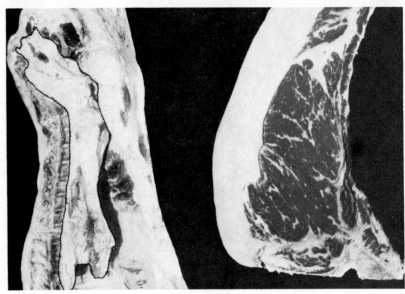

Wholesale Pricing of Beef Carcasses and Live Cattle Pricing

Beef Carcass Wholesale Price

Wholesale carcass price/cwt is calculated by adjusting the base quality grade price for actual yield grade by adding or subtracting $.25 for each .1 deviation in yield grade from the base price. This procedure is identical to the one for determining the live price/cwt of cattle. The base wholesale price of beef carcasses varies with daily market fluctuations so that prices need to be checked each day before beginning the carcass pricing procedures. Likewise, the base yield grade used for pricing beef carcasses may vary from time to time and should be checked before pricing beef carcasses. Wholesale carcass price adjusted for actual quality and yield grade price is used to calculate live price/cwt by multiplying it by the actual dressing percentage. The calculation of live price from actual carcass price is more accurate than that estimated on live cattle because the factors affecting it can be accurately evaluated or measured on the carcass. Retail pricing of beef will be presented and discussed in Section 18.

Veal and Calf

Veal and calf are included in this manual for the sake of a comprehensive evaluation of animals important in meat animal production. However, the discussion of veal and calf will be limited to a brief description of quality grading factors and procedure as applied to their carcasses.

Veal and Calf Quality Grade

The grading of veal and calf carcasses is a composite evaluation of conformation and quality. Conformation is an evaluation of the fleshing of the carcass. Conformation is evaluated by averaging the conformation of the various parts of the carcass and by considering not only the proportion, but also the value that each part comprises of the carcass. Superior conformation implies a high proportion of meat to bone and a high proportion of the weight of the carcass in the more valuable parts. Such carcasses are thickly fleshed. They are full and thick in relation to their length, and they have a plump, well-rounded appearance. Inferior conformation implies a low proportion of meat to bone and a low proportion of weight of the carcass in the more valuable parts. It is reflected in carcasses that are thinly fleshed and very narrow in relation to their length, and they have a very angular, thin, and sunken appearance.

Quality factors are usually evaluated in the unribbed veal or calf carcass. These factors include: (1) amount of feathering (fat intermingled within the lean (intercostal muscles) between the ribs and (2) the amount of fat streakings within and upon the inside flank muscles. In making these evaluations, the amount of feathering and flank fat streakings are considered in relation to color (veal) and maturity (calf). In other words, as color becomes darker (redder) and maturity more advanced, increasingly higher degrees of feathering and flank fat streakings are required to qualify for each grade (see Figure 10.25). The degrees of feathering and flank fat streakings are identified by the same descriptive terms as those for marbling and from lowest to highest degree they are as follows: (1) none, (2) practically none, (3) traces, (4) slight, (5) small, (6) modest, (7) moderate, (8) slightly abundant, and (9) moderately abundant. The abundant degrees of feathering and flank streaking are seldom encountered, and they are above the maximum for the high Prime grade.

While feathering and flank streakings are the major quality factors evaluated, consideration is sometimes given to such other factors as firmness of the lean; distribution of feathering; the amount of fat covering on the diaphragm or "skirt" and the amount and character of the external and kidney and pelvic fat. These latter factors are used only when they will result in a more accurate quality assessment than when using only the degrees of feathering and flank fat streakings.

Figure 10.25. Quality grade equivalent of various degrees of feathering and flank fat streakings in relation to color of lean (veal) or maturity (calf).

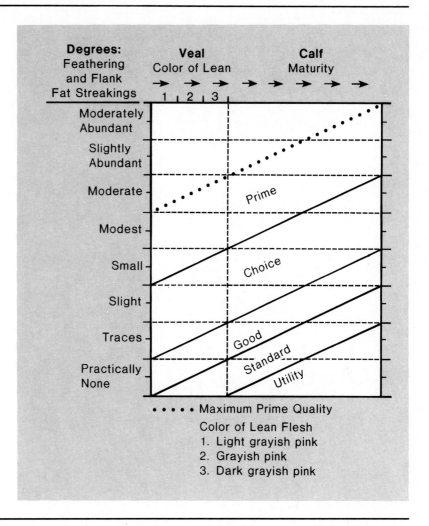

Evaluation of Beef Cattle Performance Data

The major production traits that need to be considered in a beef selection program are reproductive performance, mothering ability, growth rate, efficiency of gain, and carcass merit. While the importance of each of these traits will vary depending on the type of production program involved, the successful producer will consider all aspects of the beef production system when establishing a complete selection program. Many of the following formulas and recommendations are from the Beef Improvement Federation's 1986 Guidelines for Uniform Beef Improvement Programs.

Reproductive Performance

The first goal of every cow-calf producer should be to produce one live, healthy calf from each cow every 12 months. Thus a record of "percentage calf crop" is useful to the producer in evaluating the entire selection, management, and production system.

$$\text{Percentage calf crop} = \frac{\text{number of calves weaned}}{\text{number of cows exposed to bull or AI}} \times 100$$

It is very important to consider all females in the breeding program in order to get an accurate measure of reproductive performance. Any females that are pregnancy tested "open" should be culled from the herd to avoid the costs of maintaining a nonproducer.

Birth weight and calving ease are often interrelated factors that can affect reproductive performance. Determining an ideal birth weight is very difficult because high birth weights are associated with increased dystocia, but are also associated with increased weaning and yearling weights. Also, light weight calves at birth will generally be weaker and less thrifty, which may result in an increased death loss after birth. Thus, the producer should establish an acceptable range of birth weights and avoid selecting bulls and heifer replacements with birth weights above or below this range. In most cases, birth weights of 60–90 lb. are acceptable. This range can vary with different breeds, cattle types, and management systems. A more effective means of preventing calving difficulties is to use bulls, or progeny of bulls, that have been progeny tested for their calving ease. This information is available on many bulls and may be obtained through AI Sire Directories, Breed Associations or the owners of the bulls.

Mothering Ability

The most commonly used measure of a cow's mothering ability is the weight of her calf at weaning. Weaning weight is highly correlated with the milking ability of the cow and provides an early indication of the calf's ability to grow. To accurately compare calf weights, the weights must first be corrected to a standard age of calf. Also, since the age of the cow affects the amount of milk she produces, the weights must be adjusted to a standard age of dam. The Beef Improvement Federation recommends weighing calves between 160 and 250 days of age and correcting to a standard 205 days of age. They have also established a set of factors to adjust the age of dam to a mature cow basis. This adjustment is necessary due to the inability of a young cow to milk as heavily as a 2, 3, or 4-year old as she will as a mature cow. To calculate the 205–day adjusted weaning weight, the average daily gain (ADG) to weaning is first calculated.

$$\text{ADG}_w = \frac{\text{actual weaning weight} - \text{birth weight}}{\text{age of calf in days}}$$

When birth weight is unknown, a standard of 70 lb. is used. The 205-day adjusted weight is then calculated using the ADG_w and one of the following age of dam adjustment factors:

Age of Dam	Adjustment Factor (lb.)	
	Male	Female
2 years	+60	+54
3 years	+40	+36
4 years	+20	+18
5–10 years	0	0
11 years and older	+20	+18

205-day adjusted weaning wt. = $(ADG_w \times 205)$ + Birth weight + Age of Dam adjustment factor

Many beef breed associations have developed age of dam adjustment factors specific to their breed. Most of these are slightly different than the BIF adjustment factors in order to more accurately reflect the differences in milk production between cows of different ages within that particular breed. To accurately compare the performance of the cows in the herd, the 205-day adjusted weight should be adjusted to a common sex of calf. This adjustment is necessary because bull calves will usually weigh approximately 10% more than heifer calves and approximately 5% more than steer calves. The weights are most commonly adjusted to a steer basis by subtracting 5% from the adjusted weight of bull calves and adding 5% to adjusted weight of heifer calves. In some purebred herds, where all male calves are weaned as bulls, the adjustment is made to a bull basis by adding 10% to the adjusted weights of the heifer calves. Weaning weight records are especially important to the cow-calf producer, since this weight represents the pounds sold. Cow-calf producers may want to consider actual weaning weight more important than adjusted weaning weight, since consideration of actual weight rewards cows that calve early in the calving season and puts indirect selection pressure on reproductive efficiency. Weaning weight is also important in heifer selection because it indicates the maternal ability of the cow. Even though a ratio system (Section 4) should be used to make within herd comparisons, herd replacements should meet the following standards:

British breed heifers	400–500 lb.
British breed bulls	450–550 lb.
Exotic breed heifers	450–550 lb.
Exotic breed bulls	500–600 lb.

These standards can vary depending on environment and management system. For example, when calves have been creep fed, 50–70 lb. should be added to the above standards.

When culling the cow herd, the producer needs an estimation of the cow's producing ability. If all of the cows produce the same number of calves, this is simply the average weaning weight ratio of all calves produced. In most instances, however, the producer must compare cows with unequal numbers of calves. The Most Probable Producing Ability formula was developed to help make these comparisons.

$$MPPA = H + \frac{NR}{1 + (N-1)R} \times (C - H)$$

Where H = 100, the herd average weaning weight ratio
N = the number of calves included in the cow's average
R = .4, the repeatability for weaning weight ratio
and C = the average weaning weight ratio for all calves the cow has produced

Thus, if a cow has produced 5 calves with an average weaning weight ratio of 105, her MPPA would be calculated as follows:

$$MPPA = 100 \times \frac{(5 \times .4)}{1 + (5 - 1).4} \times (105 - 100)$$

$$MPPA = 100 + \frac{2}{1 + 1.6} \times 5 = 100 + 3.8 = 103.8$$

The following example should demonstrate the need to use MPPA when comparing cows with unequal numbers of calves.

Cow	Number of Calves	Average Weaning Weight Ratio	MPPA
A	1	90	96.0
B	3	92	94.6
C	5	94	95.3

If the cows were compared on the basis of average weaning weight ratio, A would appear to be the poorest producer. However, it is very possible that B and C, which are also relatively poor producers, have also produced a calf or calves with a ratio of 90 or less. The MPPA accounts for the difference in the number of opportunities a cow has had to express her genetic potential and allows for more accurate culling. In this example, the MPPA values indicate that A may potentially be a higher producing cow than B or C and, therefore, should be ranked above B or C when determining which cows to keep or cull.

Many producers prefer cow efficiency as an indicator of cow producing ability, especially in herds made up of various frame size cows.

$$\text{Cow Efficiency} = \frac{\text{Adjusted Weaning Weight of Calf}}{\text{Weight of Cow at Calf Weaning}} \times 100$$

Cow efficiency calculations remove some of the effect of different growth potentials in herds of this type. In other words, a 900 lb. cow that produces a 450 lb. calf is considered to be as efficient as a 1,000 lb. cow that produces a 500 lb. calf $\left(\frac{450 \text{ lb.}}{900 \text{ lb.}} = 50\% \text{ efficiency} = \frac{500 \text{ lb.}}{1000 \text{ lb.}} \right)$. When using cow efficiency, a producer should consider other performance records and total production costs and returns (cow maintenance, feeder calf prices, etc.) before making final culling decisions.

Adjusted Hip Heights

Hip heights are objective, linear measurements that provide a descriptive supplement to the other herd production records. When combined, adjusted heights and adjusted weights provide an estimate of the animal's growth and body composition. Weaning heights should be adjusted to a 205-day basis and then adjusted for the age of the dam. The age of calf adjustment factors are .033 in. per day for bulls and .025 in. per day for heifers. The age of dam adjustment factors for hip height at weaning are as follows:

Age of Dam (Years)	Height Adjustment Factor
2 and 13 or older	1.02
3 and 12	1.015
4 and 11	1.01
5 through 10	1.0 (no adjustment)

Following are the equations for calculating adjusted weaning hip heights.

Bull calves:

$$\text{Adjusted hip height} = [\text{actual height} + ((205 - \text{age}) \times .033)] \times \frac{\text{age of dam}}{\text{adjustment factor}}$$

Heifer calves:

$$\text{Adjusted hip height} = [\text{actual height} + ((205 - \text{age}) \times .025)] \times \frac{\text{age of dam}}{\text{adjustment factor}}$$

For example, the adjusted 205-day hip height of a 197-day old heifer calf that measures 41 inches, out of a 4 year-old cow would be calculated as follows:

$$\begin{aligned}
\text{Adjusted hip height} &= [41 + ((205 - 197) \times .025)] \times 1.01 \\
&= [41 + (8 \times .025)] \times 1.01 \\
&= 41.2 \times 1.01 \\
&= 41.61 \text{ inches}
\end{aligned}$$

Adjusted yearling heights are calculated by simply adjusting to a 365 day basis. These adjustments for bulls and heifers are as follows:

Yearling bulls:

$$\text{Adjusted hip height} = \text{actual height} + [(365 - \text{age in days}) \times .033]$$

Yearling heifers:

$$\text{Adjusted hip height} = \text{actual height} + [(365 - \text{age in days}) \times .025]$$

For example, the adjusted 365-day hip height of a bull which measures 49 inches at 375 days of age would be:

$$\begin{aligned}
\text{Adjusted hip height} &= 49 + [(365 - 375) \times .033] \\
&= 49 + [\quad -10 \times .033] \\
&= 49 - .33 \\
&= 48.67 \text{ inches}
\end{aligned}$$

Tables 11.1 and 11.2 relate hip heights of bulls and heifers to the body type or frame scores previously discussed in Section 4. The proper method for measuring hip height in cattle is illustrated in Figure 4.2.

Growth Rate and Feeding Efficiency

Group feeding weaned calves for 140 days gives an adequate indication of their ability to grow. All calves within a group should be fed the same ration, but they do not have to be full-fed. Thus, a group of bulls would probably receive a higher energy ration than a group of replacement heifers.

The collection of individual feed efficiency data during this test period would be extremely beneficial, but the high costs of labor and facilities to obtain such information limits its use. Some bull test stations do, however, furnish these data. It should be remembered that gain on test and feed efficiency are both influenced by management, level of nutrition and environmental conditions. Thus, accurate comparisons of these records can be made only within a test group. Rate and efficiency of gain on test are important in bull selection as this test period relates to the finishing period of the feedlot phase of production.

Table 11.1 Relationship of Bull Hip Height in Inches to Frame Score.[1]

Frame score	Age in months																
	5	6	7	8	9	10	11	12	13	14	15	16	17	18	19	20	21
1	33.5	34.8	36.0	37.2	38.2	39.2	40.2	41.0	41.8	42.5	43.1	43.6	44.1	44.5	44.9	45.1	45.3
2	35.5	36.8	38.0	39.2	40.2	41.2	42.2	43.0	43.8	44.5	45.1	45.6	46.1	46.5	46.8	47.1	47.3
3	37.5	38.8	40.0	41.2	42.3	43.3	44.2	45.0	45.8	46.5	47.1	47.6	48.1	48.5	48.8	49.1	49.2
4	39.5	40.8	42.1	43.2	44.3	45.3	46.2	47.0	47.8	48.5	49.1	49.6	50.1	50.5	50.8	51.0	51.2
5	41.6	42.9	44.1	45.2	46.3	47.3	48.2	49.0	49.8	50.4	51.1	51.6	52.0	52.4	52.7	53.0	53.2
6	43.6	44.9	46.1	47.2	48.3	49.3	50.2	51.0	51.8	52.4	53.0	53.6	54.0	54.4	54.7	55.0	55.1
7	45.6	46.9	48.1	49.3	50.3	51.3	52.2	53.0	53.8	54.4	55.0	55.6	56.0	56.4	56.7	56.9	57.1
8	47.7	48.9	50.1	51.3	52.3	53.3	54.2	55.0	55.8	56.4	57.0	57.5	58.0	58.4	58.7	58.9	59.1
9	49.7	51.0	52.2	53.3	54.3	55.3	56.2	57.0	57.7	58.4	59.0	59.5	60.0	60.3	60.6	60.9	61.0

[1]Beef Improvement Federation, 1986.

Table 11.2. Relationship of Heifer Hip Height in Inches to Frame Score.[1]

Frame score	Age in months																
	5	6	7	8	9	10	11	12	13	14	15	16	17	18	19	20	21
1	33.1	34.1	35.1	36.0	36.8	37.6	38.3	39.0	39.6	40.1	40.6	41.0	41.4	41.7	41.9	42.1	42.3
2	35.1	36.2	37.1	38.0	38.9	39.6	40.3	41.0	41.6	42.1	42.6	43.0	43.3	43.6	43.9	44.1	44.2
3	37.2	38.2	39.2	40.1	40.9	41.6	42.3	43.0	43.6	44.1	44.5	44.9	45.3	45.6	45.8	46.0	46.1
4	39.3	40.3	41.2	42.1	42.9	43.7	44.3	45.0	45.5	46.1	46.5	46.9	47.2	47.5	47.7	47.9	48.0
5	41.3	42.3	43.3	44.1	44.9	45.7	46.4	47.0	47.5	48.0	48.5	48.9	49.2	49.5	49.7	49.8	50.0
6	43.4	44.4	45.3	46.2	47.0	47.7	48.4	49.0	49.5	50.0	50.5	50.8	51.1	51.4	51.6	51.8	51.9
7	45.5	46.5	47.4	48.2	49.0	49.7	50.4	51.0	51.5	52.0	52.4	52.8	53.1	53.4	53.6	53.7	53.8
8	47.5	48.5	49.4	50.2	51.0	51.7	52.4	53.0	53.5	54.0	54.4	54.8	55.1	55.3	55.5	55.6	55.7
9	49.6	50.6	51.5	52.3	53.0	53.8	54.4	55.0	55.5	56.0	56.4	56.7	57.0	57.3	57.4	57.6	57.7

[1]Beef Improvement Federation, 1986.

Yearling weight is the most accurate single measure of a calf's economic value, since it combines the gain prior to weaning, which is highly associated with maternal ability, with the gain from weaning to a year of age, which is highly correlated with increased efficiency of gain and cutability. Yearling weight is calculated as follows, using the 205-day weight adjusted for age of dam and the yearling average daily gain (ADG_y):

$$ADG_y = \frac{\text{actual yearling weight} - \text{actual weaning weight}}{\text{number of days between weights}}$$

$$\text{365-day adjusted wt.} = (ADG_y \times 160) + \text{205-day weight adjusted for age of dam}$$

Yearling weight is the best performance parameter for bull selection as it relates to the market weight of the steers produced. Also, since the heritability of yearling weight is moderately high, considerable progress can be accomplished by selecting for this trait. A ratio system should be used in making comparisons within a herd, but superior replacements should meet the following standards for 365-day adjusted weight:

British breed heifers	600–700 lb.
British breed bulls	950–1050 lb.
Exotic breed heifers	650–750 lb.
Exotic breed bulls	1050–1200 lb.

Calculation of 205- and 365-Day Adjusted Weights:

The 205- and 365-day adjusted weights for a bull calf, out of a 3-year-old cow, that weighed 80 lb. at birth, 600 lb. at 200 days, and 1110 lb. at 370 days are calculated as follows:

$$\text{205-day adj. wt.} = \left(\left(\frac{600 \text{ lb.} - 80 \text{ lb.}}{200 \text{ days}}\right) \times 205 \text{ days}\right) + 80 \text{ lb.} + 40 \text{ lb.}$$

$$= \left(\frac{520}{200} \times 205\right) + 80 + 40$$

$$= (2.6 \times 205) + 80 + 40$$

$$= 533 + 80 + 40$$

$$= 653 \text{ lb.}$$

$$\text{365-day adj. wt.} = \left(\left(\frac{1110 \text{ lb.} - 600 \text{ lb.}}{370 \text{ days} - 200 \text{ days}}\right) \times 160 \text{ days}\right) + 653 \text{ lb.}$$

$$= \left(\frac{510}{170} \times 160\right) + 653$$

$$= (3 \times 160) + 653$$

$$= 480 + 653$$

$$= 1133 \text{ lb.}$$

Many producers prefer to develop their bulls and heifers on lower energy, higher forage diets. These producers may prefer to use long yearling weights (452 or 550 days) as an alternative to the conventional adjusted 365 day yearling weights. Computation of adjusted long yearling weights is similar to that of adjusted 365 day weight.

$$\text{550-day adj. wt.} = \left[\frac{\text{actual final wt.} - \text{actual weaning wt.}}{\text{days between weights}} \times 345\right] + \text{205-day adjusted wt.}$$

Adjusted 452-day weights are calculated by substituting 247 for 345 in the previous equation. BIF recommends that final weights should not be taken at less than 500 days for 550-day weights or at less than 400 days for 452-day weights.

Carcass Composition

Although the important carcass characteristics are discussed in Section 10, it should be emphasized that the composition of the final beef product is important not only to the packer who buys the market animal and to the feedlot operator who sells the cattle, but also to the cow-calf producer. To maintain a successful marketing program, the cow-calf operator must produce a calf that is acceptable to all segments of the beef cattle and meat industry. Hence, the cow-calf producers should make every attempt to follow the calves through the entire production system. Carcass information can be obtained from the U.S.D.A. Beef Carcass Evaluation Service for a nominal fee on a per head basis.

Estimated Breeding Values and Expected Progeny Difference

The *estimated breeding value* (EBV) of an animal is a prediction of its value as a parent. It is not the intent of this manual to describe all of the genetic and computational aspects of breeding value. However, an understanding of this concept is important to all producers because breeding value is what purebred producers sell and commercial producers purchase in the form of seedstock.

Improvements in computer technology have provided a method for improving the prediction of an animal's breeding value through the analysis of the animal's, as well as its relatives' performance records. By utilizing all of the records available, the accuracy of an animal's estimated breeding value is enhanced. This not only provides a valuable tool for within herd selections, but it also increases the ability to compare the genetic merits of animals in different herds. EBVs are also adjusted for the amount of information (records) used in the computation. This adjustment allows for comparisons to be made between individuals with differing numbers of progeny records.

The working definition of an individual's breeding value is twice the difference between the average performance of a large group of progeny from that individual and the population (breed) average. Since breeding values are generally presented in ratio form (Section 4), an animal that produced an offspring that performed equal to the population average would have an estimated breeding value (EBV) of 100. Likewise, if the progeny performed 2% better than the population average, the estimated breeding value (EBV) would be 104, or twice the difference. EBVs are generally calculated for birth, weaning, and yearling weights, as well as for maternal ability.

The accuracy of the estimated breeding value is also important. Accuracy for a trait can generally vary from .00 to 1.00, with 1.00 being perfect accuracy. As the accuracy of an EBV increases, so does its reliability. The accuracy of an EBV increases as the number of records included in its calculation increases. As an example, a yearling EBV for a bull, calculated using only the individual's and parents' performance, would have a much lower accuracy than a yearling EBV for a bull whose individual, parent, and progeny records were all included in the calculation.

Another type of breeding value estimate is the *expected progeny difference* (EPD). The EPD is based on existing progeny records and is an estimate of how future progeny of a sire will perform. EPD information is the most accurate method of comparing the breeding value of bulls within a breed. Unfortunately, this information is available only in breeds that have a National Sire Evaluation Program.

Most of these breeds presently provide EPD information for birth weight, weaning weight direct (weight due to growth), weaning weight maternal (weight due to milk production, also referred to as milk EPD), and yearling weight. Individual breeds may offer more (hip height, scrotal circumference, calving ease) or less information depending on their analysis system. In addition, many breeds are rapidly working on estimating EPDs on carcass traits, such as ribeye area, backfat, and marbling score.

Whereas EBVs are generally presented in ratio form, EPDs are presented in the actual unit of measurement, which is generally pounds. One must remember that EPDs can only be used to compare bulls and not to predict how many pounds a bull will add to a particular herds average for weaning or yearling weights. For example, if bull A had a weaning EPD of +30 pounds and bull B had a weaning EPD of +20 pounds, progeny of bull A would be expected to have a 10 pound weight advantage when compared to progeny of bull B. This does *not* mean that calves from bull A will weigh 30 pounds more than the herd average.

EPDs have several advantages over other performance data that can be used in selection. First and most importantly, they are the most accurate predictors of progeny performance. Secondly, EPDs provide an accurate description of an individual animal's or a herd's strengths and weaknesses in various performance traits. In addition, they are expressed in actual units of measure and are easy to relate and comprehend. Because of these advantages, EPDs allow for greater specificity in multi-trait selection.

Increasing the accuracy of selection decisions is essential for the beef producer to overcome the long generation interval and relatively low heritability estimates that hamper the rate of selection response. National sire evaluation programs and increased use of on farm testing and record keeping are valuable to improving beef cattle selection programs.

Specification Based Selection Programs

When selecting cattle it is important to realize that certain situations will require different types of animals. All animals have traits that may make them superior under one set of circumstances; yet under different circumstances, these same traits may be a liability. For example, a bull that produces heavy milking daughters would not be desirable to use when feed limitations exist for the cow herd. Conversely, a bull with a very low milk EPD would not be desirable for producing replacement heifers, but he might be very acceptable for use in a terminal crossbreeding program where all progeny are slaughtered. The development of EPDs has greatly expanded the use of specification selection because of their accuracy of predicting progeny performance in several traits and their accuracy of describing the strengths and weaknesses of the cow herd.

When selecting cattle, ask the following questions:

1. How are the selected bulls (heifers) to be used? (purpose)
2. Under what conditions (feed, labor, present herd status) are the bulls (heifers) expected to perform? (situation)
3. Based on the purpose and the situation, what traits are most important? (selection priorities)

The purpose and situation are collectively referred to as the *scenario*. Once you understand the scenario, you can accurately determine which traits are the priorities for selection. With that information, choose the correct bull (heifer) for that specific situation and purpose. For example, consider selection of yearling Simmental bulls for the following scenario:

- Three-breed rotational crossbreeding
- 1,100 lb. Hereford X Angus cows as well as the virgin heifers
- This particular herd is low in milk production
- Feed is plentiful
- Labor is limited during calving season
- Calves are marketed at weaning

To meet the criteria of this scenario, relatively high priority should be placed on calving ease and low birth weight EPD because the bulls will be mated to virgin heifers and relatively small cows and because labor is limited during calving season. The next priority should be milk because this particular herd is known to be deficient in this trait. Thus, bulls should be selected with above average milk EPDs. Although growth is important in any herd, it would not be the highest priority in this particular situation. Bulls near Simmental breed average for yearling weight EPD would still improve the growth of this herd.

To illustrate how selection priorities can differ depending on the scenario, consider another example scenario, provided for selection of yearling Angus bulls:

- Three-breed rotational crossbreeding
- 1,200 lb. Polled Hereford × Limousin cows, no heifers
- Pasture is adequate to support slightly more milk than the cows are producing
- Labor is plentiful
- Steers and surplus heifers are fed to slaughter

For this scenario, growth (weaning weight direct and yearling weight EPDs) would be the highest priority, then milk, and finally calving ease or birth weight the least.

Cattle producers are fortunate to have several technologically advanced selection tools to aid in making selection decisions. It is critical that producers realize the importance of selecting for an optimal level of performance in a balance of traits. By doing this, purebred producers can provide seedstock to the commercial industry that has the predictable genetics necessary to match specified production systems.

Visual Evaluation of Breeding Beef Cattle

Decisions made in the selection of breeding stock are perhaps more important in beef than in any other species. This is due primarily to the longer generation interval which decreases the rate of progress from selection. Hence, the producer can neither make rapid changes in type, nor make rapid recovery from selection mistakes. Secondly, the relatively high initial cost of breeding stock requires that they have the longevity to stay in the breeding herd for many years to help dilute the initial investment. Therefore, the genetic influence of the selected cattle will remain in the herd for a relatively long period of time.

Structural Correctness

Breeding cattle must be structurally and reproductively sound in order to remain productive for many years in the breeding program. They must also move freely and be able to cover many acres of pasture for both nutritional and breeding purposes.

The bull in Figure 12.1 is correct in his skeletal struture. He has smoothness, balance, and straightness of lines. He is sloping in his shoulder, straight and strong in his top, and level from his hooks to pins. This bull also stands squarely on all legs, is strong in his pasterns, and has the proper set to his hind legs.

The steer in Figure 12.2 is structurally incorrect. He is very straight in his shoulder and buckled over at the knees. The steer is also post-legged (too straight) behind and moves with a short, choppy stride. These are serious faults, especially with breeding stock. Such cattle are restricted in their mobility, and they are prone to injuries, especially in the stifle joint. In contrast, the bull in Figure 12.3 is droopy rumped, sickle-hocked (too much set to hocks), and back at the knees. This bull will set under when he walks. While these conditions are not desirable, they are not as serious faults as the problems shown in Figure 12.2.

Figure 12.1. Illustration showing a structurally correct bull.

Figure 12.2. Illustration of a structurally incorrect steer that is straight shouldered, buck kneed and post-legged.

Figure 12.3. Illustration of a structurally incorrect bull that is droopy rumped, sickle hocked and calf kneed.

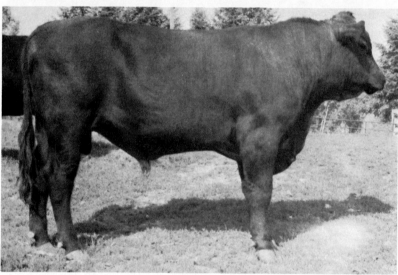

When viewed from the front, the feet should point straight forward both at the walk and when the animal is standing in a normal position (Figure 12.4). The steer in Figure 12.5 toes out in front—a condition that is also referred to as splay-footed. The feet should be big and round with a deep heel, and the toes should be even-sized.

From the rear, the legs should be equally wide at the hocks and the pasterns, and then toe out slightly from the pasterns to the ground. The animal should walk straight forward, flexing its hock rather than rolling at the hocks. All joints should be well defined and show no swelling or puffiness. The heifer in Figure 12.6 is close at the hocks (cow-hocked), while the bull calf in Figure 12.7 is wide at the hocks (bow-legged).

Cattle should also be smooth and laid in tightly at the shoulder. This is especially important in large framed cattle with heavy birth weights. Coarse, open-shouldered calves will usually cause increased calving problems.

Figure 12.4. Illustration showing correct front leg structure.

Figure 12.5. Illustration showing a splay-footed (toes out) steer.

Figure 12.4   Figure 12.5

Figure 12.6. Illustration showing a heifer that is close at the hocks (cow hocked).

Figure 12.7. Illustration of a bull calf that is wide at the hocks (bow-legged).

Figure 12.6   Figure 12.7

Figure 12.8. Illustration of a feminine appearing cow.

Sex Character

As was discussed in Section 11, increasing reproductive rate is very important in improving the economic return of the beef cow-calf enterprise. While reproductive traits are difficult to visually appraise, there are certain criteria that should be emphasized when selecting a bull or female breeding stock.

Females should, in general, have a feminine, angular appearance (Figure 12.8) that shows medium refinement about the head, neck, and shoulders. A female should have a long, clean neck, be sharp over the withers, and be set wide at the pin bones. It may be desirable for large framed heifers to droop slightly from the hooks to the pins to increase calving ease. The heifer in Figure 12.9 is narrow at her pin bones, indicating a small pelvic area which could lead to calving problems. Yearling heifers should show adequate and normal vulva and udder development. The cow in Figure 12.10 is not feminine. She is coarse, fat, and has the appearance of a poor producer.

Bulls should be masculine and rugged about the head and neck and show prominent muscling in the arm and forearm. Producers should be wary of bulls that develop these secondary sex characteristics early in life because this may indicate early maturity and an increased predisposition to waste fat. However, these secondary sex characteristics are desirable in bulls that are one year of age or older.

The circumference and shape of the scrotum are also important in evaluating a bull's potential fertility because they are related to sperm production. Most yearling bulls will have a scrotal circumference of 25 to 40 cm. Yearling bulls that are to be used in rotational crossbreeding systems should have at least 34 cm scrotal circumference, and yearling terminal sires should have at lest 32 cm. Figure 12.11 shows proper scrotal shape, with a distinct neck and fully developed testicles descending to the hock level. In contrast, the scrotum shown in figure 12.12 is tapered, which may indicate undersized testicles. If the bull is overfed, fat may be deposited in the scrotum and will indicate a scrotal circumference that is not representative of testicular size.

Size and Scale

Selection for increased frame size results in later maturing, faster growing cattle that are leaner at a given weight and produce more pounds of edible meat per day of age than small-framed cattle. Unfortunately, some of the extremely large framed cattle may have calving problems, and they reach puberty later. These cattle also have greater mature weights and require more feed for maintenance than smaller cattle. Therefore, a commercial cow-calf producer generally uses a combination of different frame size cattle to maximize his production efficiency. In other words, he probably would prefer moderate frame-size cows to help minimize his maintenance feed costs and then use a larger framed bull to add increased growability to the calf crop. Methods for measuring frame size are discussed in Sections 4 and 11.

Figure 12.9. Illustration showing a heifer that is narrow at the pin bones.

Figure 12.10. Illustration of a coarse, fat cow that lacks angularity and femininity.

Figure 12.11. Illustration showing excellent testicular development.

Figure 12.12. Illustration showing poor testicular development.

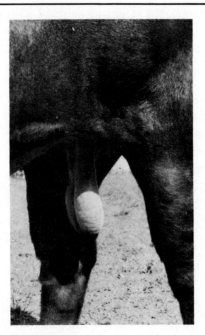

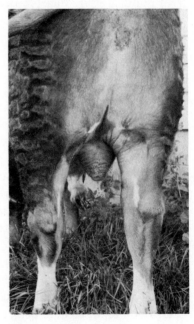

Figure 12.11.

Figure 12.12.

Muscle

As is the case with many of the traits that are evaluated in cattle, there seems to be an optimum amount of muscle. Both too little and too much muscle are undesirable. The bull in Figure 12.13 is very desirable in muscle structure and quantity. He shows good expression of muscling down his top and is square and thick through his rump. He is also long and deep in his quarter, yet shows adequate thickness of muscling. The bull in Figure 12.14 is narrow down his top, tapers over his rump, and is extremely narrow and

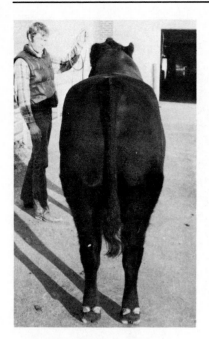

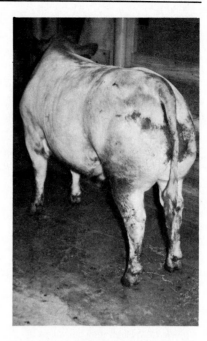

Figure 12.13. Illustration showing desirable muscle structure.

Figure 12.14. Illustration showing an extremely light muscled bull.

Figure 12.15. Illustration showing a coarse, short, bunchy muscle structure.

light muscled in his quarter. In contrast, the steer in Figure 12.15 is too heavily muscled. He is very short and bunchy in his muscle, which may be indicative of early maturity. Use of breeding animals with these characteristics may result in increased calving difficulties.

Condition

Selection of large-framed, late maturing cattle usually results in trimmer cattle that have less condition. However, it is important that cattle have some fleshing ability to cheapen winter maintenance feed costs. Nevertheless, the over-conditioning of breeding stock, especially young heifers and bulls, can be damaging to their subsequent reproductive performance. Research has also shown over-conditioning of heifers to be detrimental to their milk producing potential. On the other hand, cows that are too thin at calving time require more time to begin cycling after calving. Cows that are thin at breeding time have reduced conception rates and tend to calve later in the breeding season. Figure 12.16 shows cows of various body condition scores (described in Section 4). Producers should design their feeding and management programs to have the cows in body condition score 5 or 6 at the start of the breeding season.

Capacity

High performing cattle, those that gain rapidly and efficiently, generally have more chest and body capacity than slower gaining cattle. They have adequate spring and depth of rib, are wide through the chest floor, and are long bodied. One must be careful not to confuse excess fat or condition with extra capacity, since this area of the body is highly disposed to fat deposition and additional fat tends to make the calf look deep bodied with a full spring of rib.

Breed Character

For the purposes of this manual, sufficient breed character to qualify a bull or heifer for registry with the particular breed association will be considered acceptable. Since breed character is a subjective trait and difficult to visually appraise, many of the breed associations have adopted blood typing procedures to help maintain breed purity.

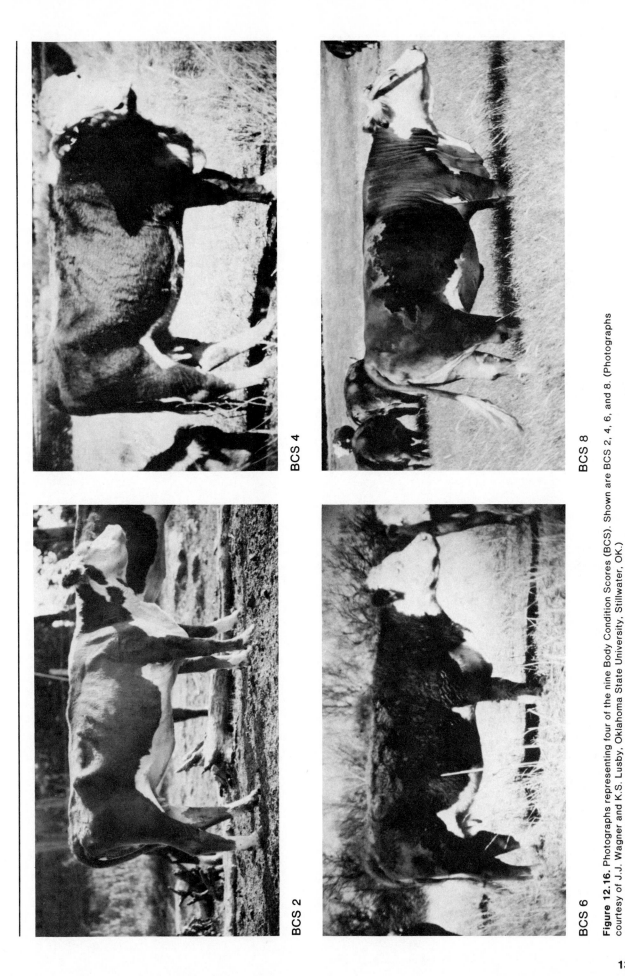

BCS 2

BCS 4

BCS 6

BCS 8

Figure 12.16. Photographs representing four of the nine Body Condition Scores (BCS). Shown are BCS 2, 4, 6, and 8. (Photographs courtesy of J.J. Wagner and K.S. Lusby, Oklahoma State University, Stillwater, OK.)

Live Lamb Evaluation, Grading, and Pricing

Live market lamb evaluation is essentially an estimation of important carcass characteristics. The specific characteristics evaluated are those that provide an indication of amount of fat and/or muscle, as well as quality grade, which, in turn, determines carcass value. Live value can then easily be calculated from estimated carcass value. A definition, brief description, ranges, and the mechanics used in estimating each carcass characteristic will be presented in this section. The student should familiarize him or herself with the normal ranges and the mechanics involved for evaluation of each characteristic for efficient use of class time.

Evaluation

Weight

Definition: Live weight is the actual weight of the lambs at the time of evaluation.

Extreme Range:	60–200 lb.
Normal Range:	90–150 lb.
Average:	120 lb.

These weight ranges are applicable to wether, ewe, and ram lambs of intermediate to large type sheep.

Live and carcass weight will be actual weights. Carcass weight (either hot or chilled) can be estimated from live weight by the dressing percentage procedure described below. Hot carcass weight can be calculated by multiplying chilled carcass weight by 102¾%. If hot carcass weight is available and chilled carcass weight is needed, multiply hot carcass weight by 97¼%. The information presented below for each characteristic is most applicable to intermediate to large type lambs that are of normal market weight of approximately 90 to 140 lb.

Dressing Percentage

Definition: (Chilled carcass weight ÷ live weight) × 100.

Extreme Range:	40–60%
Normal Range:	45–58%
Average:	53% (shorn lambs)

The factors that have the greatest effect on dressing percentage in lambs are: (1) fill (i.e., the contents of the stomach compartments and intestines). Dressing percentage and fill are inversely related; (2) weight of pelt (skin and fleece) because as fleece length increases, dressing percentage decreases; (3) degree of muscling, and (4) degree of fatness of the lamb. Heavily muscled lambs dress higher than light muscled lambs. Fatness has the least effect on dressing percentage. Only for the extremes in degree of fatness is dressing percentage affected and then it generally is affected by less than 1%. Dressing percentage is lowest in young, light weight lambs and increases as they increase in age and weight. As lambs increase in age and weight, viscera becomes a progressively smaller proportion of the body and, therefore, dressing percentage increases. Dressing percentages of shorn lambs for each quality grade are shown in Table 13.1.

Table 13.1   Dressing Percentage of Shorn Lambs by Quality Grade.*

Quality Grade	Range (shorn)	Av. (shorn)
Prime	50–58%	54%
Choice	48–56%	53%
Good	45–52%	50%
Utility	44–50%	47%

*Wooled lambs will have 1 to 5% lower dressing percentage (average 2 to 3) than shorn lambs.

Fat Thickness

Definition: Method 1.Depth of fat in tenths of inches over the ribeye muscle at the 12th rib. Consists of the average of the measurement at the midpoint of the lateral length of the right and left ribeye muscle as shown in Figure 13.1

   Method 2. An average of 4 measurements—one over the center of each ribeye as in method 1 and one at the thickest point of fat covering laterally over the rib on the right and left side (Figure 13.1). Method 2 will average about .2 in. more fat than method 1.

	Method 1	**Method 2**
Extreme Range:	.0–.9	.1–1.1
Normal Range:	.05–.5	.1–.8
Average:	.25	.5

The minimum fat thicknesses (method 1) necessary to maintain a fresh appearance, bloom, and to prevent excessive carcass shrink and discoloration is .1 inch.

Figure 13.1. Illustrations showing the fat thickness measurement on a lamb carcass at the 12th rib interface of method 1 (top) and method 2 (bottom). In method 1 the fat is measured over the center of the left and right ribeye muscle and then averaged. In method 2 the fat is measured over the center of the left and right ribeye muscle plus measurements taken laterally from the eye muscle on both sides at the point where the fat thickness is greatest. These four measurements are then averaged.

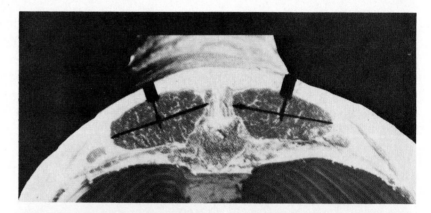

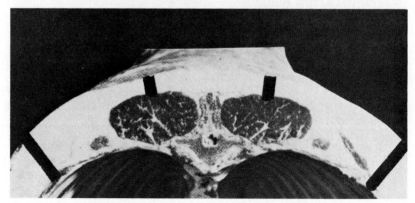

Fat thickness at the 12th rib (method 1) is one of the factors used to calculate yield grade. As fat thickness increases, yield grade increases in numerical value (toward 5.0), but percentage boneless, closely trimmed retail cuts decreases. Fat thickness is an assessment of external fat on the carcass; thus, as it increases, it lowers retail yield. Method 1 fat thickness is used to calculate yield grade; however, the average of 4 measurements (method 2) is actually a better predictor of total carcass fat than is method 1.

A side and top view of a lamb in Figure 13.2 illustrate the 12th rib site for estimating fat thickness and ribeye area. Method 1 (A, top view) and method 2 (A & B, top view) correspond to the fat measurement over the center of each eye muscle (A) and the center of each eye muscle, plus the lateral fat measurements (A & B), as illustrated at the 12th rib interface of the lamb carcass in Figure 13.1. On live lambs, points A are located at the 12th rib approximately 1½ in. laterally from the dorsal midline (dotted line), and points B are 3 to 4½ in. laterally from the dorsal midline (Figure 13.2).

Figure 13.2. Side view of a lamb showing the location of the 12th rib site for backfat and ribeye area estimation. The rear view shows the dorsal midline side for estimating 12th rib fat thickness using method 1 (A) and method 2 (A & B).

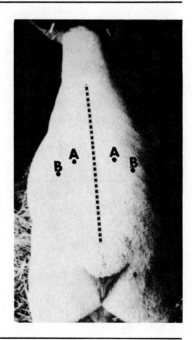

Ribeye Area:

Definition: Average area, in square inches, of the right and left ribeye (longissimus) muscle. It is measured after the carcass is ribbed between the 12th and 13th rib (Figure 13.3).

Extreme Range:	1.0–3.8 in.^{2}
Normal Range:	1.5–3.3 in.^{2}
Average:	2.4 in.^{2}

Ribeye area is correlated with total carcass lean, but not to a very high degree. Nevertheless, ribeye area is widely used as an indicator of lamb carcass muscling because it can be accurately measured with relative ease once the carcass has been ribbed at the 12th rib. It is the largest muscle in the carcass. It is also the most valuable muscle in the carcass because it is the major muscle in the chops and roasts of the wholesale loin and rack.

A photograph of ribeye area as indicated by the darkened outline of the longissimus muscle is shown in Figure 13.3. Eye muscle depth (dorsal-ventral dimension) and width (lateral dimension) should be observed on live lambs at the loin-rack junction (12th rib) to estimate ribeye area. In Figure 13.3 these two dimensions essentially determine area of the eye muscle. Either the right or left side of the live lamb can be used to estimate ribeye area, but in lamb carcasses where both sides are exposed, the average of right and left eye muscle areas is estimated or measured because sometimes the two sides differ in area.

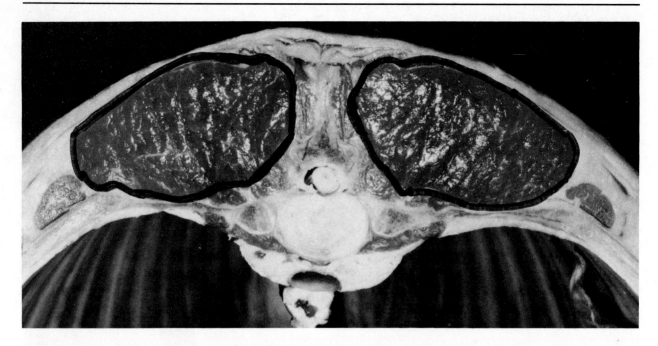

Figure 13.3. Illustration of a lamb carcass showing the 12th rib interface and the outline (dark line) of the perimeter of the right and left eye muscle.

Kidney and Pelvic Fat

Definition: The internal carcass fat associated with the kidney and pelvic cavity, expressed as a percentage of chilled carcass weight.

Extreme Range:	.5–9.0%
Normal Range:	1.5–6.0%
Average:	3.0%

Percentage kidney and pelvic fat (KP) is one of the factors used to calculate yield grade. As percentage KP increases, yield grade increases in numerical value (toward 5.0), but the percentage of boneless, closely trimmed retail cuts decreases. Percentage KP is an assessment of internal fat in the carcass and as it increases, it lowers retail yield.

A reasonable estimate of percentage KP may be obtained from the 12th rib fat thickness estimate as outlined in Table 13.2 because it is difficult to evaluate on live lambs. Fat thickness estimated by method 1 is used for the relationship to percentage KP.

Overall Conformation

Definition: A subjective evaluation of the relative distribution of muscling, especially in the leg, loin, rack, and shoulder regions. Degrees of conformation are expressed in terms of one-thirds of a quality grade (i.e., U.S. Prime⁺, Prime⁰, Prime⁻, Choice⁺, etc.).

Extreme Range:	High Prime–low Utility
Normal Range:	High Prime–low Good
Average:	Average Choice

Conformation is the manner of formation of the animal with particular reference to the relative development of the muscular and skeletal systems, although it is influenced, to some extent, by the quantity and distribution of external finish. Conformation is evaluated by averaging the conformation for the entire

Table 13.2   Estimated Percentage Kidney and Pelvic Fat from Estimated 12th Rib Fat Thickness.

Estimated 12th Rib Fat Thickness (method 1)	% Kidney and Pelvic Fat
.05 .10 } .15	1.0–2.5%
.20 .25 } .30	2.5–3.5%
.35 .40 } .45	3.5–5.0%
.50 .55 } .60	5.0–6.5%
≥ .65	≥ 7.0

lamb, giving consideration not only to the proportion that each part comprises of the total weight, but also to the desirability of each part compared to other parts. Best conformation implies a high proportion of edible meat to bone and a high proportion of the weight in the demanded cuts. It is reflected in lambs that are wide and thick in relation to their length and that have a plump, full, well-rounded appearance. Inferior conformation implies a low proportion of the weight in the demanded cuts and is reflected in lambs that are narrow in relation to their length and that have an angular, thin sunken appearance. External fat in excess of that normally left on retail cuts is not considered in evaluating conformation.

Leg Conformation

Definition: The degree of muscling in the leg expressed in terms of one-thirds of a conformation grade.

Extreme Range:	High Prime–low Utility
Normal Range:	High Prime–low Good
Average:	Average Choice

Leg conformation will seldom differ by more than one-third grade from the final quality grade. Thus, one can readily estimate leg conformation from estimated quality grade.

Leg conformation is one of the factors used to calculate yield grade. Since lamb carcasses are not ribbed in commercial practice, leg conformation is used as the assessment of muscling rather than ribeye area. Legs that are thick through the widest part when viewed from the rear, and plump and bulging when viewed from the side are assigned high conformation grades (toward Prime), whereas those that are narrow and tapering are assigned low conformation grades (toward Utility). Leg conformation is only a fair assessment of total carcass muscling, but it is used in yield grade calculation because it is easily obtainable even on live lambs.

Since leg conformation is a measure of muscling, yield grade increases in numerical value (toward 5.0) as leg conformation decreases (toward Utility), but the percentage of boneless, closely trimmed retail cuts decreases. Conversely, as leg conformation increases (toward Prime) yield grade decreases in numerical value (toward 1.0), but the percentage of boneless, closely trimmed retail cuts increases.

Maturity

Definition: Maturity is an estimation of the chronological age of the live lamb and is determined by assessing the physiological age of bone and muscle characteristics in the carcass. Carcasses must have a break joint present on at least one of the two front cannon bones (metacarpals) to be identified as lamb. The color, moistness, and porosity of the break joint—as well as shape of the ribs and color of the inside flank muscles—are used to assess maturity in lamb carcasses.

> Extreme Range: A–B
> Normal Range: A–B

At the same chronological age, ewe lambs will be physiologically (bone and muscle characteristics) more mature than wether lambs, and ram lambs will be physiologically less mature than wethers. Large framed, growthy lambs will be less mature at any given chronological age than small framed or small, short-bodied lambs.

Live Lamb Grading

Lamb grading involves two separate and distinct procedures. The grading procedures include determination of the quality grade (U.S. Prime, U.S. Choice, U.S. Good and U.S. Utility) and yield grade (1, 2, 3, 4 and 5). Each of these grading systems will be discussed in more detail in Section 14.

Quality Grade

Carcass quality grade is based upon a composite evaluation of conformation, maturity, and quality of the lean flesh. Quality of the lean flesh is evaluated by the quantity of fat streakings on the inside flank muscles, firmness of the lean flesh, and external fat, and U.S. Prime and U.S. Choice carcasses have a minimum degree of external fatness requirement. The requirement of a minimum external fat thickness is necessary to ensure maintenance of carcass quality during normal refrigerated storage. Carcasses with a very thin or no fat covering have excessive shrink, discolor, and dehydrate during even normal length storage periods. Fat thickness in excess of that normally left on retail cuts (about ¼ inch) is objectionable. Since degree of flank fat streakings and firmness of the lean flesh and external fat cannot be determined on live lambs, estimation of quality grade on live lambs is essentially based upon an evaluation of conformation and finish (degree of fatness). Amount of finish is related to degree of marbling, which, in turn, is related to degree of flank fat streakings, although these interrelationships are low. However, for lack of better criteria, degrees of flank fat streakings are used to predict quantity of marbling, which, in turn, is predicted in the live lamb from the estimate of fatness. The estimate of fatness is also directly related to the other two quality factors (i.e., degree of firmness of the lean flesh and external fat, and the quantity of fat on the external surfaces of the carcass).

Actual maturity is seldom known under normal marketing conditions, but lambs, yearling, and older sheep (mutton) are identified by mouthing and determining age by the teeth. Conformation of live lambs is an evaluation of relative distribution of muscling especially in the high priced leg and loin regions. Heavy muscled legs are deep, thick and plump. A heavy muscled loin is wide, deep, and full. Muscling in the loin should carry forward into the rack and shoulder regions. A high proportion of muscle to fat and/or bone is desirable and contributes to a high conformation grade.

Since amount of finish is related to quantity of flank fat streakings and/or marbling and a high degree of these qualitative factors is desired, it might be concluded that high grading lambs have to be very fat. Fortunately this is not the case to ensure Choice or Prime grading lambs. The amount of fat and degree of conformation are combined in assessing live lamb grades. Grade is estimated to the nearest ⅓ (i.e., U.S. Prime⁺, U.S. Prime⁰, U.S. Prime⁻, U.S. Choice⁺, etc). Photographs of the quality grades of lamb are presented in Figure 13.4.

Figure 13.4. Photographs of the four quality grades of lambs.

Prime

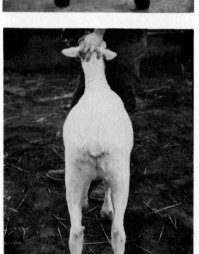
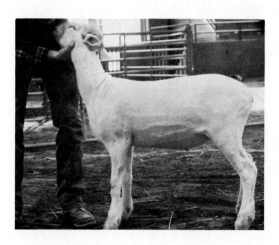

Choice

Good

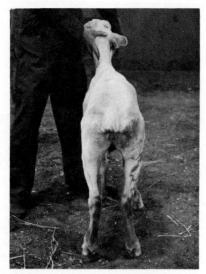
Utility

Yield Grade

Yield grade identifies lambs for differences in yield of boneless, closely trimmed, retail cuts from the leg, loin, rack, and shoulder. Yield grade is frequently used synonymously with cutability. The yield of boneless, closely trimmed, retail cuts (cutability) is usually expressed as a percentage of carcass weight (i.e., 45, 46, 47%, etc.). However, the percentage figure is converted to a yield grade number between .1 and 5.9. A yield grade of 1.0 is equivalent to 49.0%, whereas a 5.9 yield grade is equivalent to 40.2% boneless, closely trimmed retail cuts from the leg, loin, rack, and shoulder.

The factors evaluated to determine yield grade are: (1) fat thickness (method 1) at the 12th rib which is adjusted up or down depending upon the distribution of fat over all external surfaces of the lamb; (2) percentage KP; and (3) leg conformation grade. In order to establish a base to estimate yield grade on lambs, a preliminary yield grade of 4.0 is used as the base. This yield grade is equivalent to a lamb with .3 in. of fat (12th rib, method 1), a leg conformation grade of average Choice, and a % KP of 3.5. The final yield grade is determined by adjusting the preliminary yield grade as follows:

1. Each .05 in. of adjusted fat thickness (12th rib) is equivalent to .33 yield grade (each .01 in. = .066 yield grade). Thus, for each .05 in. fat over the base of .30 in., add .33 yield grade; and for each .05 less than .30 in., subtract .33 yield grade.
2. Each 1.0% KP is equivalent to .25 yield grade. Thus, for each 1.0% KP above the base of 3.5%, add .25 yield grade; and for each 1.0% below 3.5%, subtract .25 yield grade.
3. Each ⅓ leg conformation grade is equivalent to .05 yield grade. Thus, for each ⅓ leg conformation grade above the base of average Choice, subtract .05 yield grade; and for each ⅓ leg conformation grade below average Choice, add .05 yield grade.

From the previous discussion it is obvious that the major factor affecting yield grade is 12th rib fat thickness, since each .05 in. of fat thickness raises or lowers yield grade by .33. Leg conformation grade has little affect, because 1 full grade difference (low Choice vs. low Prime) only affects final yield grade by .15. KP percentage and is intermediate in its affect on yield grade. Because % KP is difficult to estimate on live lambs, it is determined from the 12th rib fat thickness estimate from Table 13.2 as described previously.

The following two examples illustrate the procedures used to estimate yield grade on live lambs.

	Lamb A	Lamb B
Fat thickness (12th rib), in.	.15	.40 (method 1)
Leg conformation grade	Av. Choice	Av. Prime

Lamb A has .15 in. less fat than the base of .3 in. (.3–.15 estimated fat thickness = .15 in. difference). Since each .05 in. is equivalent to .33 yield grade and the difference is 3, .05's in., the adjustment of base yield grade (4.0) for fat thickness is .99 or when rounded 1.0 yield grade (.33 × 3 = .99 yield grade). Since Lamb A is less fat than the base, the yield grade adjustment for 12th rib fat thickness is subtracted from the base yield of 4.0 (4.0 − 1.0 = 3.0) to obtain a PYG of 3.0 after adjusting the base for the difference in fat. Since lamb A has a leg conformation grade of average Choice and that is the base for leg conformation grade, no adjustment of yield grade is necessary for leg conformation grade in this lamb. Lamb A was estimated to have .15 in. of 12th rib fat thickness; and since % KP cannot be directly estimated, the interrelationship shown in Table 13.2 is used. Thus, lamb A is expected to have about 2.0% KP (from Table 13.2 when estimated to have .15 in. of 12th rib fat). Lamb A then has 1.5% less KP fat than the base of 3.5% [3.5 (base) − 2.0% (estimated) = 1.5% (difference)]. Each 1.0% KP is equivalent to .25 yield grade; therefore, 1.5% (difference) × .25 (for each 1.0% yield grade) = .375 (adjustment) or when rounded .38 yield grade is the adjustment. Since the % KP of lamb A was estimated to be below the base

Figure 13.5. Illustrations showing lambs representative of each of the five yield grades.

Yield Grade 1

Yield Grade 2

Yield Grade 3

Yield Grade 4

Yield Grade 5

of 3.5%, the .38 yield grade adjustment is subtracted from the yield grade previously adjusted for 12th rib fat thickness and which did not need to be adjusted for leg conformation grade. Thus, $3.0 - .38 = 2.62$, or when rounded, 2.6 is the yield grade of lamb A.

Lamb B has .1 in. more fat than the base; therefore, 2, .05's $\times$ .33 = .66 is the adjustment or $4.0 + .66 = 4.66$ yield grade after adjusting for fat thickness. Leg conformation grade of lamb B is 1 full grade above base, therefore 3, ⅓'s $\times$ .05 = .15 adjustment or $4.66 - .15 = 4.51$ after adjusting for both fat thickness and leg conformation grade. Next find the % KP for a lamb with .4 in. of 12th rib fat in Table 13.2. The percentage is 4.5% which is 1.0% above the base of 3.5%. Therefore, 1.0% $\times$ .25 = .25 yield grade is the adjustment or $4.51 + .25 = 4.76$ and when rounded, the yield grade for lamb B is 4.7 after adjusting for all 3 yield grade factors.

During the calculation of yield grade, you may carry 2 digits to the right of the decimal, but always round down to the .1 yield grade for the FYG.

Photographs representative of each of the yield grades of lambs are presented in Figure 13.5.

Calculation of Live Price of Lambs

In order to price live lambs, the student must estimate dressing percentage, carcass quality grade and calculate yield grade. The quality grade is estimated in order to select the correct carcass price/cwt. To illustrate the live lamb pricing procedure, the following carcass prices/cwt were chosen for the examples shown below.

Quality Grade	Carcass Price/cwt
U.S. Prime	$135
U.S. Choice	$133
U.S. Good	$125
U.S. Utility	$100

The base yield grade of 4.0 was arbitrarily chosen in these examples for calculating live price/cwt, but any other yield grade base could be used. For every .1 yield grade deviation from 4.0 (above or below), add or subtract $.25/cwt to or from the carcass price.

To illustrate how live price/cwt is determined, let us again refer to the yield grade estimates of lambs A and B. In order to complete the calculation of live price, the following estimates that were recorded during the evaluation are provided for this purpose.

	Lamb A	Lamb B
Dressing %	50.0	52.0
Quality grade	Av. Choice	Low Prime

Lamb A had a final yield grade of 2.6 which is 1.4 yield grade below the base of 4.0. Since each .1 yield grade is equivalent to $.25/cwt, lamb A is worth $3.50 ($.25 $\times$ 14, .1's yield grade = $3.50) more than the base carcass price of $133.00/cwt for Choice lambs or $136.50/cwt of carcass. Since lamb A was estimated to have a dressing percentage of 50, the live price/cwt of this lamb would be $68.25 ($136.50 $\times$ 50%) or $68.30/cwt when rounded to the nearest $.10.

Lamb B had a final yield grade of 4.7 which is .7 yield grade above the base of 4.0. Since each .1 yield grade is equivalent to $.25/cwt, lamb B is worth $1.75 ($.25 $\times$ 7, .1's yield grade = $1.75) less than the base carcass price of $135.00 for Prime lambs or $133.25/cwt of carcass. Lamb B was estimated to have a dressing percentage of 52; thus, the live price/cwt of this lamb would be $69.29 ($133.25 $\times$ 52%) or $69.30/cwt when rounded.

Since carcass price varies with daily market fluctuations, the prices need to be checked each day before beginning the pricing procedures. Likewise, the base yield grade used for pricing lambs may vary and should be checked each time lambs are priced.

Estimating Carcass Traits of Live Market Lambs

The major carcass traits evaluated in market lambs are fat thickness at the 12th rib (BF), ribeye area (REA), yield grade (YG), and quality grade (QG). Making an accurate estimate of BF is extremely important, since BF is the primary factor used in estimating kidney and pelvic fat (%KP), dressing percentage, YG, and QG. The relationship of weight to frame and thickness is useful in estimating BF and REA on market lambs. Lightweight lambs are generally leaner but lighter muscled than heavyweight lambs; therefore, the evaluator should narrow the normal ranges for these traits according to the weight of the lamb. For example, a large framed, black-faced lamb, weighing less than 110 lb. will rarely have over a 2.5 in.^{2} REA or .20 in. of BF. Likewise, the same type of lamb, weighing over 130 lb. will rarely have less than 2.2 in.^{2} of REA or .15 in. of BF. There are also significant breed differences to account for when evaluating market lambs. At the same weight, ewe breeds (most of the white-faced breeds) will generally be fatter and lighter muscled than the ram breeds (black-faced breeds).

Table 13.3	Fat and Muscle—Quality Grade Interrelationship.	
Fat and Muscle	**Quality Grade**	
.05 – .15 – Light Muscle	Choice⁻	– Choice⁰
.05 – .15 – Heavy Muscle	Choice⁰	– Choice⁺
.15 – .30 – Light Muscle	Choice⁰	– Choice⁺
.15 – .30 – Heavy Muscle	Choice⁺	– Prime⁻
.30 – .45 – Light Muscle	Choice⁺	– Prime⁻
.30 – .45 – Heavy Muscle	Prime⁻	– Prime⁺

Quality grading market lambs is similar to quality grading cattle with two major exceptions. First, since nearly all market weight lambs will grade at least low Choice, the range of grades is much narrower for lambs. Secondly, conformation, or muscle, plays a role in quality grading lambs. The guidelines in Table 13.3 should help to establish some relationships of fat and muscling to quality grade.

In market lambs, as in market steers, there is considerable individual variation in quality grade due to influence of factors other than fat thickness. Therefore, these guidelines should be used as a general guide and should not be taken as set standards.

Lamb C (Figure 13.6, upper two photographs) is a 120 lb. ewe lamb and appears very muscular with an average amount of fat. She stands wide, has a very thick, plump leg, and a thick muscular top. From the side, C has a long, bulging stifle. While C is trim at the twist and dock, fat can be detected in her breast and flank. She is also starting to square out over her top, especially over the forerib. She will have about .25 in. of BF and approximately 3.0% KP. She should have about 2.6 in.^{2} of REA and an average Prime leg conformation grade. These estimates would give lamb C a yield grade of 3.4 and a quality grade estimate of low Prime.

Lamb D (Figure 13.6, middle two photographs) is a 110 lb. wether lamb and appears to be very lean with average muscling. Lamb D is very trim through the breast, flank and twist, and also appears lean over the rib and loin edge. While D stands wide behind and has a muscular shape to his top, he does not have as much bulge and thickness as C. D will have about .15 in. of BF and 2.0% KP. He will have about 2.3 in.^{2} of REA and a high Choice leg conformation grade. These estimates will give lamb D a yield grade of 2.6 and a quality grade of average Choice.

Lamb E (Figure 13.6, lower two photographs) is also a 110 lb. wether that appears to be fat and light muscled. From the side, E appears to have about the same amount of fat as C. However, when viewed from behind, it is easy to see that E is much fatter than C. Lamb E is deep and wasty in his twist and very square over his top. He is very fat over the rib and loin edge, and shows virtually no turn to his top. E is also flat and narrow in his leg and short and tapered in his stifle. E will have about .35 in. of BF and 4.0% KP. He will have about 2.0 in.^{2} REA and an average Choice leg conformation grade. These estimates will give lamb E a yield grade of 4.4 and a quality grade of low Prime.

Figure 13.6. Photographs showing rear and side view of three market lambs illustrating differences in muscle, fat, frame, and thickness. These photographs are intended to aid the student in his/her initial attempt at estimation of carcass characteristics in live lambs.

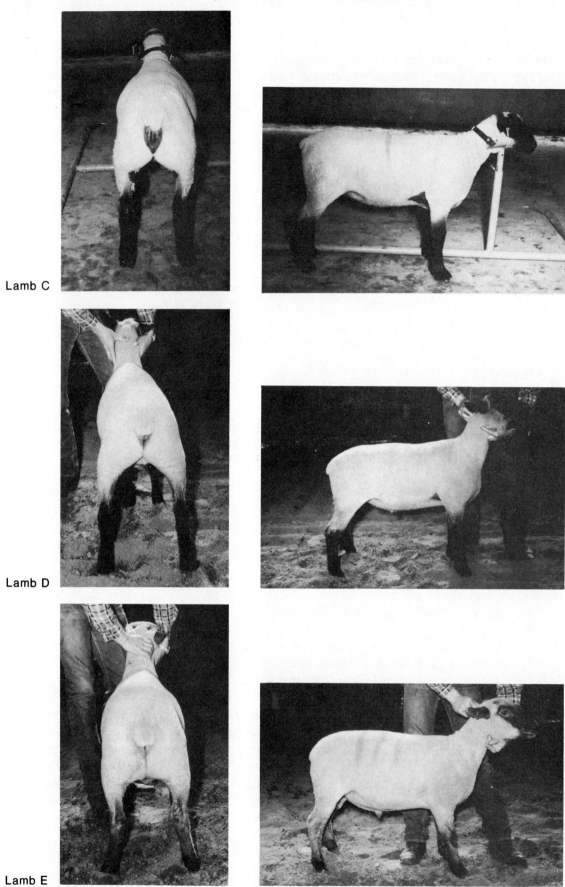

Lamb C

Lamb D

Lamb E

Lamb Carcass Evaluation, Grading, and Pricing

SECTION

14

Lamb Carcass Evaluation

Before beginning the evaluation, the carcasses must be identified as to their sex condition or class and their maturity group or kind. The classes or sex groups of sheep are ewe (female), wether (castrate male), and ram (male). The classes are then further subdivided by kind or maturity groups into lambs, yearling mutton, and mutton. Each of the kinds or maturity groups contains ewes, wethers, and rams; however, normally wethers are marketed before they reach the mutton stage. Thus, the bulk of mutton carcasses are from old ewes and rams. It is necessary to identify kind and class of sheep carcasses prior to grading so that one can apply the correct set of standards and grades because they differ slightly among classes and especially among the different kinds. The various kinds, classes, and appropriate grades of each are presented in Table 14.1. Slaughter and feeder sheep are included in Table 14.1, but only slaughter sheep will be discussed in this section.

The subsequent discussion will describe the procedure for identifying classes and kinds of sheep.

Table 14.1   Market Kinds, Classes and Grades of Sheep.

Kind	Class	Grade Quality	Yield
SLAUGHTER SHEEP			
Lambs	Ewe	PRIME, CHOICE, GOOD, UTILITY	1, 2, 3, 4, 5
	Wether	PRIME, CHOICE, GOOD, UTILITY	1, 2, 3, 4, 5
	Ram	PRIME, CHOICE, GOOD, UTILITY	1, 2, 3, 4, 5
Yearling Mutton[1]	Ewe	PRIME, CHOICE, GOOD, UTILITY	1, 2, 3, 4, 5
	Wether	PRIME, CHOICE, GOOD, UTILITY	1, 2, 3, 4, 5
	Ram	PRIME, CHOICE, GOOD, UTILITY	1, 2, 3, 4, 5
Mutton[2]	Ewe	CHOICE, GOOD, UTILITY, CULL	1, 2, 3, 4, 5
	Wether	CHOICE, GOOD, UTILITY, CULL	1, 2, 3, 4, 5
	Ram	CHOICE, GOOD, UTILITY, CULL	
FEEDER SHEEP			
Lambs	Ewe	PRIME, CHOICE, GOOD, UTILITY, CULL	
	Wether	PRIME, CHOICE, GOOD, UTILITY, CULL	
	Ram	PRIME, CHOICE, GOOD, UTILITY, CULL	
Yearlings	Ewe	PRIME, CHOICE, GOOD, UTILITY, CULL	
	Wether	PRIME, CHOICE, GOOD, UTILITY, CULL	
	Ram	PRIME, CHOICE, GOOD, UTILITY, CULL	

1. Lamb, Yearling Mutton and Mutton are graded without regard for ewe, wether or ram characteristics. However, carcasses from males that have thick heavy necks and shoulders typical of rams are discounted in grade in accord with the extent to which these characteristics are developed. Such discounts may vary from less than one-half grade in carcasses from young lambs in which such characteristics are barely noticeable to as much as two full grades in carcasses from mature rams in which such characteristics are very pronounced.
2. Mutton carcasses not eligible for the Prime grade.

Figure 14.1. A. In the left illustration the metacarpal on the left shows the break joint while that on the right shows the spool joint. The break joint is the cartilaginous area of the epiphyseal-diaphysis junction while the spool joint is the epiphysis of the metacarpal. **B.** The illustration on the right shows break joints (arrows) on a lamb carcass.

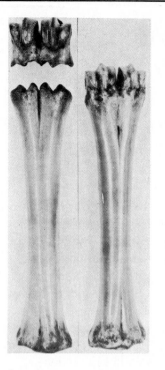

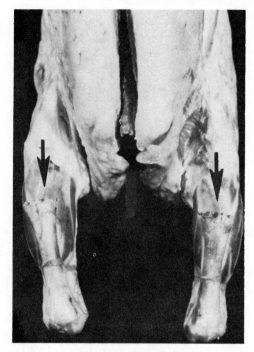

A   B

Determination of Kind

The kinds or maturity groups are identified as follows:

1. Lamb carcasses are approximately 2 to 14 months of age. They have the characteristic "break joint" on at least one of their front shanks. The other fore shank may have an imperfect break joint, a spool joint, or the entire fore shank may be missing, having been removed during slaughter. In addition to the above break joint requirements, the color, moistness, and porosity of the break joint(s) also are evaluated to determine maturity of the carcass. The color of the flank muscles on the inside of the carcass varies from slightly dark pink to slightly dark red. The ribs vary from quite round in shape to moderately flat, and they usually have some redness on their exposed surfaces.
2. Yearling mutton carcasses are approximately 12 to 25 months of age, and they either have "spool joints" on both front shanks, or one spool joint and one imperfect break joint, or imperfect break joints on both front shanks. The color of the flank muscles on the inside of the carcass varies from slightly dark red to moderately dark red. The ribs are moderately wide and tend to be flat, and they range from slight redness to no redness on their exposed surfaces.
3. Mutton carcasses are older than 24 months of age, and they always have spool joints. The color of the flank muscles on the inside of the carcass varies from dark red to very dark red. The ribs are wide, flat, and the color of mature bone.

The break joint is the epiphyseal cartilaginous area of the cannon bone (metacarpal) and because this epiphyseal area is not ossified in young sheep, it breaks at this location when pressure is applied (hence, the name—break joint). In older sheep the epiphyseal area ossifies and fuses to the diaphysis of the metacarpal and cannot be broken (Figure 14.1A). The spool is actually the distal epiphysis of the metacarpal as can be seen in Figure 14.1A. A break joint can also be obtained on the metatarsal (hind shank cannon bone) in lambs. In fact, a break joint can be obtained on both the proximal as well as distal end of the metacarpal and metatarsals and also on the ulna and tibia of lambs. Perfect break joints are shown on the distal metacarpals in Figure 14.1B.

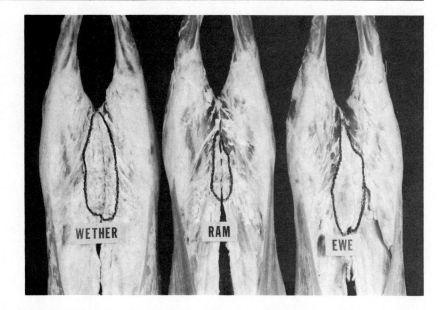

Figure 14.2. Illustrations from left to right showing the cod (wether), scrotal (ram), and udder (ewe), respectively, outlined by a dark line.

WETHER   RAM   EWE

The perfect break joint has all the ridges of the joint intact and is well defined as shown in Figure 14.1A on the left. In an imperfect break joint, a portion of the ridges may be missing or damaged because of an imperfect break. The Federal Meat Grader considers an imperfect break joint the same as a spool joint, and they also assume that if the fore shank(s) is (are) removed during slaughter that they were spool joints no matter what the age.

While the shape of the ribs is one of the criteria used by the Federal Meat Grader to assess stage of maturity, the color of ribs is not, although the color of the ribs still provides the student with a good indicator of maturity. The exposed surfaces of the ribs are red in young sheep (lambs) because the marrow in them is involved in the manufacture of red blood cells. As the sheep grows older, the marrow loses the capacity to make red blood cells and the marrow becomes yellow and, therefore, the ribs become more bone-like in color.

Determination of Class

The classes of sheep can be identified as follows:

1. Ewes are identified by the presence of the udder. In mutton carcasses, the udder may be wet (yellowish brown exudate), but if it is very wet, it will be removed at the time of slaughter. In lambs and yearlings, the udder is present and it is a relatively long, smooth fat deposit (Figure 14.2).
2. Wether carcasses are identified by the presence of cod fat. In contrast to the udder, cod fat is rough, and irregular and usually is a much smaller deposit of fat than the udder (Figure 14.2).
3. Ram carcasses will have much less fat in the scrotal area than either wethers or ewes. The fat that is present is irregularly shaped, much like a wether. Ram carcasses usually have wide, heavy shoulders and thick necks, and these areas of the carcass are usually more prominent in wethers than in ewe lambs (Figure 14.3).

The evaluation of slaughter sheep usually is confined to lambs. Thus, the subsequent discussion will be restricted to lamb carcasses.

Weight

Hot carcass weight is almost always obtained on lamb carcasses just prior to chilling, and chilled carcass weight is usually calculated from hot carcass weight in commercial practice because chilled weight is not obtained until the lamb carcasses are shipped from the slaughtering plant. In practice, hot carcass

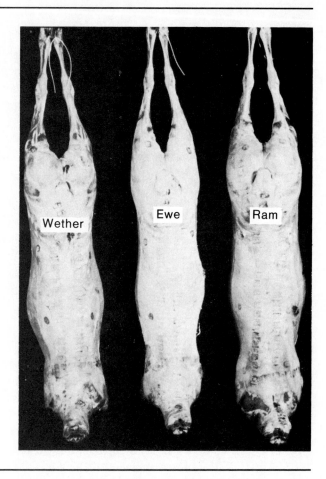

Figure 14.3. Illustrations from left to right showing the body contour of a wether, ewe and ram lamb carcass, respectively.

weight is shrunk 2¾% (hot carcass wt. × .9725 = chilled carcass wt.) to obtain chilled carcass weight. When chilled carcass weight is obtained and hot carcass weight is not, the latter can be calculated from chilled weight by multiplying chilled carcass wt. by 102.75%.

Dressing Percentage

Chilled carcass weight is divided by live weight and multiplied by 100 to obtain dressing percentage.

Ribbing Lamb Carcasses

Lamb carcasses are seldom ribbed (cut between the 12th and 13th rib to expose the ribeye muscle and fat thickness) in commercial practice. The grade standards for both quality and yield grades of lamb and mutton are designed for use on unribbed carcasses. However, to facilitate the maximum learning experience in meat evaluation courses, lamb carcasses are usually ribbed to expose the ribeye muscle and actual fat thickness. Because the carcass does not need to be ribbed to quality grade lambs, they should be quality graded prior to ribbing which is consistent with commercial practice. Following the quality grading, the carcasses should be ribbed and then yield graded. Ribeye area, although not used in yield grading, is usually determined on the ribbed carcass and is an important characteristic in lamb carcass evaluation.

To rib lamb carcasses, count from the first rib to locate the 12th rib. It is not recommended to count from the last rib because some lambs have 14 ribs and others 13. After the 12th rib is located, make a small knife cut through the intercostal muscles immediately cranial to the 13th rib adjacent to the backbone on both the right and left side of the backbone. The knife cut is made from the inside of the carcass to the outer surface of the subcutaneous fat. Then the carcass is turned so the dorsal surface (back) is facing the individual doing the ribbing. Insert the knife (either right or left side) into the cut made previously from the inside with the cutting edge of the blade away from the backbone and follow the caudal surface of the

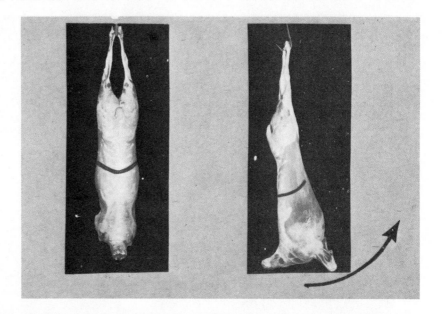

Figure 14.4. Illustration showing the ribbing procedure on lamb carcasses.

12th rib cutting the intercostal muscles, but leave approximately 2–3 in. of the flank muscles attached to the hindsaddle. This procedure is then repeated on the opposite side. If the original knife cut was made close to the 13th rib, the knife can be drawn through the cartilaginous disc between the 12th and 13th rib to separate fore- and hindsaddle. If the knife cannot be drawn through the cartilage disc, the backbone can be "broken" at the cartilaginous disc by bending the foresaddle upward as indicated by the arrow in Figure 14.4. If the backbone doesn't break after 1 or 2 attempts of this bending procedure, a saw should be used to saw through the backbone.

Ribeye Area

Ribeye area is not used in determining either the quality or yield grade because lambs are usually not ribbed commercially. However, because the ribeye muscle is the largest muscle in the carcass and the major muscle in the rack (rib) and loin (two of the most valuable wholesale cuts in the carcass), it is estimated on live lambs and usually measured during lamb carcass evaluation. The area of both the right and left eye muscle is estimated or measured because they sometimes differ in area (Figure 14.5). Ribeye area of the right and left side usually does not differ by more than .1 or .2 in.^{2}. The right and left areas are averaged to obtain ribeye area for each carcass (example: 2.3 on left, 2.5 on right = 2.4 in.^{2} of ribeye area as shown in Figure 14.5).

Area may be measured directly on the carcass with a grid or from a tracing of the right and left eye muscle by a compensating planimeter. The procedure for determining ribeye area on lamb carcasses by the grid method is identical to the one described for pork carcasses in section 6 because the same grid (20 dots/in.^{2}) is used, except the area of the right and left ribeye is obtained for lambs and then averaged.

Lamb Carcass Grading

Lamb carcasses may be either quality graded, yield graded, or both. Quality grade is an estimation of palatability-indicating characteristics (i.e., tenderness, juiciness and flavor), while yield grade is an estimation of boneless, closely trimmed, retail cuts from the leg, loin, rack, and shoulder. The subsequent discussion will provide a description of the mechanics involved in each of the two grading systems.

Quality Grade

Lamb carcass quality grade is based upon a composite evaluation of conformation, maturity, and quality of the lean flesh. Quality of the lean flesh is evaluated by the quantity of fat streakings on the inside flank muscles, firmness of the lean flesh, and external fat. U.S. Prime and U.S. Choice carcasses also have

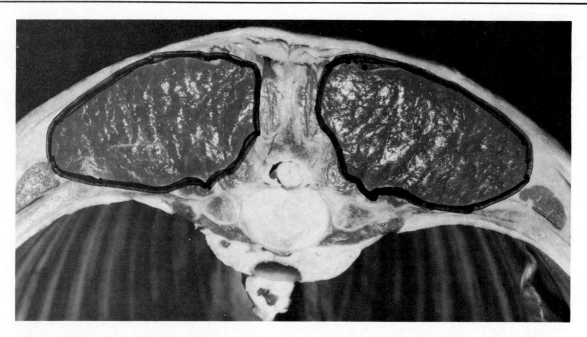

Figure 14.5. An illustration showing ribeye area on the left and right side of a lamb carcass. The perimeter of the eye muscle is outlined with a dark line.

a minimum requirement for degree of external fatness. The quality grades of lamb carcasses are: U.S.D.A. Prime, Choice, Good, and Utility as shown in Table 14.1. Very few lambs grade U.S. Utility and most lamb carcasses grade either U.S.D.A. Prime or Choice.

Conformation is an assessment of overall muscling in the lamb carcass with emphasis on the greatest development of muscling in the highest priced primal cuts which range in order of value from the leg, loin, rack (rib), and shoulder. Conformation is the manner of formation of the carcass with particular reference to the relative development of the muscular and skeletal systems, although it is also influenced, to some extent, by the quantity and distribution of external finish. However, external fat in excess of that normally left on retail cuts (approximately ¼ inch) is not considered in evaluating conformation. The conformation descriptions refer to the thickness of muscling and to an overall degree of thickness and fullness of the carcass. The conformation of a carcass is evaluated by averaging the conformation of the component parts, giving consideration not only to the proportion that each primal cut is of the carcass weight, but also to the general desirability of each primal cut as compared with other primal cuts. Superior conformation implies a high proportion of edible meat to bone and a high proportion of the weight of the carcass in the more demanded primal cuts. It is reflected in carcasses which are very thickly muscled, very wide and thick in relation to their length, and which have a very plump, full, and well-rounded appearance. Inferior conformation implies a low proportion of edible meat to bone and a low proportion of the weight of the carcass in the more demanded primal cuts. It is reflected in carcasses which are very thinly muscled, very narrow in relation to their length, and which have a very angular, thin, and sunken appearance. The minimum conformation required for the U.S.D.A. Prime, Choice, and Good quality grades is presented in Table 14.5. Carcass conformation is identified by the quality grade designations themselves as: U.S. Prime, Choice, etc. and are usually further subdivided into Prime⁺, Prime⁰, Prime⁻, Choice⁺, etc. The leg is the most easily and accurately evaluated wholesale cut for determination of carcass conformation, since it is usually covered by less fat than the other wholesale cuts. Hence, more emphasis is placed upon the leg in assessing carcass conformation than any other area of the carcass. In addition to the leg, conformation is evaluated in the loin, rack, and shoulder regions. However, since these wholesale cuts are usually covered with fat, the task of assessing muscling is more difficult than for the leg. In evaluating conformation grade of the loin, rack, and shoulder regions of the carcass, muscle development and the amount of fat normally left (¼ inch) on retail cuts from these areas of the carcass should be assessed. An example of conformation representative of the midpoint of the U.S. Prime, Choice, Good, and Utility grades is shown in Figure 14.6.

Figure 14.6. Illustrations showing lamb carcass conformation representative of the midpoint of the Prime, Choice, Good and Utility grades.

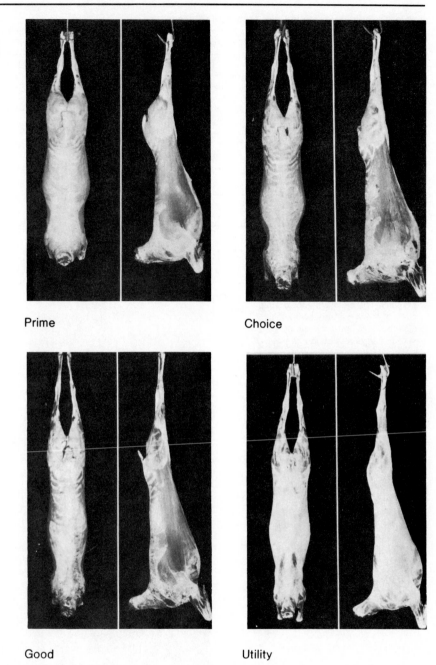

Prime

Choice

Good

Utility

Maturity is an assessment of the physiological age of the animal. Lamb carcasses usually are less than one year of age, and the effects upon palatability characteristics within this 12 month age period are negligible. Lambs are categorized as either A or B maturity by the federal meat grading standards, but both of these maturities (A and B) are young in contrast to yearling carcasses which are from 1 to 2 year old sheep. Nevertheless, B maturity lambs are generally referred to as old lamb carcasses as can be seen in Table 14.2 and Figure 14.11. Maturity is determined by an assessment of bone and muscle characteristics. The bones include the break joint(s) and the shape of ribs, while muscle characteristics include an evaluation of the color of the inside flank muscles. The ridged surface of the break joint(s) is quite red, moist, and porous in A maturity and becomes progressively less red, drier, and harder with advancing maturity in the B group. These bone and muscle characteristics for A and B maturity lamb carcasses are presented in Table 14.2 and are illustrated in Figures 14.7, 14.8, and 14.9. A maturity is subdivided into A^-, A^0, A^+ and the same for B maturity. A^- and B^- maturities are the youngest, and A^+ and B^+ are the oldest of the respective maturities.

Table 14.2   Maturity Indicators in Lamb Carcasses.

| Characteristics | Maturity Group | |
	A (young)	B (old)
Ribs	Moderately narrow, slightly flat	Slightly wide, moderately flat
Break joint(s)	Moderately red, moist and porous	Slightly red, slightly dry and hard
Color of inside flank muscles		
U.S. Prime	Slightly dark pink	Light red
U.S. Choice	Moderately dark pink	Moderately light red
U.S. Good	Dark pink	Slightly dark red

Figure 14.7. An illustration showing a break joint representative of A (left) and B (right) maturity. The red color of A maturity appears dark in contrast to the lighter (whiter) slightly red color B break joint. The moister, more porous surface of the A maturity break joint versus the drier, harder B maturity break joint surface also is apparent.

Figure 14.8. Illustrations showing the shape of the ribs of lambs representative of A (left) and B (right) maturities. The ribs of the A maturity carcass are narrower and rounder than the wider, flatter ribs of the B maturity carcass. The redder (dark appearing) color on the exposed surface of the ribs is also apparent in the A maturity carcass compared to the white appearing rib surfaces of of the B maturity carcass.

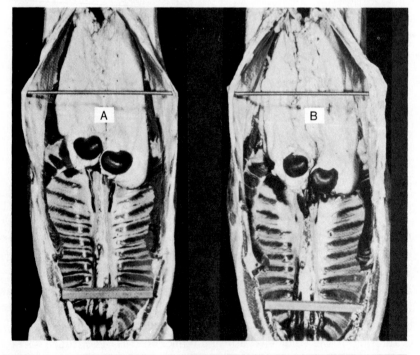

Figure 14.9. Illustrations showing the color of the inside flank muscles of A (left) and B (right) maturities. The pinker color of the A maturity is lighter appearing than the darker color of B maturity.

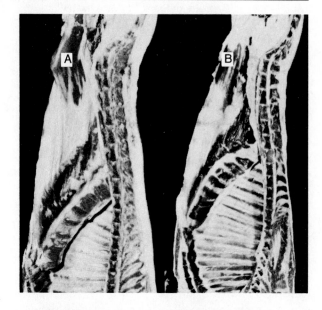

Figure 14.10. Illustrations showing high, intermediate and low degrees of flank fat streakings in the primary (P) and secondary (S) flank.

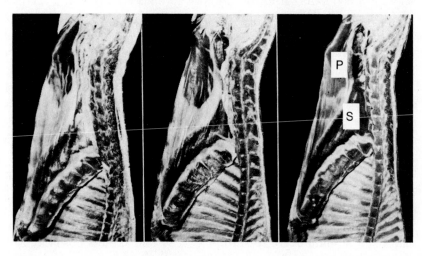

High   Intermediate   Low

Flank Fat Streakings are fat deposits visible on the inside surfaces of the primary and secondary flank muscles (Figure 14.10). Flank fat streakings usually are more extensive in the secondary flank than in the primary flank muscles. Flank fat streakings are used to predict marbling, since lamb carcasses are not ribbed in commercial practice to expose the ribeye muscle marbling. Thus, there are no standards for marbling in lamb carcasses and flank fat streakings are used instead. Within each quality grade, the requirements for flank fat streakings increase progressively with evidence of advancing maturity as shown in Figure 14.11. The degrees of flank fat streakings used by the federal lamb quality standards correspond in terminology and number to the degrees of marbling used in beef carcass quality grading. There are 10 degrees and they are shown from lowest to highest degree in Table 14.3.

Examples of high, intermediate, and low degrees of flank fat streakings are illustrated in Figure 14.10. Except for the devoid degree of flank fat streakings, each of the other degrees is further subdivided into high (+), typical (⁰) and low (−). Thus from highest to lowest each of the degrees greater than devoid is +, ⁰, and −, respectively.

Table 14.3   Degrees of Flank Fat Streakings

Devoid
Practically Devoid
Traces
Slight
Small
Modest
Moderate
Slightly Abundant
Moderately Abundant
Abundant

Firmness of the lean flesh and external fat is an evaluation of the firmness of the lean flesh and the external fat. It is generally assessed in the flank region of the carcass by using the hand to check the firmness. Firmness is highly influenced by carcass fatness; thus, the fattest lambs are the firmest in their lean and fat, and lambs with a very thin covering of fat have the softest lean and fat. Because fatness generally increases from U.S. Good to U.S. Prime grade carcasses, a minimum degree of firmness of the lean flesh and external fat is required to qualify for each of these grades. The degrees of firmness of the lean flesh and external fat from lowest to highest degree and the minimum degree to be eligible for the U.S. Prime, Choice, and Good quality grades are presented in Table 14.4.

The minimum degree specified in Table 14.4 for each quality grade is required to qualify for the respective grade; however, no credit is applied to the carcass no matter how much it may exceed the minimum degree of firmness of the lean flesh and external fat specified.

A Minimum Degree of External Fatness is required on U.S. Prime and Choice carcasses. This requirement is designed to protect the carcasses from excessive shrink, discoloration, and dehydration during normal cooler storage and handling. To be eligible for the U.S. Prime and Choice quality grades, lamb carcasses must have at least a very thin covering of external fat over the top of the shoulders and over the outside of the center portion of the legs. In addition, the back (sirloin, loin and rack) must have at least a thin covering of fat (i.e., the muscles of the back may be no more than plainly visible through the fat). A thin fat covering over the back is approximately equivalent to .1 inch (method 1) at the 12th rib. Carcasses that otherwise qualify for the U.S. Prime and Choice grade, but with less than the minimum degree of external fat specified automatically qualify for the U.S. Good grade. However, most carcasses have more than the minimum degree of external fat so that fatness normally is not a factor in the determination of quality grade of lambs.

Table 14.4   Degrees of Firmness of the Lean Flesh and External Fat and the Minimum Degree Required for Each Quality Grade

Degrees from Lowest to Highest

Very Soft
Moderately Soft
Tends to be Moderately Soft
Slightly Soft   (minimum for U.S. Good)
Tends to be Slightly Soft
Tends to be Slightly Firm   (minimum for U.S Choice)
Slightly Firm
Tends to be Moderately Firm (minimum for U.S. Prime)
Moderately Firm
Tends to be Firm
Firm
Tends to be Extremely Firm
Extremely Firm

Table 14.5 Minimum Conformation Qualifications for Each Quality Grade of Lamb Carcasses.

| Quality Grade | Conformation | | | |
	Overall	Legs	Back[a]	Shoulders
U.S. Prime	tends to be thickly muscled throughout; moderately wide and thick in relation to length	moderately plump and full	moderately wide and thick	moderately thick and full
U.S. Choice	slightly thick muscled throughout; tends to be slightly wide and thick in relation to length	slightly plump and full	slightly wide and thick	slightly thick and full
U.S. Good	slightly thin muscled throughout; moderately narrow in relation to length	slightly thin and tapering	slightly narrow and thin	slightly narrow and thin

[a]The back includes the loin and rack (rib) portion of the carcass.

Final Quality Grade

Final quality grade (FQG) is determined by combining conformation, maturity, and flank fat streakings. In addition, lambs in the U.S. Prime and Choice grades must have at least the minimum external fat required, and carcasses in the U.S. Prime, Choice, and Good grades must have at least the minimum degree of firmness of the lean flesh and external fat to be eligible for the respective quality grade (Table 14.4).

One generally calls the conformation first when quality grading lamb carcasses. The call is made to the nearest $\frac{1}{3}$ grade (i.e., Prime$^+$, Prime^0, Prime$^-$, Choice$^+$, etc.). The minimum conformation and muscling required for the U.S. Prime, Choice, and Good quality grade is presented in Table 14.5. Next the maturity call is made to the nearest $\frac{1}{3}$ degree (i.e., A$^-$, A^0, A$^+$) and the same for B maturity. Then the degree of flank fat streakings is called to the nearest $\frac{1}{3}$ degree. The minimum degree of flank fat streakings required for each quality grade is then determined from Figure 14.11 for each degree of maturity. As can be seen from the diagonal lines in the figure, the minimum degree required increases progressively with advancing maturity even within a maturity group (i.e., from A$^-$ to A^0 to A$^+$) and similarly for B maturity. Finally, the degrees of firmness of the lean flesh and external fat and degree of external fatness are determined.

The preliminary quality grade (PQG) is actually determined by combining the degree of flank fat streakings and carcass maturity as shown in Figure 14.11. If the conformation corresponds to the PQG, and if the carcass has at least the minimum degree of firmness of the lean flesh and external fat, as well as at least the minimum degree of external fatness specified by the U.S. Prime and Choice grade, then the FQG is the same as the PQG. Because the grade factors vary among lamb carcasses, adjustment of the

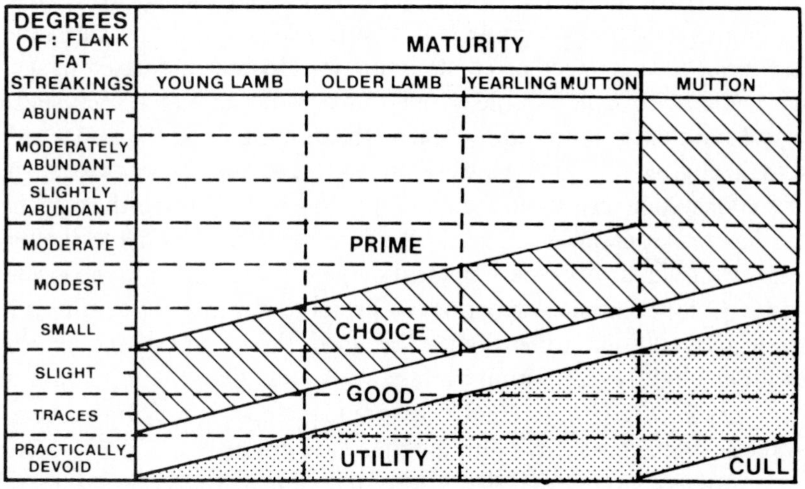

Figure 14.11. A diagram showing the relationship of maturity and flank fat streaking for quality grading lamb carcasses.

PQG obtained from Figure 14.11 is described for each quality grade below. In all instances in carcass evaluation courses and exercises the FQG is designated to ⅓ of a grade (i.e., Prime⁺, Prime⁰, Prime⁻, Choice⁺, etc.).

Adjustments in the Prime Grade. Regardless of the extent to which the conformation of a carcass may exceed the minimum requirements for Prime, a carcass must have minimum Prime quality to be eligible for the Prime grade. However, a development of quality superior to that specified as minimum for the Prime grade may compensate, on an equal basis, for a development of conformation inferior to that specified as minimum for Prime as indicated in the following example: A carcass which has evidence of quality equivalent to the midpoint of the Prime grade (one degree of flank fat streakings more than required as the minimum for Prime) may have conformation equivalent to the mid-point of the Choice grade and remain eligible for Prime. However, in no instance may a carcass be graded Prime which has a development of conformation inferior to that specified as minimum for the Choice grade. In addition, to be eligible for Prime, the lean flesh and external fat of lamb carcasses must not be less than tends to be moderately firm. Lamb carcasses with less than the minimum degree would be graded U.S. Choice, provided they had the minimum firmness of lean flesh and external fat for the U.S. Choice grade. Also, to be eligible for Prime, a carcass must have at least a very thin covering of external fat over the top of the shoulders and the outside of the center parts of the legs, and the back must have at least a thin covering of fat, that is, the muscles of the back may be no more than plainly visible through the fat. Carcasses with less than this amount of external fat would grade U.S. Good.

Adjustments in the Choice Grade. A development of quality which is superior to that specified as a minimum for the Choice grade may compensate, on an equal basis, for a development of conformation which is inferior to that specified as minimum for Choice as indicated in the following example: A carcass which has evidence of quality equivalent to the midpoint of the Choice grade may have conformation equivalent to the midpoint of the Good grade and remain eligible for Choice. However, in no instance may a carcass be graded Choice which has a development of conformation inferior to that specified as minimum for the Good grade. Also, a carcass which has conformation at least one-third grade superior to that specified as minimum for the Choice grade may qualify for Choice with a development of quality equivalent to the lower limit of the upper third of the Good grade. Compensation of superior conformation for inferior quality is limited to one-third grade of deficient quality. In addition, to be eligible for Choice, the lean flesh and external fat of lamb carcasses must not be less than tends to be slightly firm. Lamb carcasses with less than the minimum degree would be graded U.S. Good, provided they had the minimum firmness of lean flesh and external fat for the U.S. Good grade. Also, to be eligible for Choice, a carcass must have at least a very thin covering of external fat over the top of the shoulders and outside of the center parts of the legs, and the back must have at least a thin covering of fat; that is, the muscles of the back may be no more than plainly visible through the fat. Carcasses with less than this amount of external fat would grade U.S. Good.

Adjustments in the Good Grade. A development of quality which is superior to that specified as minimum for the Good grade may compensate, on an equal basis, for development of conformation which is inferior to that specified as minimum for Good as indicated in the following example: A carcass which has evidences of quality at least one-third grade superior to that specified as minimum for the Good grade may have conformation equivalent to the minimum for the upper one-third grade of the Utility grade and remain eligible for Good. However, in no instance may a carcass be graded Good which has a development of conformation inferior to the minimum for the upper one-third of the Utility grade. Also, a carcass which has conformation at least one-third grade superior to that specified as minimum for the Good grade may qualify for Good with a development of quality equivalent to the lower limit of the upper third of the Utility grade. Compensation of superior conformation for inferior quality is limited to one-third grade of deficient quality. In addition, to be eligible for Good, the lean flesh and external fat of lamb carcasses must not be less than slightly soft. Lamb carcasses with less than the minimum degree would be graded U.S. Utility.

The Utility Grade. The Utility grade includes those lamb carcasses whose characteristics are inferior to those specified as minimum for the Good grade.

Carcasses representative of the midpoint of the U.S. Prime, Choice, Good and Utility grades are shown in Figures 14.12, 14.13, 14.14 and 14.15, respectively.

Figure 14.12. An illustration of a lamb carcass representative of the midpoint U.S. Prime quality grade.

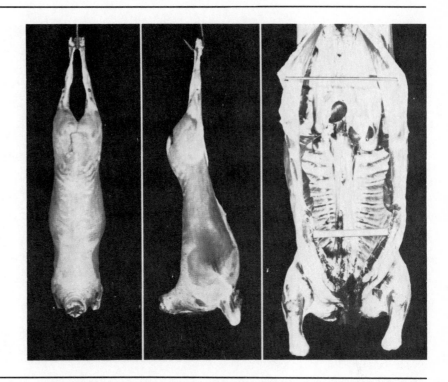

Figure 14.13. An illustration of a lamb carcass representative of the midpoint U.S. Choice quality grade.

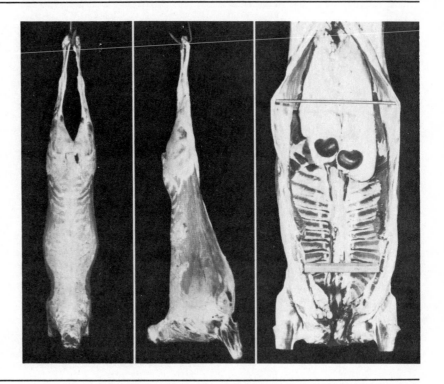

Figure 14.14. An illustration of a lamb carcass representative of the midpoint U.S. Good quality grade.

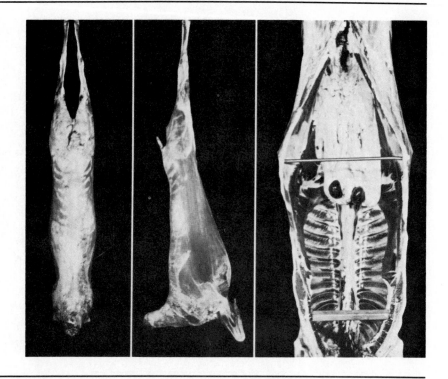

Figure 14.15. An illustration of a lamb carcass representative of the midpoint U.S. Utility quality grade.

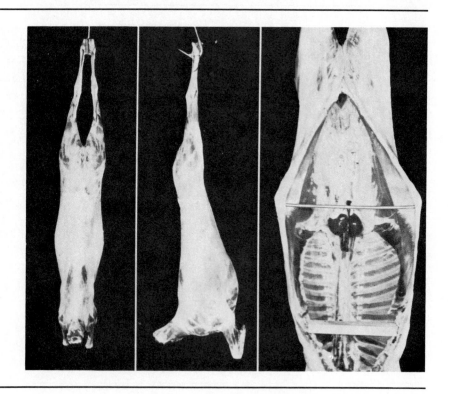

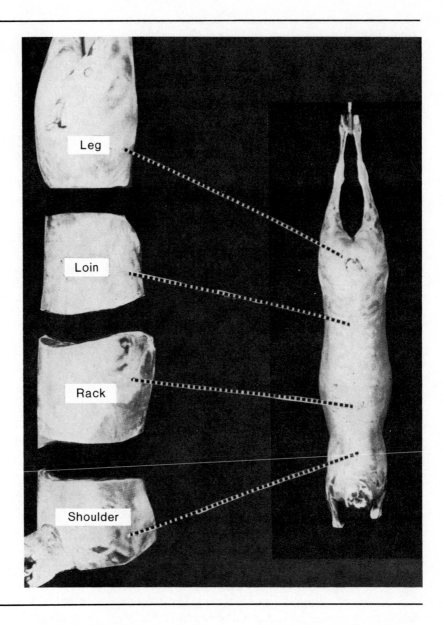

Figure 14.16. An illustration of a lamb carcass and the four major primal cuts, the leg, loin, rack and shoulder of the carcass.

Yield Grade

Yield grade is based upon the yield of boneless, closely trimmed (approximately .3 in.) retail cuts from the leg, loin, rack, and shoulder. These four wholesale cuts (Figure 14.16) represent 80% of the carcass weight and approximately 90% of carcass value. Approximately ⅔ of the carcass value is in the hindsaddle (essentially leg and loin). Because of the high proportion of value in the leg, loin, rack, and shoulder, these wholesale cuts are used to calculate retail cuts rather than the entire carcass. However, the correlation between the retail cuts from the leg, loin, rack and shoulder and those from the entire carcass is very high (generally in excess of .9). This relationship indicates that more than 80% of the variation in total retail cuts of the carcass is accounted for by leg, loin, rack, and shoulder retail cuts. Furthermore, the wholesale breast is much more difficult to cut into retail cuts than the leg, loin, rack, and shoulder because it contains considerable seam fat which is time-consuming and difficult to remove.

Cutting retail cuts from the carcass is the ultimate in determining its value, but this is impossible to obtain on all carcasses in everyday practice. Hence the U.S. Dept. of Agriculture has developed the yield grade procedure after studying yields from a number of lambs of different weights, degrees of fatness, and muscling combinations.

Table 14.6 Conversion Table Used to Convert Yield Grade to Retail Cut Percentage and Vice Versa.

Yield Grade	% Retail Cuts	Yield Grade	% Retail Cuts	Yield Grade	% Retail Cuts	Yield Grade	% Retail Cuts	Yield Grade	% Retail Cuts	Yield Grade	% Retail Cuts
.1	50.9	1.0	49.0	2.0	47.2	3.0	45.4	4.0	43.6	5.0	41.8
.2	50.5	1.1	48.9	2.1	47.1	3.1	45.3	4.1	43.4	5.1	41.7
.3	50.3	1.2	48.7	2.2	46.9	3.2	45.1	4.2	43.3	5.2	41.5
.4	50.1	1.3	48.5	2.3	46.7	3.3	44.9	4.3	43.2	5.3	41.3
.5	50.0	1.4	48.3	2.4	46.5	3.4	44.7	4.4	43.0	5.4	41.1
.6	49.8	1.5	48.2	2.5	46.3	3.5	44.6	4.5	42.8	5.5	41.0
.7	49.6	1.6	48.0	2.6	46.2	3.6	44.4	4.6	42.6	5.6	40.8
.8	49.4	1.7	47.8	2.7	46.0	3.7	44.2	4.7	42.4	5.7	40.6
.9	49.2	1.8	47.6	2.8	45.8	3.8	44.0	4.8	42.2	5.8	40.4
		1.9	47.4	2.9	45.6	3.9	43.8	4.9	42.0	5.9	40.2

Yield grades have been developed for lamb and mutton carcasses, and they are numbered from 1 through 5. Yield grade 1 represents the highest yield of retail cuts, while yield grade 5 designates the lowest yield. The yield grades are applied without regard to quality grade. Yield grades 1 and 5 are open end grades, but based on the cutting and trimming methods used in developing the standards, yield grades 2, 3, and 4 each include a range of 1.8% in expected yields of boneless, closely trimmed, major retail cuts.

The interconversion of yield grade and percentage boneless, closely trimmed retail cuts is presented in Table 14.6.

The yield grade of a lamb or mutton carcass is determined by considering three characteristics: (1) the amount of external fat at the 12th rib (method 1), (2) the amount of kidney and pelvic (KP) fat, and (3) the conformation grade of the legs.

The official standards include the following regression equation for determining the yield grade of lamb or mutton carcasses:

$$\text{Yield grade} = 1.66 - (.05 \times \text{leg conformation grade numerical value})$$
$$+ (.25 \times \text{percentage kidney and pelvic fat})$$
$$+ (6.66 \times \text{adjusted 12th rib fat thickness in hundreds of inches})$$

However, this equation is seldom used in actual practice for determining yield grade. The working formula method is used in commercial practice and the details of this method will be described below.

Adjusted 12th Rib Fat Thickness. The amount of external fat is the most important yield grade factor because it is a good indicator of the amount of fat that is trimmed away in making retail cuts. In carcasses with a normal distribution of external fat, this factor is evaluated in terms of the actual thickness of fat over the center of the right and left ribeye muscle between the 12th and 13th ribs (Figure 14.17, method 1). On unribbed carcasses, as in commercial practice, fat thickness is obtained by probing and then only when disagreements arise, because with practice, fat thickness can be quite accurately estimated. This measurement may be adjusted, as necessary, to reflect unusual amounts of fat on other parts of the carcass. In determining the direction and the amount of this adjustment, particular attention is given to the amount of external fat on the rump, over the top and sides of the shoulder, and over and in the breast, flank, and cod or udder. In a carcass that is relatively fatter than indicated by the actual fat thickness over the ribeye, the measurement is adjusted upward. Conversely, in a carcass that is relatively less fat than indicated by the actual fat thickness over the ribeye (method 1), the measurement is adjusted downward. In many carcasses no adjustment is necessary; however, an adjustment of as much as .1 in. is not uncommon. Adjustments are made in increments of .05 in. of fat thickness. In some carcasses, a greater adjustment may

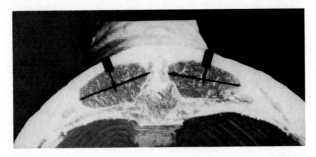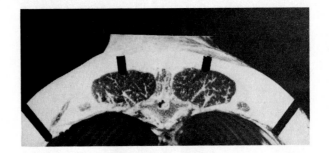

Figure 14.17. Illustrations showing the location of the fat thickness measurement at the 12th rib interface for method 1 (left) and method 2 (right).

be necessary. As a guide in making these adjustments, the standards for each yield grade include an additional related measurement—body wall thickness, which is measured 5 inches laterally from the middle of the backbone between the 12th and 13th ribs. The body wall thickness for each yield grade is as follows:

Yield Grade	Body Wall Thickness
1	.5 inch
2	.7 inch
3	.9 inch
4	1.1 inch
5	>1.1 inch

As the amount of external fat increases, the percentage of retail cuts decreases, and each .05 in. change in adjusted fat thickness over the ribeye changes the yield grade by one-third (.33) grade.

Kidney and Pelvic Fat. The amount of KP fat is evaluated subjectively and expressed as a percentage of carcass weight. A 60 lb. carcass with 3.5% KP fat would have 2.1 lb. of fat in the kidney and pelvic regions or just over 1 lb. on the right and left side. Thus, to arrive at percentage KP fat, estimate the fat in pounds and divide by chilled carcass weight. Heart fat is not considered because it is a negligible quantity of fat in lamb carcasses. Illustrations of two lamb carcasses differing in percentage KP are presented in Figure 14.18.

Figure 14.18. Illustrations of two lambs carcasses showing the kidney (K) and pelvic (P) fat. The carcass on the left has 2.5% KP fat while that on the right has 5.5%.

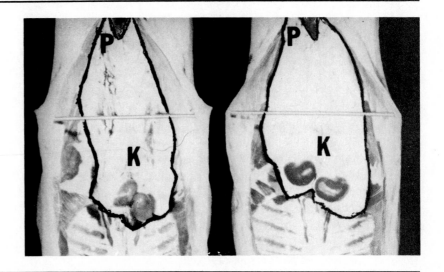

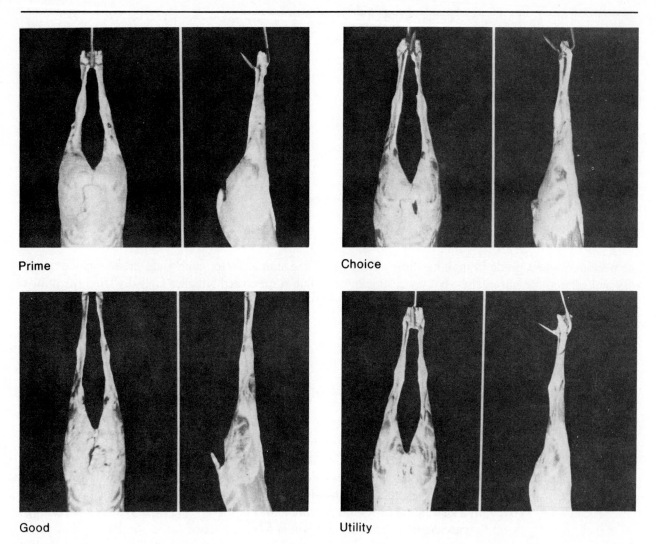

Prime

Choice

Good

Utility

Figure 14.19. Illustrations showing rear and side view of leg conformation grades representative of midpoint Prime, Choice, Good, and Utility.

Leg Conformation is subjectively evaluated in terms of ⅓ quality grades. Illustrations of lambs with midpoint U.S. Prime, Choice, Good, and Utility leg conformation grades are presented in Figure 14.19.

Determining Final Yield Grade

In determining final yield grade (FYG), a base yield grade of 4.0 is used. The base yield grade of 4.0 is equivalent to a lamb with .3 in. of adjusted fat thickness over the right and left eye muscle at the 12th rib, 3.5% KP fat and average Choice (Ch⁰) leg conformation grade. To determine FYG for lambs differing from the base values for 12th rib adjusted fat thickness, % KP fat and leg conformation grade, the following procedure or working formula is used.

Start with the base yield grade of 4.0 and:

1. For each .05 in. of adjusted fat thickness above the base of .3 in., add .33 yield grade; and for each .05 in. of adjusted fat thickness below the base of .3 in., subtract .33 yield grade. If one chooses to estimate fat thickness to the nearest .01 in., then the yield grade adjustment is .066 for each .01 in. above or below the base of .3 in.
2. For each 1.0% KP fat above the base of 3.5%, add .25 yield; and for each 1.0% KP fat below the base of 3.5%, subtract .25 yield grade.
3. For each ⅓ leg conformation grade above the base of Choice⁰, subtract .05 yield grade; and for each leg conformation grade below the base of Choice⁰, add .05 yield grade.

The base or preliminary yield grade (PYG) of 4.0 is adjusted for each of the above 3 factors if they differ from the base to arrive at FYG. Hundredths of a yield grade are carried throughout the determination of yield grade, but FYG of each lamb is rounded to the nearest tenth yield grade. Remember in commercial practice that only whole yield grade numbers from 1 to 5 are actually "rolled" on the carcass.

From the preceding discussion, it can be seen that 12th rib fat thickness has the greatest affect on FYG, leg conformation grade has the least affect, and percentage KP is intermediate.

The following example illustrates the procedure of the FYG calculation:

	Adjusted 12th Rib Fat Thickness	% KP Fat	Leg Conformation Grade
Carcass values	.2 inch	2.5%	P⁻
Adjustment factors	−.66	−.25	−.1
PYG = (4.0	−.66) = 3.34	−.25	−.1 = 3.0 FYG

Examples of the five yield grades of lamb carcasses are shown in Figures 14.20 through 14.24.

Wholesale Pricing of Lamb Carcasses and Live Lamb Pricing

Lamb Carcass Wholesale Price

Wholesale carcass price/cwt is calculated by adjusting the base quality grade price for actual yield grade by adding or subtracting $.25 for each .1 deviation in yield grade from the base price. This procedure is identical to the one described for determining the live price/cwt of lambs. The base wholesale price of lamb carcasses varies with daily market fluctuations so that prices need to be checked each day before beginning the carcass pricing procedure. Likewise, the base yield grade used for pricing lamb carcasses may vary from time to time and should be checked each time pricing is done. Wholesale carcass price adjusted for actual yield and quality grade is used to calculate live price/cwt by multiplying it by actual dressing percentage. The calculation of live price from actual carcass wholesale price is more accurate than that estimated on live lambs because the factors affecting it can be accurately evaluated or measured on the carcass. Retail pricing of lamb will be presented and discussed in Section 18.

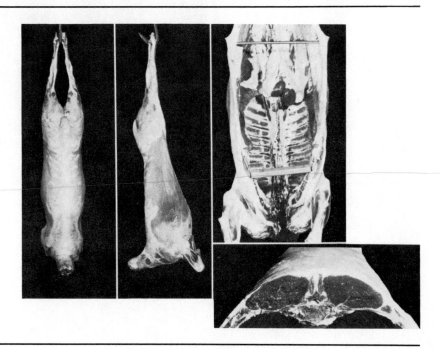

Figure 14.20. A lamb carcass and data representative of yield grade 1.
External Fat Thickness, .05 Inch.
Kidney and Pelvic Fat, 1.5 Percent
Leg Conformation Grade, Low Prime
Yield Grade, 1.7

Figure 14.21. A lamb carcass and data
representative of yield grade 2.
External Fat Thickness, .10 Inch
Kidney and Pelvic Fat, 3.0 Percent
Leg Conformation Grade, Average Prime
Yield Grade, 2.4

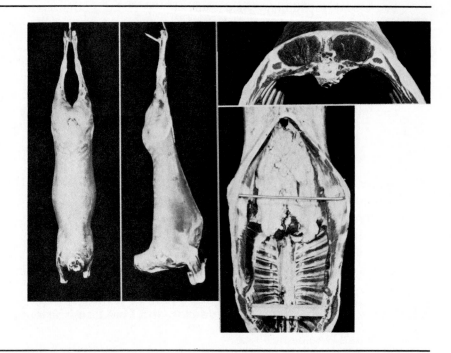

Figure 14.22. A lamb carcass and data
representative of yield grade 3.
External Fat Thickness, .25 Inch
Kidney and Pelvic Fat, 3.5 Percent
Leg Conformation Grade, Low Choice
Yield Grade 3.6

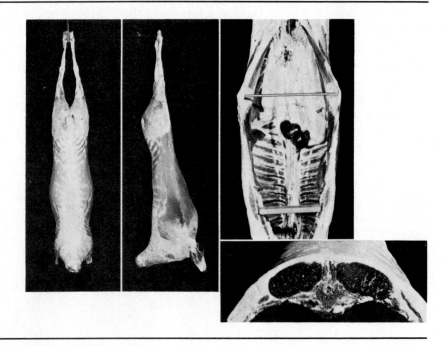

Figure 14.23. A lamb carcass and data representative of yield grade 4.
External Fat Thickness, .35 Inch
Kidney and Pelvic Fat, 4.5 Percent
Leg Conformation Grade, High Choice
Yield Grade, 4.6

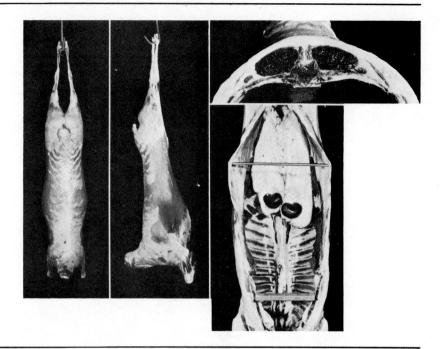

Figure 14.24. A lamb carcass and data representative of yield grade 5.
External Fat Thickness, .45 Inch
Kidney and Pelvic Fat, 5.5 Percent
Leg Conformation Grade, Average Choice
Yield Grade, 5.5

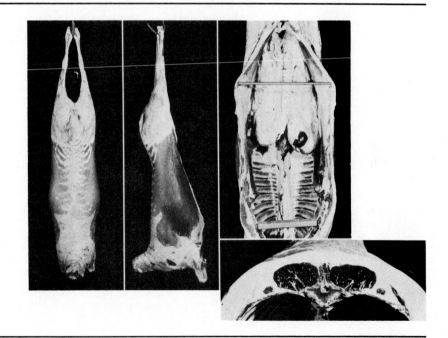

Evaluation of Sheep Performance Data

When discussing the performance traits of sheep, one must consider that each breed was developed for a distinct purpose. The "ewe" breeds were developed for maternal traits and the "ram" breeds were developed for paternal traits. Thus, in selecting replacements for a ewe breed, the producer should emphasize reproductive efficiency, milk production, and wool production as performance traits in the selection program. In the case of a ram breed, the producer should emphasize growth rate and carcass cutability. However, even in this type of specialized situation, a breeder must be aware of the total production system. In other words, a person raising a ram breed of sheep must not only select for production and carcass traits, but must also maintain high levels of reproductive efficiency and maternal abilities within his ewe flock to be a successful producer.

Reproductive Efficiency

Selection for multiple births is a practical method of selection for increased reproductive efficiency. Even though the heritability of multiple births is low, the variability for the trait is large and progress through selection can be made. Twin and triplet lambs should be identified and replacements should be selected from this group. The producer should also note ewe lambs that reach puberty during the first year because these lambs will generally be the most fertile and have a greater lifetime lamb production.

Wool Production

The most accurate measure of wool production is clean fleece weight. However, since clean fleece weight and grease fleece weights are highly correlated, it may be more practical to measure grease fleece weights. Although the quantity and quality of the wool produced vary among breeds, the meat-type breeds should be expected to produce approximately 6 to 8 lb. of wool, and the wool breeds over 12 lb. of wool, annually. It should be remembered that wool production is negatively related to growability and the carcass traits. Thus, heavy selection pressure for all of these traits will result in slow selection progress.

Birth Weight

Birth weight is the first indicator of future growth rate. Lambs with heavier birth weights tend to grow more rapidly. However, lambing problems may occur with the larger, heavier lambs at birth. Acceptable birth weights will vary between breeds and type of birth (number born).

Weaning Weight

As with cattle and swine, lamb weaning weight is an excellent indicator of the ewe's milk producing ability, as well as an early indicator of growth potential. The three most popular times for weaning lambs are at 60 days, 90 days, or 120 days. Weaning weights taken at 60 days directly reflect the milk producing ability of the ewe. Use of these weights to select ewe lambs is acceptable, but selecting ram lambs at this time would not be desirable because they have not yet expressed their potential to grow and gain efficiently. Weaning at 90 days is the most popular age. This age allows for relatively accurate selection of both ram and ewe lamb replacements. Although some of the dam effect is removed, as compared to 60 day weights, the milk producing ability of the dam still has a significant influence on this weight. In addition, the extra 30 days allows potentially fast gaining lambs more time to overcome a poor start that may have occurred due to sickness or a poor producing dam. By 120 days, much of the dam effect is removed; thus, these weights would favor the lambs that have the ability to grow on their own. This time would be excellent for ram lamb selection, but some of the indication of the future milk producing ability of the ewe lambs has now been masked by her growability.

Weaning weights should be corrected to a standard age, and then adjusted for sex, type of birth and rearing, and age of dam. The following method should be used to correct to a standard age.

$$\text{90-Day Corrected Weight} = \left(\frac{(\text{Weaning Weight} - \text{Birth Weight})}{(\text{Days of Age at Weaning})} \times 90\right) + \text{Birth Wt.}$$

If birth weight is unknown, the following method may be used:

$$\text{90-Day Corrected Weight} = \frac{(\text{Weaning Weight})}{(\text{Days of Age at Weaning})} \times 90$$

The adjusted weight is calculated as follows:

$$\text{Adjusted Weight} = \text{Corrected Weight} \times \text{Adjustment Factor}$$

The adjustment factors recommended by the National Extension Sheep Committee are listed in Table 15.1.

Example Calculations of Adjusted Weights:

Ram twin raised as twin
Weight at 85 days = 95 lb.
Birth Weight = 10 lb.
Age of Dam = 2 years
Dam's Fleece Weight = 10 lb.

$$\text{Corrected 90-Day Weight} = \left(\left(\frac{95 - 10}{85}\right) \times 90\right) + 10 = 100 \text{ lb.}$$

$$\text{Adjusted 90-Day Weight} = 100 \text{ lb} \times 1.09 = 109 \text{ lb.}$$

Lamb Index

In ram breed flocks, lambs should be compared by the ratio system (Section 4), using the adjusted weaning weights of the lambs. In ewe breed flocks, the producer may want to use a lamb index to make within the flock comparisons. The following index was developed by the National Extension Sheep Committee.

For single births:
Lamb Index = Adjusted Weight + (.6 × Dam's fleece weight)

For multiple births:
Lamb Index = (Adjusted Weight × 1.10) + (.6 × Dam's fleece weight)

This index emphasizes multiple births, growth rate, and wool production. Thus, the use of a lamb index for selection of replacements may be more accurate, from a total production standpoint, than using adjusted weights alone.

Ewe Index

To compare ewes within the flock, the producer should utilize a ewe productivity index. The following index, recommended in *The National Uniform Sheep Selection Program,* encompasses the ewe's reproductive efficiency, milking ability, and wool production.

Table 15.1   Adjustment Factors.

	3 to 6 Years Old	2 Years Old or Over 6 Years	One Year Old
Ewe Lamb			
Single	1.00	1.09	1.22
Twin—Raised as Twin	1.11	1.20	1.33
Twin—Raised as Single	1.05	1.14	1.28
Triplet—Raised as Triplet	1.22	1.33	1.46
Triplet—Raised as Twin	1.17	1.28	1.42
Triplet—Raised as Single	1.11	1.21	1.36
Wether			
Single	.97	1.06	1.19
Twin—Raised as Twin	1.08	1.17	1.30
Twin—Raised as Single	1.02	1.11	1.25
Triplet—Raised as Triplet	1.19	1.30	1.43
Triplet—Raised as Twin	1.14	1.25	1.39
Triplet—Raised as Single	1.08	1.18	1.33
Ram Lamb			
Single	.89	.98	1.11
Twin—Raised as Twin	1.00	1.09	1.22
Twin—Raised as Single	.94	1.03	1.17
Triplet—Raised as Triplet	1.11	1.22	1.35
Triplet—Raised as Twin	1.06	1.17	1.31
Triplet—Raised as Single	1.00	1.10	1.25

For ewes giving birth to singles and raising singles:

$$\text{Ewe Index} = \text{Adjusted Weaning Weight of Lamb} + (3 \times \text{Fleece Weight})$$

For ewes having multiple births and raising one or more lambs:

$$\text{Ewe Index} = \text{Sum of Adjusted Weaning Weights of Lambs} + (3 \times \text{Fleece Weight})$$

For example, a ewe that yielded 8 lb. of wool and raised a single, ram lamb that had an adjusted 90-day weight of 85 lb. would have a ewe productivity index calculated as follows:

$$\begin{aligned} \text{Ewe Index} &= 85 + (3 \times 8) \\ &= 85 + 24 \\ &= 109 \end{aligned}$$

Ewes that raise no lambs receive no index and should be culled from the flock. The ewe index values from ewes which raise lambs should be calculated into ratio form (Section 4) and then utilized in making culling decisions for the flock.

Growth Rate

Weaning weight can be used to estimate growability, but a more accurate measure of a lamb's growth potential is a post-weaning growth trial. Post-weaning rate of gain reflects directly on a lamb's ability to grow and has a higher heritability than pre-weaning gain. The handling of the lambs prior to the trial has a large effect on performance during the trial. Therefore, compensatory gain, by lambs which have been held off feed, becomes a problem in making accurate comparisons among lambs from varied background. There is also a problem in marketing those lambs that performed unsatisfactorily on test, since they will have surpassed the desired market weights.

Purebred producers may want to consider yearling or 16-month weights in selecting a new ram. These weights have the highest heritability of the growth traits and are the most accurate measure of a lamb's growability. Unfortunately, this system also has the problem of marketing the older rams that had unsatisfactory performance.

Carcass Traits

The specific carcass traits that are important to the sheepman are discussed in Section 14. The producer should keep in mind that producing lambs that have acceptable carcass quality is rather easily accomplished, and for that reason the major carcass concern is cutability. The most practical method of selecting for an increased lean-to-fat ratio is selecting for rate of gain. The fastest gaining lambs will generally be more efficient and, at a given weight, will usually be more muscular and leaner than the slower gaining lambs.

National Sheep Improvement Program

The National Sheep Improvement Program (NSIP) was developed to provide sheep producers with a means of genetically evaluating their animals for maternal, growth, and wool traits on a within-flock basis. Two programs are available, one for purebred flocks and one for commercial flocks. In both programs, genetic merit values are reported as flock expected progeny differences (FEPD) in units consistent with the trait being evaluated. It is imperative for producers to realize that FEPDs can only be used to compare animals within a flock. This is in contrast to beef cattle EPDs which can be used across herds.

The maternal traits evaluated by NSIP are (1) number of lambs born per ewe lambing and (2) pounds of lamb weaned per ewe exposed. In the growth traits, NSIP has the capability to genetically evaluate five different age-weight categories (30, 60, 90, 120 and 240 days). Each producer can select up to three of these age-weight categories for evaluation within their flocks. Producers interested in improving the quality and quantity of wool production can select up to three traits for evaluation: (1) clean or grease fleece weight, (2) staple length, and (3) fiber diameter.

The NSIP and its development of FEPD for within flock comparisons are the first steps in the development of a national program for sheep improvement. As the program grows and more records are collected, sufficient across flock pedigree relationships will be developed to permit across-flock genetic evaluations similar to those present in the beef industry.

Specification Based Selection Programs

When selecting sheep it is important to realize that certain situations require different types of animals. All animals have traits that may make them superior under one set of circumstances; yet under different conditions, these same traits may be of little value. For example, if a ram was being selected for generating crossbred replacement ewes, wool production, milking ability and multiple births would receive high selection priority. However, if the ram was being selected for use as a terminal sire to generate market lambs, these traits would be less important, and the growth and carcass traits would receive the highest priorities.

When selecting sheep one should ask the following questions:

1. How are the selected rams (ewes) to be used (selection purpose)?
2. Under what conditions are the rams (ewes) expected to perform (selection situation)?
3. Based on the purpose and the situation, what traits are most important (selection priorities)?

The selection purpose and situation are collectively referred to as the scenario. Once you understand the scenario, you can accurately determine which traits are the priorities for selection. With that information, you should then be able to choose the correct ram (ewe) for that specific situation and purpose.

In sheep, the selection purpose tends to be rather breed specific. The white-faced breeds are generally considered to be maternal line or ewe breeds. The number of lambs born, the pounds of lamb weaned per ewe, and the clean or grease fleece weight should receive high selection priority for the maternal line breeds.

In contrast, the black-faced breeds are considered to be paternal line or ram breeds. Growth rate and carcass merit receive higher consideration in the paternal line breeds.

As an example, consider the selection of Suffolk rams for the following scenario:

- Terminal sire
- Used on white-faced, crossbred ewes
- All lambs fed to slaughter

The scenario calls for a paternal line sire; therefore, adjusted 120 day weight, post-weaning gain, leanness and muscling should receive top selection priority. Multiple birth, as well as 30 day and 60 day weights, should receive moderate consideration, and the wool traits should receive little or no consideration.

Consider another example scenario for the selection of Dorset rams:

- Purebred farm flock
- Ewe lambs kept as replacements, a few ram lambs sold to other flocks, wethers sold as club or feeder lambs
- Feed and labor resources are high

This scenario calls for more of a dual-purpose (maternal and paternal) type of ram; therefore, a balance of traits is necessary. Adjusted 60-day weight should receive high selection priority as should twinning. Post-weaning growth rate, muscling, and quantity of wool produced should receive moderate selection consideration in this scenario.

Visual Evaluation of Breeding Sheep

The profitable breeding sheep is structurally and reproductively sound, highly productive, and can gain rapidly and efficiently. Since it is a ruminant, the sheep should produce large quantities of wool and meat on a high roughage diet. The ideal sheep should also be adaptable to changes in environment and management systems.

Skeletal Correctness

A skeletally correct sheep is straight in its lines and stands correctly on its feet and legs. The legs should be straight, strong, and set wide apart on the corners of the body. The pasterns should be strong and fairly straight, yet still cushion and flex at the walk. The feet should be straight and sound with the weight distributed equally on all toes. It is important for the sheep to walk with a long, free, easy stride. This will allow the sheep to be adaptable to range conditions and should add to its durability and longevity. A long sloping shoulder, a level rump, and a correct positioning of the feet and legs are essential to allow freedom of movement. The ram in Figure 16.1 is ideal in his skeletal structure. He has smoothness of shoulder, straightness of lines, and the ideal set of the front and rear legs. Some common problems of the front legs are buck knees, calf knees, weak pasterns, as well as the splay-footed and pigeon-toed conditions. On their hind legs, sheep can be "post-legged" (too straight in the angle of the hocks), "sickle-hocked" (too set in the angle of the hocks), or weak on their pasterns. From the rear, sheep may stand "cow-hocked" (hocks too close together) or "bow-legged" (hocks too wide apart). These same skeletal problems are found in swine and cattle and are illustrated in Sections 8 and 12.

Figure 16.1. Illustration of a structurally correct ram that is very long bodied, long-legged and should by very large framed at maturity.

Frame

The emphasis placed on size and scale varies with the breed of sheep. Slaughter lambs are normally marketed at a moderate weight (100–130 lb.). Therefore, it is more economical for the commercial producer to maintain moderate size ewes and breed them to large framed, fast growing rams to produce the desired weight market lamb. This practice creates the need for the two distinct types of breeds of sheep, the "ram" breeds and the "ewe" breeds, which are discussed in Section 15.

In most purebred breeds, especially "ram" breeds, additional frame, scale, and size for age is preferred. Such sheep are tall, late maturing, and long bodied.

Capacity

A productive sheep should be boldly sprung in the upper rib and deep ribbed. The lamb should also stand wide and have ample width through the chest floor. As in the other species, be wary of excess fat and condition creating an illusion of increased capacity.

Body Composition

The ideal lamb is heavily muscled and has a minimum amount of fat. The lamb should be thick and meaty through the loin, rump, and leg (thigh) regions. Since the hindsaddle (leg and loin) contains the highest priced retail cuts, the lamb should have a high percentage of its weight in this area. The loin should

Figure 16.2. Illustration of a very lean, muscular lamb that has desirable shape down his top.

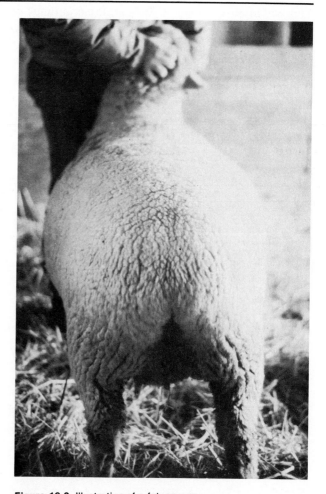

Figure 16.3. Illustration of a fat, square-topped lamb.

be deep as well as wide, and the leg should have all of the necessary dimensions to indicate a large quantity of muscle. The lamb should also be expressively muscled in the forearm and be fully sprung in the rib or rack.

The lamb should be trim in the breast, middle, flank, and twist; and it should not be full and smooth behind the shoulders in the fore-rib, or heart girth. Fullness in this area indicates excess fat and condition. The lamb should also be trim over the ribs and the edge of the loin and have a muscular shape to its top.

The lamb in Figure 16.2 has a desirable lean to fat ratio. This lamb has a muscular shape to its top as compared to the fat, square-topped lamb shown in Figure 16.3.

Head, Neck and Shoulders

A late maturing sheep has a relatively long neck and head. It should also have a broad forehead and ample width between the eyes. A ram should have a strong, masculine head (Figure 16.4), while a ewe's head should be more refined and feminine (Figure 16.5).

The sheep must be able to see. Sound sheep should show no signs of inherited eye defects, such as entropian (inverted eyelid) or ectropian (loose, gaping eyelid). Breeds of sheep with wool on the head should be free from wool in the eye channel. The ram in Figure 16.6 is open-faced and would have no problem with excess wool. In contrast, the ewe in Figure 16.7 is close-faced and wool blind.

The shoulders should be expressively muscled, yet they should be joined neatly at the top and blend in smoothly with the neck. Coarse, prominent shoulders can cause lambing difficulties and should be discriminated against.

Figure 16.4. Illustration of a masculine head.

Figure 16.5. Illustration of a feminine head.

Figure 16.6. Illustration of an open-faced ram.

Figure 16.7. Illustration of a close-faced, wool blind ewe.

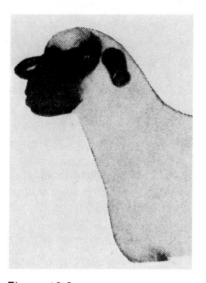

Figure 16.7

Figure 16.6

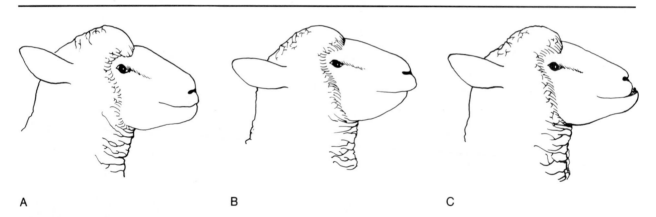

A   B   C

Figure 16.8. Illustrations showing correct (sheep A) and incorrect jaw structures (overshot jaw or parrot mouth, sheep B, and undershot jaw or monkey mouth, sheep C).

The sheep must also have a sound mouth. Ideally, the jaws should meet squarely and the incisor teeth in the lower jaw should be centered on the dental pad in the upper jaw. A "scratched" mouth refers to a mouth in which the teeth miss the dental pad, but the jaws are in the proper position. While this situation is not desirable, it usually causes no major problems. However, jaw defects are highly heritable and they may prevent the sheep from gathering adequate forage in a pasture situation. Jaw defects should be highly discriminated against. Figure 16.8 illustrates correct (sheep A) and incorrect jaw structures (overshot jaw or parrot mouth, sheep B and undershot jaw, sheep C).

Breed Character

More emphasis is placed on breed character in sheep evaluation than in any other species. However, it is beyond the scope of this manual to discuss the differences in breed character. This is due to the subjectivity involved in measuring breed character and its questionable economic importance.

Fleece

Since the main objective of this manual is evaluation of the meat animal species, the authors have not included an in-depth discussion of wool grading and evaluation. Wool, on the other hand, is a valuable secondary product of the mutton breeds of sheep, and for that reason should be considered in sheep evaluation.

In the mutton breeds of sheep, the ideal fleece is tight, dense, and has a long staple. It should be uniform in grade (diameter of the wool fiber) and should be free of coarse or hairy wool in the britch (thigh).

Black fibers, in black-faced breeds, and kemp fibers in white-faced breeds should be discriminated against. These types of fibers will not take a dye and thus lower the quality of the wool.

In some breeds, especially Suffolks, portions of the belly have no wool. This is referred to as "barebelly" and is not desirable because it results in lower wool production.

Selection of Feeder Livestock

The principles of feeder livestock selection are essentially the same as those involved in selecting breeding stock. In all species, the feeder animal must be able to grow rapidly and efficiently and, at slaughter time, produce a carcass with acceptable quality and high cutability. Thus, desirable feeder livestock have adequate frame and body capacity, acceptable structural correctness, and the potential to maintain a high lean-to-fat ratio up to market weight. They should have the ability to produce muscle without laying down excess fat. It is also of utmost importance that the feeder animals of all species are thrifty, healthy, and free of any internal or external parasites. Thriftiness refers to the ability of a feeder animal to gain weight rapidly and efficiently, and it is an economically important trait in feeder animals of all species.

Feeder Pig Selection

In selecting feeder pigs, one must consider the grade, health, structural soundness, and sex of the pigs. These factors affect the performance of the pigs during the finishing period and, therefore, have a direct influence on the profitability of the feeder operation.

Grade

The U.S.D.A. grades of feeder pigs are U.S. No. 1, U.S. No. 2, U.S. No. 3, U.S. No. 4, U.S. Utility, and U.S. Cull. Except for Cull these grades correspond to the U.S.D.A. grades of slaughter hogs (Section 5) and are an estimation of a feeder pig's slaughter grade at a market weight of 220–260 lb. The U.S. Utility and U.S. Cull grades consist of unthrifty pigs. The differentiation between the U.S. Utility and U.S. Cull grades is based entirely on differences in thriftiness. The grade of a feeder pig, therefore, is a combined evaluation of its thriftiness and slaughter potential. Hence, a U.S. No. 1 feeder must be a thrifty pig with sufficient muscle, length, and leanness to produce a U.S. No. 1 carcass at 220–260 lb. The U.S.D.A. grades of feeder pigs are shown in Figure 17.1.

Health

The importance of purchasing healthy, disease-free feeder pigs cannot be overemphasized. Thrifty pigs with smooth haircoats generally have a lower death loss and greater feedlot performance than unthrifty pigs. The buyer should also avoid ruptured or crippled barrows, gilts, and boars—as well as castrates that are not properly healed. Purchasing feeder pigs from a reputable producer or dealer will help the buyer avoid many of the above problems.

Structural Soundness

Structural correctness is included in the evaluation and selection of feeder pigs for two very important reasons. First, structural faults are a source of stress for market hogs, especially those fed on concrete, and can, therefore, impair the performance of the pig. Also, since the market barrows and gilts produced in a swine operation are half sibs or sibs of the gilts selected as replacement females, structural unsoundnesses in the market animals are a direct reflection of the structural problems in the breeding herd. This second reason, while perhaps not as important to the feeder, is very important to the swine industry as a whole. Therefore, the old adage that "a barrow needs only be correct enough to walk to the truck to go to slaughter" is certainly a fallacy.

Figure 17.1. Illustrations representative of each of the feeder grades of pigs, except for U.S. Cull.

U.S. No. 1

U.S. No. 2

U.S. No. 3

U.S. No. 4

U.S. Utility

Sex of Pig

In the swine industry, only gilts and barrows are fed as market hogs. Because of "boar odor" and several management problems associated with boars, they are not fed out as market animals. From a feeding standpoint, barrows and gilts each have certain advantages over the other. Gilts are generally leaner and heavier muscled and thus produce carcasses with higher percentages of muscle. Gilts also tend to convert feed more efficiently as they require less feed per unit of gain than barrows. On the other hand, barrows grow more rapidly and reach market weight in a fewer number of days.

Ideal Type

The ideal type feeder pig as described by a panel of experts at the 1978 National Feeder Pig Show is large framed and structurally sound, being flat over his top and rump and correct on his feet and legs. He is long bodied, especially from flank to flank and long in his rump. He is also long in his muscle pattern in contrast to being tightly wound and bunchy in muscling. The pig has a big skeleton and a large total body dimension with little fat. He has the necessary frame and structure of a late maturing pig and can be fed to heavy weights without laying down excess fat or developing structural problems.

Feeder Cattle Selection

When selecting cattle to feed, it is important for the feeder to understand the effects of age, weight, sex, feeder grade, body condition, and frame size on feedlot performance. Many types, kinds, and sizes of cattle are usually available for feeding, creating a wide variety of options for the feedlot operator. However, these various types of feeder cattle necessitate different management systems, requiring the feedlot operator to either select feeder cattle that are suitable to his feeding and management system or adapt his management practices to fit the type of cattle available.

Age Groups

To determine the proper feeding regimen for a group of cattle, the feeder needs to know the age of the cattle. Calves and yearlings are the most commonly available age groups of cattle. Calves generally make more efficient gains than yearlings due to the composition of gain of the calves. Because they are less mature, they deposit a higher percentage of muscle and less fat than the yearlings. Calves normally cost more per hundredweight than yearlings, but since calves are lighter in weight, they cost fewer total dollars per head. Another advantage of feeding calves is that during the early phases of the feeding period they can be grown on cheaper feeds such as forages and crop residues. Yearling feeder cattle have higher average daily gains and require fewer days on feed. Therefore, they have a more rapid turnover rate which allows for a more rapid return on investment. In other words, a feeder who feeds yearlings may be able to feed three groups of cattle a year, whereas with calves, he may be able to feed only one and a half groups of cattle a year. Unfortunately yearlings require more feed per pound of gain and in addition they are often in shorter supply than calves.

Under certain conditions, it may be economical to feed older cattle such as cull cows. Not only do these cattle out gain calves and yearling feeders, but it may also be possible to improve the slaughter grade of thin cows, thus increasing the price received per hundredweight. However, since the composition of gain on these cattle is primarily fat, the feed required per pound of gain is considerably higher than for yearlings and calves.

Weight Groups

Feeder cattle markets report prices by weight groups as well as age groups. Lighter weight cattle generally bring a higher price per hundredweight than heavier cattle and they have the same feeding advantages as calves. Actually, the light cattle usually are calves and they weigh less than 500 lb. In areas where roughage and crop residue supplies are plentiful, these light weight cattle are popular for stocker programs. Such programs utilize the cheaper feed sources to grow calves to approximately 700 lb. at which time they are sent directly to feedlots or resold to feedlot operators for finishing. Heavy weight cattle weigh 700 lb. or more and are usually yearlings; therefore, they have the same advantages and disadvantages as yearlings. These cattle are ready to be placed on a high concentrate, finishing ration and require fewer days on feed than light weight cattle to reach the desired slaughter endpoint.

Sex or Classes

Steers and heifers make up the majority of the young cattle on feed. The differences between the performance of steers and heifers depends upon whether they are fed to a constant slaughter grade (same approximate degree of finish) or are fed for an equal period of time. When fed to a constant slaughter grade, heifers will weigh approximately 80% as much as steers of the same frame size because of the heifers' earlier rate of maturity. They also require fewer days on feed to reach this slaughter endpoint. There is, however, very little difference in the performance levels, especially in feed efficiency, between steers and heifers when fed to the same degree of finish. On the other hand, if steers and heifers are fed for the same period of time, steers gain faster and more efficiently than heifers. This is due almost entirely to the differences in composition of gain during the latter stages of the finishing period.

While heifers and steers are still preferred by most cattle feeders, there are definite advantages to feeding young bulls (bullocks). Bullocks gain faster, require less feed per pound of gain, and have higher cutability than steers or heifers. However, feeding bullocks does have some disadvantages. They are discriminated against somewhat in slaughter price, but this problem tends to be subsiding in many areas. They also require a higher level of management because they are more active and do more fighting and riding than steers. In addition to these problems, to maintain tenderness in the meat, bulls need to be marketed at 18 months of age or less. However, due to their lateness of maturity, bullocks seldom have sufficient marbling at this age to grade U.S. Choice.

Grade

The U.S.D.A. Feeder Cattle Grades were revised in 1979 in order to make the standards more descriptive of the types of feeder cattle being produced and more accurate in predicting feedlot performance potential. The factors used to grade feeder cattle are thriftiness, frame size, and thickness of muscling.

Thriftines refers to the health of an animal and its ability to gain weight and fatten normally. Unthrifty cattle, regardless of frame size and muscle thickness, are graded Inferior.

Thickness of muscling refers to the development of the muscle system in relation to skeletal size. At a constant fat thickness, thicker cattle have a higher ratio of muscle to bone and will thus have a more desirable yield grade. Feeder cattle are classified by thickness as No. 1, No. 2, or No. 3. Illustrations representing these degrees of thickness are shown in Figure 17.2.

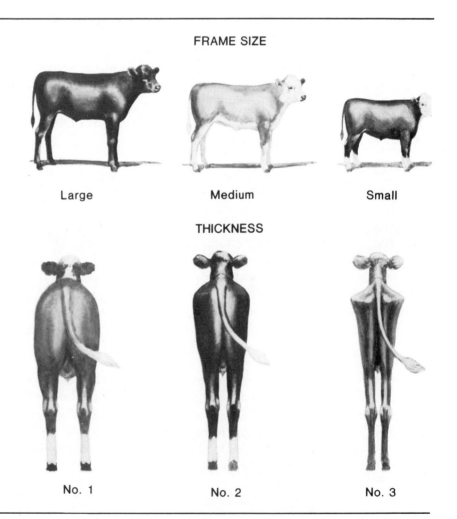

Figure 17.2. Illustrations representing the degrees of frame and thickness used in grading feeder cattle.

FRAME SIZE

Large   Medium   Small

THICKNESS

No. 1   No. 2   No. 3

Frame size refers to the animal's height and length in relation to its age. Frame size is an indicator of the animal's growability and mature size. The effects of frame size on feedlot performance are discussed in more detail later in this section. Grade classifications for frame size are Large, Medium, and Small. These are also illustrated in Figure 17.2.

Each thrifty feeder calf is given a frame classification and a muscle classification. These two factors are then combined to give the calf a feeder grade. The U.S.D.A. grades of feeder cattle are listed below.

Large Frame, No. 1	Medium Frame, No. 1	Small Frame, No. 1
Large Frame, No. 2	Medium Frame, No. 2	Small Frame, No. 2
Large Frame, No. 3	Medium Frame, No. 3	Small Frame, No. 3

Inferior

Body Condition

The body condition of cattle is an important factor to consider when selecting feeder animals. At constant weights, thin cattle will have more frame and generally gain faster and more efficiently than fat feeder cattle. Therefore, thrifty, thin feeder cattle will usually bring higher prices per hundredweight than fat feeder cattle.

Frame Size

Large framed cattle gain more efficiently (require less feed per pound of gain) at a given weight than smaller framed cattle, but the larger framed cattle must be fed to heavier weights to grade U.S. Choice. Research data indicate that there is virtually no difference in the feed efficiency of cattle of different frame sizes when they are all fed to the same approximate degree of finish. Therefore, it is much more important for the feedlot operator to recognize the size of cattle being fed and feed them only to the desirable degree of finish (presently to assure the low Choice quality grade) rather than try to feed all cattle to a certain slaughter weight.

A system for classifying cattle according to frame size (Wisconsin body-type score) was discussed in Section 4. The slaughter cattle in Figure 17.3 are representative of some of the various body-types. Table 17.1 gives estimates of the weights at which steers and heifers of the various body-types should have sufficient fat to grade low Choice.

Figure 17.3. Illustration showing slaughter steers representing 4 of the 7 body-types of steers fed in the Wisconsin type studies. These steers represent body-types 7, 5, 3, and 1, respectively, from left to right.

Table 17.1   Approximate Weights at Which Steers and Heifers of Various Frame Size Should Grade Low Choice.

	Body-Type Score						
	1	2	3	4	5	6	7
Steers, lb.	750	850	950	1050	1150	1250	1350
Heifers, lb.	600	680	760	840	920	1000	1080

Feeder Lamb Selection

Choice and Prime slaughter lambs can be produced on their mother's milk and grass. However, seldom are 100% of the lambs ready for slaughter at weaning. In regions that are capable of producing high yielding crops, there is sufficient feed available to either creep feed for more rapid growth or finish out the balance of the lamb crop for slaughter. Many native (farm states) feeder lambs are the result of poor management because they are parasitized, bucks are not castrated and tails are not docked. In areas of grass, hay and, small grain production, some thrifty feeder lambs are available.

Approximately 70% of the breeding sheep are located in the western range country where the sheep rancher does not produce harvested crops of corn or other high energy feeds. Therefore, when the lambs are weaned it is common to sell the whole lamb crop at one time. It varies from year to year but 20 to 40% of the lambs are sold as feeders and the rest are sufficiently fat to be sold for slaughter. Thus, the bulk of thrifty feeder lambs originate in the western range states. These states are also among the leading states in lambs on feed primarily because of the prohibitive costs of transporting lambs to other areas of the country. Few producers make a living by feeding lambs today, and their greatest problem is obtaining a sufficient number of lambs.

Because the present carcass quality grade standards permit any breed or shape of lamb to qualify for the U.S. Choice grade when finished for slaughter, and because of the limited supply of lambs, lamb feeders purchase almost any available lamb because they can make a profit on the feed. Feeder lambs are purchased between 65 and 90 lb. in weight and they are 5 to 8 months of age. They are fed 60 to 90 days and marketed at 100 to 140 lb. in weight. Many of the heavier weight lambs are overfat and are thus discounted in price.

Feeder Grades

The U.S.D.A. grades of feeder lambs are Prime, Choice, Good, Utility, and Cull. These standards have not been revised in sometime and many feeder lambs are purchased without reference to these standards. In Michigan, for example, all feeder lambs are sold as feeders without any reference to grade.

Several weight divisions are used to categorize feeder lambs. Light weight feeder lambs weigh 60 to 75 lb.; medium weights 75 to 85 lb.; and heavy weights over 85 lb.

Other feeder lamb terminology:

1. Natives are lambs produced in the farm states. Their breeding varies from all white face to all black face breeding. It takes an excellent sheepman to treat these lambs for parasites, dock, castrate, and get them on feed without large losses.
2. Western lambs come from various parts of the west and often the state of origin is used. Feeders are available from the southwestern states and California earlier in the season than those from the northwest. White-faced Texas lambs are primarily of fine wool Rambouillet breeding. White-faced lambs from the northwest may be either Columbia or Rambouillet sired lambs. Black-faced western lambs are sired by Suffolk or Hampshire rams, and they are out of white-faced ewes. Black-faced lambs are preferred as feeders because they are more muscular and faster growing than most white-faced lambs.

Sex of Lamb

In the past wethers have been preferred as feeder lambs because they generally gain faster and more efficiently and produce carcasses with higher cutability than ewe lambs. Ram lambs are superior to both wether and ewe lambs in feedlot performance and carcass traits, but until recently, they have been discounted in slaughter price. This is no longer true at most markets; therefore, more and more producers are not castrating male lambs, but marketing them instead as ram lambs. While feeding ram lambs may increase the management requirement for a feeding operation, they may also increase the profitability of the operation because of their faster and more economical gains.

Wholesale and Retail Pricing of Pork, Beef, and Lamb

Wholesale Pricing

Wholesale prices are established for beef and lamb carcasses because they are usually merchandized in carcass form. On the other hand, pork carcasses are almost always merchandized as wholesale or primal cuts; consequently, wholesale prices are established for each cut. However, when wholesale pork carcass price needs to be determined, it is calculated from the weighted combined price of each wholesale cut, which will be described later. This procedure was used to arrive at wholesale pork carcass price for the live pricing procedures presented in Sections 5 and 6. Wholesale prices are also established for the primal cuts of beef because merchandizing of beef primals is increasing in popularity. The wholesale price of beef and lamb carcasses, as well as the primal cuts of beef and pork, are established primarily by supply and demand. These wholesale prices are used throughout the livestock industry to determine the live price of hogs, cattle, and lambs as described in Sections 5, 9 and 13, respectively.

The wholesale price per cwt of beef and lamb carcasses and the combined wholesale or primal cut price per cwt of pork differs from the live price per cwt of each species only by the factor of the dressing percentage of the respective species. Thus, a steer carcass that has a wholesale price of $112.50/cwt with a dressing percentage of 62 has a live price of $69.80/cwt ($112.50 × .62 = $69.80) when rounded to the nearest $.10. Likewise, a lamb and pork carcass with dressing percentages of 50 and 72 would have live prices per cwt that are 50% and 72%, respectively, of the wholesale carcass price per cwt. Because of this relationship, the total live value (live weight × live price per cwt) is equal to the total carcass value (chilled carcass weight × wholesale carcass price per cwt). This relationship is shown in the following example. A Choice, yield grade 3.2, 700 lb. steer carcass with a wholesale price of $112.00/cwt has a total carcass value of $784.00 (700 lb. × $112.00). If the dressing percentage of this steer is 60, the live price per cwt is $67.20/cwt ($112.00 × .60) and the total live value of this steer equals $784.00 [1167 lb. live wt. (700 ÷ .60) × $67.20]. Thus, total carcass value and total live value of this steer both equal $784.00. These relationships also apply to live hog and lamb total dollar values vs. pork carcass and lamb carcass total dollar values.

Since the total dollar value of live animals equals the total dollar value of the wholesale carcass, it appears from this conventional marketing procedure that the slaughterer has not covered his costs, much less made any profit. He has to pay the same amount of money for the animal that the carcass is worth when he sells it to the retailer. However, the slaughterer recovers the cost of his operation plus he makes a profit from the sale of by-products. By-products include the items shown in Table 18.1.

By-product value fluctuates slightly from time to time, and it differs between species. By-product value was not taken into account in any of the pricing procedures presented in this manual; however, some livestock buying procedures add a by-product value credit to the live price of the animal.

Table 18.1   Some By-Products of the Livestock Slaughter Industry.

Hides	Fat	Stomachs	Pharmaceuticals	Cheek meat
Skins (hogs)	Bones	Intestines	Livers	Brains
Hair (hogs)	Lungs	Esophagi	Hearts	Sweetbreads
Pelts	Spleens	Kidneys	Tongues	Ox tails
Blood				

Table 18.2 An Example of Pork Wholesale Carcass Price Per Cwt Calculations for a 240 lb. Hog Dressing 72%.

Primal Cut	% of Carcass	Carcass wt. (lb.)	Wt. of Each Wholesale Cut (lb.)	Price/lb.	Total Value
Ham	21.0	172.8	36.3	$ .92	$ 33.40
Loin	19.0	172.8	32.8	$1.03	$ 33.78
Picnic shoulder	8.8	172.8	15.1	$ .61	$ 9.27
Boston shoulder	7.2	172.8	12.4	$ .79	$ 9.80
Belly	16.8	172.8	29.5	$ .61	$ 18.00
Spareribs	3.5	172.8	6.0	$ .86	$ 5.16
Jowl	3.0	172.8	5.2	$ .46	$ 2.39
Neckbones	2.1	172.8	3.6	$ .26	$ .94
Feet	2.1	172.8	3.6	$ .24	$ .86
Tail	.2	172.8	.3	$ .17	$ .05
Fat trim	12.0	172.8	20.7	$ .08	$ 1.66
Lean trim	4.3	172.8	7.4	$ .83	$ 6.14
Total	100.0		173.0	—	$121.45

The wholesale prices for beef and lamb carcasses and the wholesale cuts of pork are taken from the "yellow sheet" and/or the "blue sheet" for pricing live animals. The yellow sheet is published by the National Provisioner and the blue sheet is published by the U.S.D.A. and they are the basis of all price quotations used in the livestock and meat industry. These sheet prices are established on the basis of supply and demand.

The basis of establishing wholesale beef and lamb carcass price is determined by the combination of weight, class or sex, yield, and quality grade as described in Sections 9 and 13. However, in the case of pork, the wholesale carcass price is determined in actual industry practice from the weighted total value of all of the wholesale cuts, not by percentage muscle as described in Sections 5 and 6. Percentage muscle is a relatively new innovation and has not been adopted by the industry as the basis for pricing. Even more recent is the "lean guide to pork value" method of pricing live hogs as described in Sections 5 and 6. However, the current industry procedure for determining pork carcass price per cwt is illustrated in Table 18.2 and will be described briefly. For purposes of the example, a 240 lb. hog with a dressing percentage of 72 is used; thus, chilled carcass weight is 172.8 lb. (240 lb. × .72). The percentage of carcass weight of each wholesale cut is shown in column two of Table 18.2. The weight of each wholesale cut (column 4) is obtained by multiplying chilled carcass weight (column 3) by the percentage that each wholesale cut represents of the carcass (column 2). The wholesale prices per pound of each wholesale cut (column 5) were taken from a yellow sheet but a blue sheet also could be used. Total dollar value of each wholesale cut (column 6) is obtained by multiplying its weight (column 4) by the price per pound (column 5 in Table 18.2). The total dollar value of this 173.0 lb. carcass is $121.45 (Table 18.2). The wholesale carcass price is obtained by dividing $121.45 by 173 lb. which equals $70.20/cwt. This procedure is used to determine wholesale carcass price per cwt for pricing irrespective of whether percentage muscle, lean cuts, ham and loin, lean guide to pork value or some other method is used to calculate carcass and/or live price per cwt. The $70.20/cwt is the carcass price for a pork carcass with 53% muscle. Thus, the $70.20/cwt derived from the procedure described above is used as the basis for adjustments of carcasses with higher or lower percentages of muscle and for calculating live price per cwt as described in Sections 5 and 6.

Several factors are extremely important to the packer buyer in the pricing of live animals. The first of these factors is that of condemnation of by-products, parts of carcasses, entire carcasses, and defects in beef hides and lamb pelts (brands not readily apparent, knife cuts, etc.) so that the hides and pelts are discounted in price. Carcass and by-product value are obviously affected by these problems, and unfortunately most of them cannot be detected in the live animal prior to slaughter. If the packer buyer does not take such losses into account in purchasing live animals, his net return can be greatly affected when they occur. However, he does protect himself against such losses by estimating live price below the true live price of the animal. Thus, the losses incurred by condemnations, etc. are borne by all animals purchased, not just those for which losses result.

The second factor that greatly affects the net profit or loss to the packer buyer is his estimate of dressing percentage. To illustrate this point, assume that the packer buyer estimates a 1000 lb. U.S. Choice steer to dress 62%, whereas the actual dressing percentage is 61. The 10 lb. difference in chilled carcass weight (620 vs. 610 lb.) at $112.00/cwt equals an $11.20 loss on the steer. However, if the steer had dressed 63% rather than his estimate of 62%, he would have made $11.20 on the 1% error in his underestimation of dressing percentage. The packer buyer is as concerned about underestimation as he is about overestimation of dressing percentage because by his underestimation he would bid too low on the live price and undoubtedly lose the animal or lot of animals to a competitor. Obviously an error of 2% or more could be disastrous to his business. Thus, it is obvious that the buyer must accurately estimate dressing percentage because an error of only 1% can easily be the difference between profit and loss.

The third factor that affects the profit or loss to the packer buyer is his estimation of grade (both yield and quality) in beef cattle and lambs and percentage muscle in hogs. If quality grade was over- or underestimated, the incorrect base price would greatly affect the live price. Likewise, if yield grade or percentage muscle was incorrectly estimated, live price would be affected because the incorrect base carcass price was used to calculate it. Thus, it is obvious that an error in estimation of either quality or yield grade may result in considerable error, but if both are incorrectly estimated by very much, the profit or loss would be tremendous. While such errors undoubtedly occur every day, the days run of livestock purchases must be quite accurate in order to remain in business.

While each of these three factors can greatly affect the profit or loss column, the combined affects of all three serve to illustrate the extreme importance of a keen sense of observation, judgment, and adept mathematical calculating ability to accurately price live animals. The astute packer buyer not only makes his estimates low enough to ensure a profit, but also high enough to be competitive.

Retail Pricing

The basic principle in meat pricing is to recover costs plus realize a profit. This basic principle applies whether pricing meat at the wholesale, retail, or hotel, restaurant and institutional (HRI) establishment. Costs are both fixed and variable. Examples of fixed cost include building purchasing costs or rent, equipment, supplies (wrapping materials, labels, etc.), and labor. Variable costs include utilities, meat or livestock purchases, shrinkage, etc. In actual retail pricing procedures, the meat manager determines the cost per pound of the meat item and then calculates percentage markup which includes the fixed and variable costs plus the profit desired. The percentage markup varies for different meat items (carcasses vs. primal cuts) but markups of 15% to 50% are realistic. When markup is applied to carcasses, a normal range is 15 to 30%. The value of fat and bone removed during retail cutting are accounted for by the retailer when he establishes the markup.

Retail price per pound can be calculated from the wholesale cost per pound of the meat item by two different procedures. Probably the most commonly used procedure to calculate retail selling price per pound by the retail and HRI industries is to divide the cost of the meat item by the difference between 100% and the percentage markup. If a meat item cost $1.60 per pound wholesale, and the markup is 22%, the retail selling price is $2.05/lb. This problem is illustrated by the formula and calculations below:

$$\begin{aligned}
\text{Retail selling price} &= \frac{\text{wholesale cost of the meat item per pound}}{100\% - \%\text{ markup}} \\
&= \frac{\$1.60/\text{lb.}}{100\% - 22\%} \\
&= \frac{\$1.60/\text{lb.}}{78\%} \\
&= \frac{\$1.60/\text{lb.}}{.78} \\
&= \$2.05/\text{lb.}
\end{aligned}$$

The other procedure used by the retail and HRI industries to calculate the retail selling price is to multiply the wholesale cost of the meat item by 100%, plus the percentage markup. Thus, if the same 22% markup and $1.60/lb. wholesale cost of the meat item are used, the retail selling price is $1.95/lb. by this procedure as illustrated below:

$$\begin{aligned}
\text{Retail selling price} &= \text{wholesale cost of the meat item} \times (100\% + \% \text{ markup}) \\
&= \$1.60/\text{lb.} \times (100\% + 22\%) \\
&= \$1.60/\text{lb.} \times (1.00 + .22) \\
&= \$1.60/\text{lb.} \times 1.22 \\
&= \$1.952 \text{ or } \$1.95/\text{lb. when rounded}
\end{aligned}$$

As is obvious from the calculations above, the final retail price per pound differs between these two procedures. While both procedures are used in the meat industry, all subsequent pricing of retail meat items in this manual will be by the second method. Examples of retail pricing problems will be presented for beef and lamb carcasses and for fresh pork loins. Pork carcasses are not included in these problems because few pork carcasses are sold directly to the retailer or HRI establishment. However, pork loins are the primal cut most frequently sold fresh to both the retailer and HRI establishment.

Retail Pricing of Pork Loins

The principles of the procedure presented in this manual for pricing pork loins can be applied to the other fresh wholesale cuts of pork as well. However, processed products such as hams and bacon, for instance, have a more complex pricing system and they will not be included in this manual.

The pricing procedure presented here involves the pricing of fresh pork loins at the wholesale level from a retail point of view. The procedure involves calculating the percentage muscle and weight of the loin from hot carcass weight. The student then calculates the wholesale price per cwt that the retailer can afford to pay for the loins in order to cover costs and realize his marked up retail price. The following information is given to students in order to work these problems.

1. Hot carcass weight.
2. Loins will be assumed to be a constant 19% of hot carcass weight which, of course, is not always the case.
3. Carcasses with the base of 53% muscle yield loins that have 90% of their weight in the salable trimmed retail cuts.
4. For each .1 % muscle in the carcass above 53%, the trimmed retail cuts from the loin increase by .05% from the base of 90%. Likewise for each .1% muscle below 53% the percentage retail cuts decreases by .05%. Thus, one full percentage muscle equals a .5% change in retail cuts from the loin.
5. Prices comparable to those shown below in Table 18.3. Price quotations for fresh pork loin are given on a weight basis as are most pork wholesale cuts. These weights are: 14 lb. and down; 14 to 17 lb.; 17 to 20 lb. and 20 lb. and up.
6. A percentage markup to cover costs and profits.

Example Problem Information:

Hot carcass weight	170 lb.
Loin eye area	5.4 in.^{2}
10th rib fat thickness	.8 in.
Use prices and markup in Table 18.3	

Table 18.3   Trimmed Loin Wholesale and Retail Price Quotations.

Weight	Trimmed Retail Loin Price/cwt	Markup*		Trimmed Wholesale Loin Price/cwt
14 lb./dn.	$149.15	÷	1.22	$122.25
14/17 lb.	$146.40	÷	1.22	$120.00
17/20 lb.	$134.32	÷	1.22	$111.10
20 lb./up	$124.75	÷	1.22	$102.25

*A markup of 22% is used by the retailer in this example to cover fixed and variable costs plus profit.

First calculate the percentage muscle using the regression equation which for this carcass is 55.5% from the information given above. Always use the regression equation to calculate the percentage muscle. Then calculate the percentage adjustment of the trimmed loin retail yield using the 55.5% muscle just calculated. Since each .1% muscle equals .05% trimmed retail cuts and the difference of percentage muscle from the arbitrarily chosen base of 53% in tenths is 25 (55.5 − 53.0%), the loins from this carcass yield 91.25% salable trimmed retail cuts [90% + (25 × .05%) = 91.25%]. Next calculate the weight of the loin so that the correct price in Table 18.3 will be used. The percentage loin of the carcass was assumed to be 19%, thus 170 lb. hot carcass weight × .19 = 32.3 lb. for both loins (right and left) or 16.15 lb. each. Therefore, the price quotations for 14/17 lb. loins should be used for this example problem. The retail price of the salable trimmed portion of the loin is priced at $146.40/cwt (Table 18.3). Next convert the retail price to wholesale price of the salable portion of the loin by subtracting out the percentage markup. This is simply done by dividing retail price by 1.22 because retail price is 122% of wholesale price. Thus, $146.40 ÷ 1.22 = $120.00/cwt as presented in Table 18.3. To determine the price that the retailer can afford to pay the wholesaler for these loins, multiply the $120.00 by the salable retail cut percentage (91.25%) calculated previously to account for the percentage muscle of this carcass. Thus, $120.00/cwt × 91.25% = $109.50 which is the price the retailer can afford to pay. Always round the final price per cwt to the nearest dime ($.10).

Retail Pricing of Beef Carcasses

The principles presented in the procedure for pricing beef carcasses is equally applicable to the procedure for pricing wholesale or primal cuts. However, since some retailers continue to purchase beef carcasses the procedures presented here will be confined to those of beef carcasses. The procedures involve the pricing of beef carcasses at the wholesale level from a retail point of view. The student must determine the yield and quality grade of the carcasses and then calculate the wholesale price per cwt that the retailer can afford to pay for each carcass in order to cover costs and realize his retail price markup. The following information is provided to the student to work these problems.

1. Hot carcass weight.
2. A carcass yield grade of 3.2 has a yield of salable trimmed retail cuts of 70%.
3. For each .1 yield grade below 3.2, the percentage of salable trimmed retail cuts increases by .3%; and for each .1 yield grade above 3.2, the percentage decreases by .3%.
4. Prices comparable to those shown in Table 18.4. Price quotations for beef carcasses are normally given by quality grade and weight. However, weight has been taken into account for purposes of these problems in the determination of yield grade, and no further consideration is given to weight.
5. A percentage markup to cover costs and profits.

Example Problem Information:

Quality grade	Choice[0]
Adjusted 12th rib thickness	.5 in.
Ribeye area	12.5 in.^{2}
Hot carcass weight	675 lb.
Kidney, heart and pelvic fat	2.5%

Table 18.4   Beef Carcass Trimmed Wholesale and Retail Price Quotations.

Grade	Trimmed Retail Price/cwt	Markup*		Trimmed Wholesale Price/cwt
Prime	$200.38	÷	1.22	$164.25
Choice+	$197.03	÷	1.22	$161.50
Choice°	$195.20	÷	1.22	$160.00
Choice−	$191.84	÷	1.22	$157.25
Select	$186.36	÷	1.22	$152.75
Standard	$174.16	÷	1.22	$142.75
Commercial	$165.62	÷	1.22	$135.75
Utility	$156.77	÷	1.22	$128.50

*A markup of 122% was used by the retailer in this example to cover fixed and variable costs plus profit.

First calculate the yield grade of the carcass, which for this example is from the carcass data on page 189 equals 2.9. Then calculate the percentage of trimmed retail cuts for this carcass. Since each .1 yield grade equals .3% adjustment of retail cut percentage and the base yield grade is 3.2, the final percentage of salable trimmed retail cuts from this carcass is 70.9% (3.2 − 2.9 = 3 × .3% = .9% adjustment + 70% = 70.9%). Next select the correct price of the salable trimmed retail cuts for this carcass. Since the carcass has a quality grade of average Choice, the price is $195.20/cwt (Table 18.4). Then convert the trimmed salable portion of the carcass retail price to trimmed wholesale price per cwt by subtracting out the percentage markup. This simply involves dividing retail price per cwt by 1.22 because retail price for this example problem is 122% of wholesale price. Thus, $174.16 ÷ 1.22 = $160.00/cwt as presented in Table 18.4. To determine the price that the retailer can afford to pay the wholesaler for this carcass based on its yeild of salable retail cuts to recover costs and realize his intended profit, multiply the trimmed wholesale price per cwt by the adjusted percentage of salable retail cuts. Thus, $160.00/cwt × 70.9% = $113.44 or $113.40/cwt when rounded. Always round these calculations to the nearest $.10. For beef carcasses with a yield grade of 2.9 and quality grade of average Choice, the retailer can afford to pay the whoolesaler $113.40/cwt. It should be emphasized that the two variables in working these problems are the retail and wholesale prices and the percentage markup. The wholesale and retail prices vary daily with supply and demand. Percentage markup may also vary from time to time. However, the student will always be given the prices and percentage markup when asked to work these pricing problems.

Retail Pricing of Lamb Carcasses

The procedure for pricing lamb carcasses by the retailer are the same as those discussed for pork loins and beef carcasses. Only the prices and adjustments differ between the various species. Identical to the procedures for pork loins and beef carcasses, these problems involve the pricing of lamb carcasses at the wholesale level from a retail point of view. Thus, the student must yield and quality grade the lamb carcasses and then calculate the wholesale price per cwt that the retailer can afford to pay for each carcass in order to cover costs and realize his retail price markup. The following information is provided to the student to work these problems.

1. A lamb carcass yield grade of 4.0 has a yield of salable trimmed retail cuts of 70%.
2. For each .1 yield grade below 4.0, the percentage of salable trimmed retail cuts increases by .4% and for each .1 yield grade above 4.0, the percentage decreases by .4%.
3. Prices comparable to those shown below in Table 18.5. Price quotations for lamb carcasses are usually given by quality grade. Prices usually vary by lamb carcass weight, but the prices in Table 18.5 are for all weights within a given quality grade. If prices are given for several carcass weights for each grade, the principle presented in the example problem is the same. The student will be given carcass weight when price quotations are given for various weights.
4. A percentage markup to cover costs and profits.

Table 18.5 Lamb Carcass Trimmed Wholesale and Retail Price Quotations.

Grade	Trimmed Retail Price/cwt	Markup*		Trimmed Wholesale Price/cwt
Prime	$219.60	÷	1.22	$180.00
Choice	$216.24	÷	1.22	$177.25
Good	$203.13	÷	1.22	$166.50
Utility	$162.56	÷	1.22	$133.25

*A markup of 122% was used by the retailer in this example to cover fixed and variable costs plus profit.

Example Problem Information:

Quality grade	Choice[+]
Adjusted 12th rib fat thickness	.2
Kidney and pelvic fat	2.5%
Leg conformation grade	Prime[0]

First calculate the yield grade of the carcass, which for the above data equals 2.9. Then calculate the percentage of trimmed retail cuts for this carcass. Since each .1 yield grade equals .4% adjustment of retail cut percentage and the base yield grade is 4.0, the final percentage of salable trimmed retail cuts from this carcass is 74.4% (4.0 − 2.9 = 11 × .4% adjustment + 70% = 74.4%). Next select the correct price of the salable trimmed retail cuts from this carcass. Since the carcass has a quality grade of high Choice, the price is $216.24/cwt (Table 18.5). Then convert the trimmed salable portion of the carcass retail price per cwt to trimmed wholesale price percentage by subtracting out the percentage markup. This simply involves dividing retail price per cwt by 1.22 because retail price is 122% of wholesale price. Thus, $216.24 ÷ 1.22 = $177.25/cwt as presented in Table 18.5. To determine the price that the retailer can afford to pay the wholesaler for this carcass based on its yield of salable trimmed retail cuts, recover costs and realize his profit, multiply the trimmed wholesale price per cwt by the adjusted percentage of salable retail cuts. Thus, $177.25/cwt × .744 = $131.87 or 131.90/cwt when rounded which is the price the retailer can afford to pay the wholesaler for Choice grade lamb carcasses with a yield grade of 2.9. The final price per cwt is always rounded to the nearest $.10.

While a markup of 22% was used in the examples of all three species, this is not the case in actual practice because volume of the specific product and labor input also affects percentage markup. Certainly less labor is involved to cut pork loins into chops and roasts than the cutting and trimming of retail cuts from beef and lamb carcasses. Finally, the pricing procedures presented in this section are only one of a number of methods that are in use in the livestock and meat industry. However, the procedures and problems presented in this manual should give the students a better appreciation of the complexity of the pricing systems employed in livestock and meat industry.

Scoring System for Placing Classes

Official Placing

The instructor will lead the discussion of the differences between animals and give the official placing of the class and the cuts. A correct placing equals 50 points.

Scoring

Student placings are scored by subtraction of the cuts from 50 for incorrect placings. For an example class let us assume it was relatively easy to separate the class into a top pair and a bottom pair. Therefore, a heavy penalty of 6 is assigned between the top and bottom pair. The decision as to whether 1 or 3 placed first was a close and more difficult decision. Thus, the penalty for reversing the pair is only 3. The same explanation holds for the cut of 3 on the bottom pair.

Cuts		3	6	3
Official Placing	1 — 3 — 2 — 4 = 50			
Student Placing	3 — 1 — 4 — 2			
Deductions	3 over 1 = −3			
	3 over 4 = correct			
	3 over 2 = correct			
	1 over 4 = correct			
	1 over 2 = correct			
	4 over 2 = −3			
Total deductions	−6			

Student Score = 50 − 6 = 44

To illustrate a placing where more than a simple switch of pairs is made, the scoring procedure is shown in the example below. The official placing and cuts remain the same.

Cuts

		3	6	3		
Official Placing	1	— 3	— 2	— 4		
Student Placing	4	— 2	— 3	— 1		

Deductions	4 over 2	=	-3
	4 over 3 $= (-3)+(-6)$	=	-9
	4 over 1 $= (-3)+(-6)+(-3)$	=	-12
	2 over 3	=	-6
	2 over 1 $= (-6)+(-3)$	=	-9
	3 over 1	=	-3
Total Deductions		=	-42

Student Score $= 50 - 42 = 8$

Scoring System for Keep-Cull Classes

Culling classes consist of eight animals, four that are kept and four that are culled. Each animal in the class is assigned a point value not to exceed 20 and according to the ease or difficulty of culling or keeping. All animals incorrectly kept or culled will be penalized according to the degree of difficulty in arriving at the decision. The total penalty points are subtracted from 100 to obtain the contestant's score.

Example:

Official Culls 2, 4, 6, 8

Class A Animal No.	Point Value
1	16
2	3
3	10
4	20
5	2
6	7
7	6
8	12

1. If a student culled 2, 4, 6 and 8, the score would be 100.

2. If a student culled 1, 2, 3 and 4, the score would be 55.

   Note: The student misevaluated 1, 3, 6, 8 while culling and was penalized 16, 10, 7 and 12, respectively. His total would be: 100 − (16 + 3 + 7 + 12) = 55.

3. If the student culled 2, 4, 6 and 7, his score would be: 100 − (6 + 12) = 82.

Scoring System for Live Animal and Carcass Evaluation and Grading Classes

Scores for Fat Thickness

Deviation from Official Value (In.)

Maximum Points for Each Animal	Lambs	Cattle and Swine
10	.00 — .02	.00 — .04
9	.03 — .05	.05 — .09
8	.06 — .08	.10 — .14
7	.09 — .11	.15 — .19
6	.12 — .14	.20 — .24
5	.15 — .17	.25 — .29
4	.18 — .20	.30 — .34
3	.21 — .23	.35 — .39
2	.24 — .26	.40 — .44
1	.27 — .29	.45 — .49
0	⩾ .30	⩾ .50

Scores for Loin Eye Area

Deviation from Official Value (In.²)

Maximum Points for Each Animal	Cattle	Swine	Lambs
5	0 — .4	0 — .2	0 — .1
4	.5 — .9	.3 — .5	.2 — .3
3	1.0 — 1.4	.6 — .8	.4 — .5
2	1.5 — 1.9	.9 — 1.1	.6 — .7
1	2.0 — 2.4	1.2 — 1.4	.8 — .9
0	⩾ 2.5	⩾ 1.5	⩾ 1.0

Quality Grades for Beef, Lamb and Pork

Beef and Lamb			Pork	
Maximum Points for Each Animal (Market Division)	Maximum Points for Each Carcass (Carcass Division)	Deviation from Official Grade	Max. Points per Animal or Carcass	Deviation from Official Grade
10	10	0	10	0–.1
8	8	⅓ grade	9	.2–.3
6	5	⅔ grade	8	.4–.5
4	0	1 grade	7	.6–.7
2	0	1-⅓ grade	6	.8–.9
0	0	1-⅔ grade	5	1.0–1.1
			4	1.2–1.3
			3	1.4–1.5
			2	1.6–1.7
			1	1.8–1.9
			0	≥ 2.0

The utility grade will not be considered for pork carcasses.

Yield Grades for Beef and Lamb

Carcass Division		Market Division	
Maximum Points for Each Animal	Deviation from Official Score	Maximum Points for Each Animal	Deviation from Official Score
10	.0	15	.0 − .2
9	.1	13	.3 − .5
8	.2	11	.6 − .8
7	.3	9	.9 − 1.1
6	.4	7	1.2 − 1.4
5	.5	5	1.5 − 1.7
4	.6	3	1.8 − 2.0
3	.7	1	2.1 − 2.3
2	.8	0	≥ 2.4
1	.9		
0	≥ 1.0		

Scores for Swine Length and % Muscle

Length (In.)		% Muscle	
Maximum Points for Each Animal	Deviation from Official Values	Maximum Points for Each Animal	Deviation from Official Values
5	0 − .3	10	0 − .4
4	.4 − .7	9	.5 − .9
3	.8 − 1.1	8	1.0 − 1.4
2	1.2 − 1.5	7	1.5 − 1.9
1	1.6 − 1.9	6	2.0 − 2.4
0	⩾ 2.0	5	2.5 − 2.9
		4	3.0 − 3.4
		3	3.5 − 3.9
		2	4.0 − 4.4
		1	4.5 − 4.9
		0	⩾ 5.0

External Parts of Swine

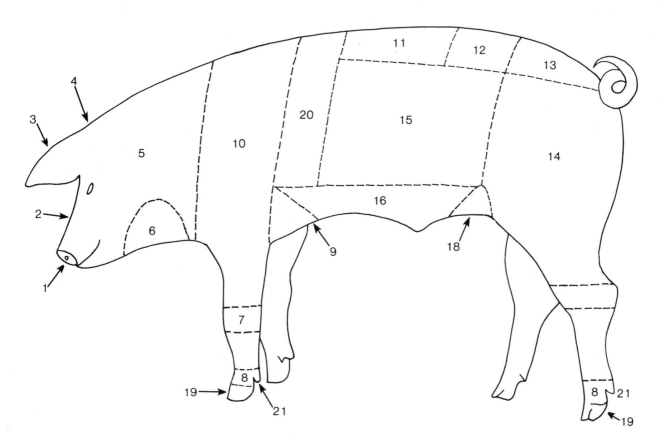

1. Nose or snout
2. Face
3. Ear
4. Poll
5. Neck
6. Jowl
7. Knee
8. Pastern
9. Fore flank
10. Shoulder
11. Back

12. Loin
13. Rump
14. Ham
15. Side
16. Belly or underline
17. Hock
18. Rear flank
19. Foot or toe
20. Forerib
21. Dew claw

External Parts of a Steer

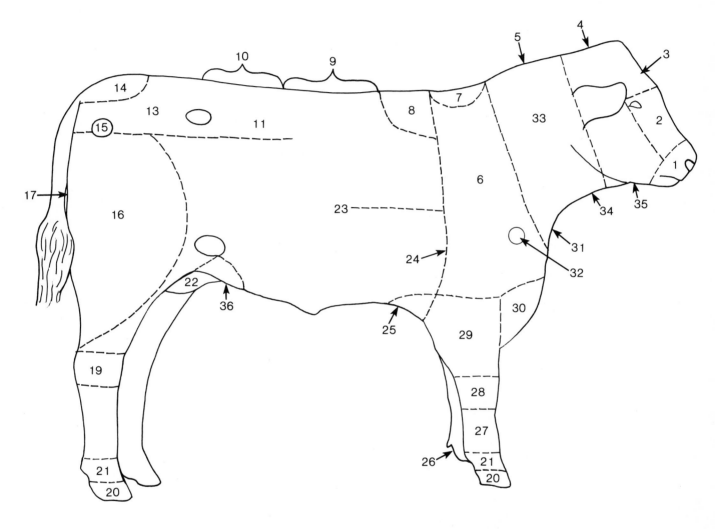

1. Muzzle
2. Face
3. Forehead
4. Poll
5. Crest
6. Shoulder
7. Top of shoulder
8. Crops
9. Back
10. Loin
11. Loin edge
12. Hooks or hips
13. Rump
14. Tailhead
15. Pins
16. Quarter or round
17. Twist
18. Stifle
19. Hock
20. Foot or toe
21. Pastern
22. Cod
23. Ribs
24. Heart girth
25. Foreflank
26. Dew claw
27. Cannon
28. Knee
29. Forearm
30. Brisket
31. Dewlap
32. Point of shoulder
33. Neck
34. Throat
35. Jaw
36. Rear flank

External Parts of Sheep

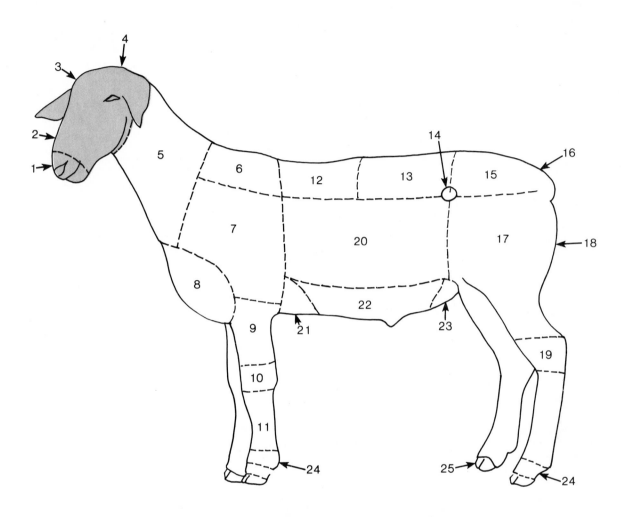

1. Muzzle	9. Forearm	17. Leg
2. Face	10. Knee	18. Twist
3. Forehead	11. Cannon	19. Hock
4. Poll	12. Back or rack	20. Middle
5. Neck	13. Loin	21. Fore flank
6. Top of shoulder	14. Hips	22. Belly
7. Shoulder	15. Rump	23. Rear flank
8. Breast or brisket	16. Dock	24. Pastern
		25. Hoof

Swine Ear Notching System

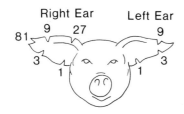

Right Ear   Left Ear

Equipment Needed:

1. Ear notching pliers

This skill teaches (The ability to _____)

1. Mark pigs for identification.
2. Understand the use of the ear notch for identification purposes.
3. Read an ear notch.
4. Properly identify pigs by litter and pig number.

Procedure:

1. Become familiar with the ear notching system.

2. Notch pig number in left ear and litter number
   in right ear.

3. All pigs in the same litter must have the same
   ear notch(es) in the right ear.

4. No pigs in the same litter should have identical
   ear notches in the left ear.

5. Place pig's ear into ear notching pliers. Take a
   full cut from the ear for each notch.

6. To ear notch the correct number, make the
   numbers representing the notches sum to the
   number desired. Example: For litter 7, make
   two notches in the "3" position plus one notch
   in the "1" position on the right ear. For pig 13,
   make one notch in the "9" position, one notch
   in the "3" position and one notch in the "1"
   position on the left ear.

NAME _____

DATE _____

GRADE _____

Give the litter and pig number for the following
pigs.

A. Litter number ____   B. Litter number ____

   Pig number _____   Pig number _____

Mark the following pigs according to the given litter
and pig number.

C. Litter number _16_   D. Litter number _35_

   Pig number __10__   Pig number __5__

Evaluation:	**Points**	
	Possible	*Earned*
1. Proper litter and pig number in (A) and (B) above. (5 pts. each)	20	_____
2. Proper notches in pigs (C) and (D). (5 pts. each)	20	_____
Ear notch live pigs or card board pig ears.		
3. Litter number properly notched in right ear.	10	_____
4. Pig number properly notched in left ear.	10	_____
5. Full cut taken for each notch.	10	_____
Total	70	_____

Swine Evaluation
Live and Carcass Estimations

Student Name _____ Number _____ Date _____

Ranges			190-270	68.0-77.0	28.0-34.0	.70-1.80				1.0-4.9	3.5-7.0	45.0-64.0				
Avg.			240	72.0	31.0	1.30				2.0	4.8	52.0				
Animal Number			Live Wt	Dressing %	Length	Av. Backfat Thick.	10th Rib Backfat	Last Rib Backfat	Muscling Score	U.S.D.A. Grade Code	Loin Eye Area	% Muscle	Marbling	Color	Firmness	Wateriness	Price Per cwt
		Comments, Notes or Description															
1	Est																
	Act																
2	Est																
	Act																
3	Est																
	Act																
4	Est																
	Act																
5	Est																
	Act																

• Indicates the location of the decimal point. This form is set up on a numerical system for computer scoring.

Avg. Group Price $ _____

Rank _____

209

Beef Evaluation
Live and Carcass Estimations

Student Name _____ Number _____ Date _____

Ranges		950–1500	55.0–67.0	.15–1.00	9.5–17.0 / 7.0–16.0		1.0–4.5	1.0–5.9				
Avg.		1150	62.0	.50	12.6	725	3.0	3.0				
Animal Number	Comments, Notes or Description	Live Wt	Dressing %	Adj. 12th Rib Fat Thick.	Ribeye Area	Hot Carcass Wt	% K.P.H. Fat	Yield Grade	Maturity	Marbling	Quality Grade Code	Price Per cwt
1	Est											
	Act											
2	Est											
	Act											
3	Est											
	Act											
4	Est											
	Act											
5	Est											
	Act											

Avg. Group Price $ _____

Rank _____

• Indicates the location of the decimal point. This form is set up on a numerical system for computer scoring.

USDA QUALITY GRADE CODE

Young		Old	
Prime+	= 22	Commercial+	= 08
Prime°	= 21	Commercial°	= 07
Prime–	= 20	Commercial–	= 06
Choice+	= 19	Utility+	= 05
Choice°	= 18	Utility°	= 04
Choice–	= 17	Utility–	= 03
Select+	= 16		
Select–	= 15		
Standard+	= 14		
Standard–	= 13		
Utility	= 12		

Lamb Evaluation
Live and Carcass Estimations

J

Student Name _____ Number _____ Date _____

Ranges	90–150	45.0–58.0	.05–.50	1.5–3.3	Gd⁻–P⁺	1.5–6.0	1.0–5.9						
Avg.	120	53.0•	.25	2.4	Ch°	3.0	3.7						
Animal Number / Comments, Notes or Description	Live Wt	Dressing %	Adj. 12th Rib fat Thick.	Ribeye Area	Leg Conform.	% K.P. Fat	Yield Grade	Maturity	Flank Streaking	Flank F & F	Confor-mation	Quality Grade Code	Price Per cwt
1 Est													
1 Act													
2 Est													
2 Act													
3 Est													
3 Act													
4 Est													
4 Act													
5 Est													
5 Act													

• Indicates the location of the decimal point. This form is set up on a numerical system for computer scoring.
• Shorn lambs.

Avg. Group Price $ _____ Rank _____

Prime+ = 22
Prime° = 21
Prime− = 20
Choice+ = 19
Choice° = 18

USDA QUALITY GRADE CODE

Choice− = 17
Choice+ = 16
Good° = 15
Good− = 14

Utility+ = 12
Utility° = 11
Utility− = 10
Cull = 09

Conversion Values to Estimate Pounds of Lean Pork (containing 10% fat) Gain Per Day on Test

(To obtain %, determine conversion values (C.V.) for each of the three traits and sum them. For measurements not listed, follow directions listed after last C.V.)

Actual Carcass Weight

LB.	C.V.
140 =	13.0620
141 =	13.0995
142 =	13.1370
143 =	13.1745
144 =	13.2120
145 =	13.2495
146 =	13.2870
147 =	13.3245
148 =	13.3620
149 =	13.3995
150 =	13.4370
151 =	13.4745
152 =	13.5120
153 =	13.5495
154 =	13.5870
155 =	13.6245
156 =	13.6620
157 =	13.6995
158 =	13.7370
159 =	13.7745
160 =	13.8120
161 =	13.8495
162 =	13.8870
163 =	13.9245
164 =	13.9620
165 =	13.9995
166 =	14.0370
167 =	14.0745
168 =	14.1120
169 =	14.1495
170 =	14.1870
171 =	14.2245
172 =	14.2620
173 =	14.2995
174 =	14.3370
175 =	14.3745
176 =	14.4120
177 =	14.4495
178 =	14.4870
179 =	14.5245
180 =	14.5620
181 =	14.5995
182 =	14.6370
183 =	14.6745
184 =	14.7120
185 =	14.7495
186 =	14.7870
187 =	14.8245

Carcass Wt. (cont.)

188 =	14.8620
189 =	14.8995
190 =	14.9370
191 =	14.9745
192 =	15.0120
193 =	15.0495
194 =	15.0870
195 =	15.1245
196 =	15.1620
197 =	15.1995
198 =	15.2370
199 =	15.2745
200 =	15.3120

(for every change of 1 lb., above 200 or below 140, add or subtract .0375)

Fat Depth

IN.	C.V.
.30 =	36.510
.35 =	36.045
.40 =	35.580
.45 =	35.115
.50 =	34.650
.55 =	34.185
.60 =	33.720
.65 =	33.255
.70 =	32.790
.75 =	32.325
.80 =	31.860
.85 =	31.395
.90 =	30.930
.95 =	30.465
1.00 =	30.000
1.05 =	29.535
1.10 =	29.070
1.15 =	28.605
1.20 =	28.140
1.25 =	27.675
1.30 =	27.210
1.35 =	26.745
1.40 =	26.280
1.45 =	25.815
1.50 =	25.350
1.55 =	24.885
1.60 =	24.420
1.65 =	23.955
1.70 =	23.490
1.75 =	23.025
1.80 =	22.560

Fat Depth (cont.)

1.85 =	22.095
1.90 =	21.630
1.95 =	21.165
2.00 =	20.700

(for every change of .05 in., above 2.00 or below .30, subtract or add .465)

Loin Muscle Area

IN.^{2}	C.V.
3.5 =	8.125
3.6 =	8.250
3.7 =	8.375
3.8 =	8.500

Loin Muscle Area—*Continued*

IN.²	C.V.	IN.²	C.V.	IN².	C.V.
3.9 =	8.625	5.1 =	10.125	6.3 =	11.625
4.0 =	8.750	5.2 =	10.250	6.4 =	11.750
4.1 =	8.875	5.3 =	10.375	6.5 =	11.875
4.2 =	9.000	5.4 =	10.500	6.6 =	12.000
4.3 =	9.125	5.5 =	10.625	6.7 =	12.125
4.4 =	9.250	5.6 =	10.750	6.8 =	12.250
4.5 =	9.375	5.7 =	10.875	6.9 =	12.375
4.6 =	9.500	5.8 =	11.000	7.0 =	12.500
4.7 =	9.625	5.9 =	11.125		
4.8 =	9.750	6.0 =	11.250		
4.9 =	9.875	6.1 =	11.375		
5.0 =	10.000	6.2 =	11.500		

(for every change of .1 in.², above 7.0 or below 3.5, add or subtract .125)

Example:	Hot Carcass Wt., lb.		Loin Muscle Area, in.²		Fat Depth, in.		
Actual Value →	170		5.0		1.0		
C.V. →	14.1870	+	10.000	+	30.000	=	54.187%

Equation adjusted to 160 lb.

$$[(81.4 + (.06)(170) + (2)(5.0) - (14.9)(1.0)] \div 160 \,(100) = 54.187\%$$

Index